HANDWRITTEN HISTORICAL DOCUMENT ANALYSIS, RECOGNITION, AND RETRIEVAL — STATE OF THE ART AND FUTURE TRENDS

SERIES IN MACHINE PERCEPTION AND ARTIFICIAL INTELLIGENCE*

ISSN: 1793-0839

Editors: **H. Bunke** (University of Bern, Switzerland)
Cheng-Lin Liu (Chinese Academy of Sciences, China)

This book series addresses all aspects of machine perception and artificial intelligence. Of particular interest are the areas of pattern recognition, image processing, computer vision, natural language understanding, speech processing, neural computing, machine learning, hardware architectures, software tools, and others. The series includes publications of various types, for example, textbooks, monographs, edited volumes, conference and workshop proceedings, PhD theses with significant impact, and special issues of the International Journal of Pattern Recognition and Artificial Intelligence.

Published

Vol. 88: *The Lognormality Principle and its Applications in e-Security, e-Learning and e-Health*
by Réjean Plamondon, Angelo Marcelli and Miguel Angel Ferrer

Vol. 87: *Fuzzy Systems to Quantum Mechanics*
by Hong-Xing Li

Vol. 86: *Graph-Based Keyword Spotting*
edited by Michael Stauffer, Andreas Fischerand Kaspar Riesen

Vol. 85: *Ensemble Learning: Pattern Classification Using Ensemble Methods (Second Edition)*
by L. Rokach

Vol. 84: *Hybrid Metaheuristics: Research and Applications*
by Siddhartha Bhattacharyya

Vol. 83: *Data Mining in Time Series and Streaming Databases*
edited by Mark Last, Horst Bunke and Abraham Kandel

Vol. 82: *Document Analysis and Text Recognition: Benchmarking State-of-the-Art Systems*
edited by Volker Märgner, Umapada Pal and Apostolos Antonacopoulos

Vol. 81: *Data Mining with Decision Trees: Theory and Applications (Second Edition)*
by L. Rokach and O. Maimon

Vol. 80: *Multimodal Interactive Handwritten Text Transcription*
by V. Romero, A. H. Toselli and E. Vidal

Vol. 79: *Document Analysis and Recognition with Wavelet and Fractal Theories*
by Y. Y. Tang

Vol. 78: *Integration of Swarm Intelligence and Artificial Neural Network*
edited by S. Dehuri, S. Ghosh and S.-B. Cho

Series in Machine Perception and Artificial Intelligence – Vol. 89

HANDWRITTEN HISTORICAL DOCUMENT ANALYSIS, RECOGNITION, AND RETRIEVAL — STATE OF THE ART AND FUTURE TRENDS

Andreas Fischer

Marcus Liwicki

Rolf Ingold

University of Fribourg, Switzerland

World Scientific

NEW JERSEY · LONDON · SINGAPORE · BEIJING · SHANGHAI · HONG KONG · TAIPEI · CHENNAI · TOKYO

Published by

World Scientific Publishing Co. Pte. Ltd.

5 Toh Tuck Link, Singapore 596224

USA office: 27 Warren Street, Suite 401-402, Hackensack, NJ 07601

UK office: 57 Shelton Street, Covent Garden, London WC2H 9HE

British Library Cataloguing-in-Publication Data
A catalogue record for this book is available from the British Library.

Series in Machine Perception and Artificial Intelligence — Vol. 89
HANDWRITTEN HISTORICAL DOCUMENT ANALYSIS, RECOGNITION, AND
RETRIEVAL — STATE OF THE ART AND FUTURE TRENDS

ISBN 978-981-120-323-7 (hardcover)
ISBN 978-981-120-324-4 (ebook for institutions)
ISBN 978-981-120-325-1 (ebook for individuals)

For any available supplementary material, please visit
https://www.worldscientific.com/worldscibooks/10.1142/11353#t=suppl

Dedicated to Prof. Em. Dr. Horst Bunke, for his pioneering research in the field of handwriting recognition.

Contents

Joan Puigcerver, Alejandro H. Toselli and Enrique Vidal

Alicia Fornés, Josep Lladós and Joana Maria Pujadas-Mora

Chapter 1

Introduction

[1,2]Andreas Fischer, [1,3]Marcus Liwicki and [1]Rolf Ingold

[1]*DIVA Group, University of Fribourg, Switzerland*
[2]*iCoSys Institute, University of Applied Sciences and Arts
Western Switzerland*
[3]*EISLAB, Luleå University of Technology, Sweden*
andreas.fischer@unifr.ch, marcus.liwicki@ltu.se, rolf.ingold@unifr.ch

Document image analysis or document recognition refers to the process of extracting valuable information from document images. Although a few optical character reading systems were already available in the 1970's, the fundamental research activities on this challenging task has mainly emerged with the development of the scanner technologies in the 1980's, which allowed affordable document image acquisition. At that time, the main applications were focused on office automation and the interpretation of printed material.

Nowadays, the technology for printed text recognition is considered as mature, even if several unsolved issues remain, typically for processing tables or mathematical formulas. However, the interest for these topics is decreasing because of the gradual reduction of paper documents used for the daily business.

In the meanwhile, a new even more challenging application area has emerged: the analysis and recognition of historical documents. Since the beginning of the new millennium, huge efforts have been made for digitizing historical documents at large scale. The main motivations for such initiatives are twofold: first, the preservation of the cultural heritage, reducing cost and avoiding additional degradations since digital information is supposed to be unalterable; and second, to make these documents available and searchable to a large community of users and notably in human sciences for scholars.

Numerous collections of historical document facsimiles have been made available on the Internet, often linked with additional descriptors and metadata, which provide additional functionalities for selecting, searching, and comparing documents according to these descriptors. However, full text transcription is rarely provided and if it is, it has usually been produced manually.

We could expect that computers should be able to do much more with these documents. It would be desirable to be able to search for historical documents by using an engine like Google, either locally on a given collection or globally working worldwide. Today, such a possibility is considered as a dream, but a dream that will become almost reality in a reasonable future. It is probably a matter of time.

The methods and tools developed for contemporary document analysis are hardly adaptable to be used in the context of historical documents. The goal of this book is to address the new issues that are raised with historical document analysis and to explore the novel research topics the scientific community is now dealing with. It presents the state of the art of several challenges involved. In order to understand the relations between these different tasks, we need to briefly remind the processing chains that are usually applied.

Figure 1.1 shows a typical processing chain composed of several important steps. In this illustration, we voluntarily exclude the image acquisition part, which often requires specific hardware and is therefore considered as a topic for itself. Here, we assume that the images are already available in gray scale or color spaces and focus our discussion on the algorithmic part.

There is not a unique processing chain that is applicable to any kind of documents. The architecture of a document analysis system is highly dependent of the targeted application and the document collection considered for it. Typically for degraded documents, a pre-processing step with sophisticated image enhancement algorithms is required before further processing. At the other end of the chain, post-processing is a matter of cost that must be accommodated to the quality requirements of the results.

However, there are typical steps between that have to be performed in a specific order which are illustrated in Figure 1.1. After the pre-processing

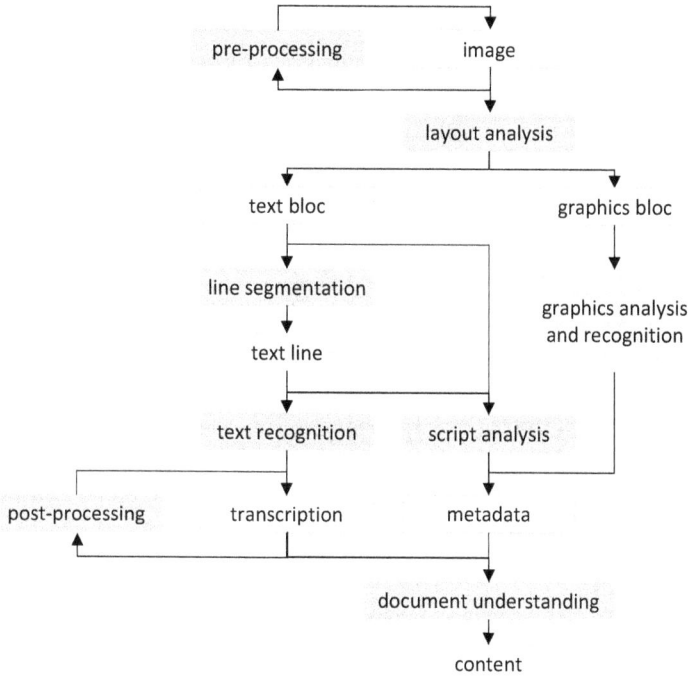

Fig. 1.1: A typical processing chain for historical documents analysis.

stage follows a very important step called layout analysis, which consists in segmenting the entire image into regions of interest. As a preliminary step, foreground and background separation is often required. Then, an important aspect is to separate text from non-text regions (such as ornaments, pictures or large initials), and then to split text blocks into text lines and even further into isolated words. Finally, relations between the regions have to be established for recovering the natural reading order or, in case of a table, to establish the horizontal and vertical alignment properties.

For several reasons, layout analysis of historical documents is much more challenging than for contemporary documents. First, as already mentioned, degradation is a major hindering for accurate analysis and image pre-processing can only hardly improve the image quality and certainly not recover the original information. Additionally, given the preciousness of parchment and paper, the presented information of historical documents is much denser than for contemporary documents. In medieval documents for instance the textual content is very often mixed with ornaments and glosses that have been added later. Classical segmentation algorithms based on spacing properties are not really applicable. Approaches based on texture analysis, inspired by natural image processing seem more appropriate. In the last couple of years, machine learning approaches and especially deep learning has made a considerable progress.

Once the images of text lines or words have been properly extracted, text recognition can be applied. Here we need to distinguish between machine printed and handwritten text. In the first case, OCR technologies are designed to perform text recognition. Most of these software tools are able to cope with almost all kind of alphabets and typefaces. For some specific needs, text recognition might not be enough; as a complementary task it might be important to recognize font variations. In that case, a font recognition module needs to be introduced, either as preliminary task (known as a priori font recognition) or after the text transcription (also named a posteriori font recognition).

Despite the regular progress made over the last two decades, handwritten text recognition has not yet reached a stage to be applicable at a large scale. One of the main reasons for this situation is the fact that characters can only hardly be isolated. Instead of recognizing individual characters (as used in OCR technologies), handwriting recognition needs to be applied on entire words or even sequences of words. This increases immensely the complexity of the task and requires more contextual knowledge, such as language models, dictionaries, or even semantic knowledge relying for instance on domain specific ontologies. To recognize handwritten words, the use of machine learning is essential; hidden Markov models (HMM) or long short-term memory networks (LSTM) seem both to be adapted to model both shape and language properties, provided that enough labeled training data is available, and this is for the moment still the main bottleneck of this technology.

However, for certain document analysis applications, full text transcription is not absolutely required. As an interesting alternative, the so called word spotting approach can be used instead. Here the goal is to recognize and locate specific keywords, reducing considerably the complexity of the task and allowing automatic and accurate indexing by these keywords.

In case of multilingual documents, sometimes by mixing different alphabets, an additional script and language analysis is required. Interestingly, the job can be performed prior to the text recognition task, by extracting relevant features from pixel data. Of course, alternatively, the language can also be recognized by comparing the OCR output with a dictionary. Such an approach is only feasible under the assumption that the text recognition result is accurate enough.

The last important processing step, often considered as optional, is called document understanding. The result of this first step toward interpretation is highly depending of the complexity of the documents and the targeted application. It relies on layout analysis and addresses the logical structure of the document. Concretely, it aims at recognizing titles and headers in order to establish the hierarchy of chapters and sections, of documents. It targets also the recognition of captions, glosses and footnotes. In addition to application-oriented research that aims to develop concrete solutions, the research community also needs to develop appropriate tools to cover its own needs. One major example of that is the development of databases with their ground-truth annotations. This is a crucial element to quantitatively evaluate algorithms and machine learning models and therefore a sound way to stimulate competitions. Providing enough annotated data is far from being trivial; in most cases the ground truth needs to be generated manually by an expert, which is boring, time consuming and therefore expensive. To simplify such work, appropriate tools are developed to automate the process as much as possible, reducing thus the human intervention essentially to the verification and correction of the proposed results.

This book reports about research activities on historical document analysis carried out during the last decade and discusses the results obtained so far. It is composed of two parts. In Part 1 (Chapters 2 to 8), we report about a series of research projects conducted by Swiss universities and largely funded by the Swiss National Science Foundation, which we summarize under the umbrella term "the HisDoc project". The main objectives of these projects was to develop tools covering the entire processing chain to allow intelligent automatic indexing of handwritten historical documents. Part 2 (Chapters 9 to 12) contains a selection of invited contributions from colleagues from other European countries to give a more global picture of the intense research activities deployed in the domain of cultural heritage preservation.

In Chapter 2, Andreas Fischer describes the effort to develop an initial database that was needed for the HisDoc project to train and evaluate automatic handwriting transcriptions. Three different datasets with great variability have been included. They differ from each other in terms of age (9th, 13th and 18th century), language (Latin, German, and English), layout structure and image quality. The chapter describes not only the ground truth features that are taken into account, but it also presents the different and complex steps that were needed to extract the relevant information. Of particular interest for its originality, we mention here the semi-automatic text alignment process that was used to establish precise links between the text transcription and the text line images.

The contribution of Chapter 3 is provided by Foteini Simistira Liwicki and presents another database developed within the HisDoc project. In contrast with the previous database, the goal of this dataset is intended for layout analysis of medieval documents. The chosen documents belong to a category with very complex layout structures due to a mixture of the original main text and marginal interlinear glosses or corrections that were added later in history. The provided annotations are composed of tight polygons surrounding text lines or graphic elements with labels to discriminate the type of text (main text, glosses or titles). Additionally to the database itself, the chapter also presents protocols and evaluation measures and reports about a competition organized at ICDAR 2017 around this complex task.

Chapter 4 is dedicated to layout analysis. Written by Mathias Seuret, this chapter discusses various techniques used for text line segmentation of medieval documents with complex and irregular layouts taken from the dataset presented in Chapter 3. The focus is put on text line segmentation and the author illustrates the complexity of the tasks and shows that there is not even a strong consensus on the form of the results: the problem can be stated as a splitting task using boundaries or specified as a pixel labeling task. As a consequence, a variety of complementary approaches, either algorithmic or based on machine learning can be applied. Good results are reported by combining a seam carving algorithm with a neural network composed of a stacked autoencoder used for feature extraction and a final pixel classifier.

Text recognition, a topic often seen as the central goal of document analysis is discussed in Chapter 5. Andreas Fischer, the author, shows the inherent difficulty of the topic when applied on historical documents. Even if fully automated transcription will remain a dream for several years, important improvements could be reported. In the HisDoc project, two approaches based respectively on hidden Markov models (HMM) and long short-term memory networks (LSTM) have been evaluated. Both methods rely on the principle that entire word recognition can be performed by combining language models from the transcription with the character models trained on the images. Furthermore, the chapter also addresses briefly the text-image alignment problem.

Chapter 6, written by Volkmar Frinken and Shriphani Palakodety, is dedicated to word spotting, an intriguing alternative to automatic transcription for content based document indexing. It provides an overview of state-of-the-art techniques and describes a complete system well-adapted for word spotting of historical handwriting that was developed during the HisDoc project. The approach is based on sliding windows for feature extraction and on LSTM models for sequence analysis. This system outperforms traditional approaches based on hidden Markov models or dynamic time warping.

The last two chapters related to the HisDoc project present practical tools, which have been developed to better support the research environment useful for the researchers themselves.

The first one, described in Chapter 7 by Marcel Gygli (formerly Marcel Würsch), called DIVAServices is a web-based platform used to access standard algorithms related to document analysis and used for data preparation and management. It includes a large variety of tools ranging from image pre-processing to public OCR and statistical evaluation tools. By sharing such an environment the researchers have no more to deal with the installation and maintenance of all these software packages and can concentrate their efforts on their own contributions.

Finally, Chapter 8, presented by Angelika Garz, describes an innovative interactive tool called GraphManuscribble. Based on a tablet computer with a stylus, it allows to quickly annotate and correct the ground truth for layout analysis of historical documents with complex structures. In a first automatic step, a document graph is computed and overlaid to the original image: the vertices correspond to points of interest extracted from a binarized or gray scale image and the edges correspond to the minimum spanning tree extracted from the Delaunay triangulation. This graph that approximately captures the visual structure of the document, is impaired by a number of incorrect or missing links which would provoke respectively under- and over-segmentation. These errors can then be effectively corrected with a few natural scribbling gestures by a human expert.

The second part of the book contains contributions of several representative research activities conducted in other European countries, which are related to the HisDoc project and aim to achieve similar goals. They describe other fascinating projects on historical analysis and their applicability in many different areas.

Chapter 9 describes a Greek national research project called OldDocPro and dedicated to the automatic indexing of machine-printed and handwritten polytonic historical documents. The main challenge comes from the complexity of the scripts containing great variety of diacritics (more than 270 classes), which the existing OCR technologies cannot manage correctly, even after thorough training. To overcome these difficulties a large specialized database has been created; its ground-truth describes the precise location of more than 100'000 words and more than 170'000 characters. This database was then used to develop several novel methods for text line segmentation, isolated character recognition as well word recognition and keyword spotting.

Chapter 10 is dedicated to a sophisticated keyword spotting system developed at the Polytechnic University of Valencia. The proposed methods are based on a probabilistic approach composed of so called pixel-level "posteriograms" and relevance probabilities estimated on segmented text lines. The methodology has been evaluated by a precision-recall trade-off model and has proven their effectiveness on several large document collections.

The contribution of Chapter 11 comes from the Computer Vision Center CVC of the Autonomous University of Barcelona, another distinguished Spanish research group. It describes a complete system dedicated to the study of historical demography based on marriage and death registers or other similar sources. This interdisciplinary work is based on the analysis of thousands of population records from various sources stored in public, ecclesiastical or private archives and targets the construction of a large knowledge base organized as a historical social network.

Last but not least, Chapter 12 considers the topic of historical document analysis from the big data perspective with the "four V" principles: Volume, Velocity, Variability and Veracity. Lambert Schomaker from the University of Groningen (Netherlands) reports about the observations made with the Monk system, an e-Science service designed for scholars, which is running for more than a decade. The contribution focuses mainly on different strategies for semi-automatic word labeling and draws very interesting conclusions extending thus the vision that is commonly shared by the scientific community dealing with historical document analysis.

PART 1

The HisDoc Project

Chapter 2

IAM-HistDB
A Dataset of Handwritten Historical Documents

Andreas Fischer

DIVA Group, University of Fribourg, Switzerland
iCoSys Institute, University of Applied Sciences and Arts
Western Switzerland
andreas.fischer@unifr.ch

2.1 Introduction

The goal of automated reading in historical manuscripts is to receive a scanned page of the manuscript as input and to produce a machine-readable transcription of all text elements of the page. Ideally, the transcription is aligned with the scanned page, such that it can be overlaid with the image similar to printed documents that have been processed by Optical Character Recognition (OCR).

In order to develop and test systems for automated reading, the data has to be prepared accordingly. Annotations are needed for layout analysis (where are text elements on the page?) as well as handwriting recognition (what is the machine-readable transcription of those elements?). Such annotations are called *ground truth* of the pattern recognition problem and have a two-fold purpose. On the one hand, they serve as learning samples for machine learning algorithms and, on the other hand, they allow to evaluate the performance of the algorithms.

In this chapter, we describe the annotated database of historical documents that was created at the beginning of the HisDoc project at IAM institute

11

of the University of Bern, Switzerland. The IAM-HistDB was one of the first comprehensive research datasets at the time and has been made publicly available to the research community.[1] It currently has over thousand registered users and has become a well-established benchmark in the field, allowing to test novel algorithms and compare them with previous work.

The remainder of this chapter is structured as follows. Section 2.2 provides pointers to related research datasets, Section 2.3 presents the contents of the IAM-HistDB in greater detail, and Section 2.4 discusses the semi-automatic method used to create the ground truth. Finally, we draw some conclusions in Section 2.5.

2.2   Related Work

In contrast to printed documents, the ground truth for handwriting recognition typically does not provide annotations at character level, i.e. it does not assign a bounding box and a transcription to each individual character. For touching and overlapping characters, especially in the case of cursive handwriting styles, it is difficult to decide where a character starts and ends. Even the segmentation into individual words may be challenging when the white space between words is small, irregular, or completely omitted.

Instead, handwriting recognition systems often operate at line level, i.e. the layout analysis module attempts to find text lines within the scanned page and the recognition module attempts to find the correct sequence of characters and words within the text line images. Accordingly, a research dataset for handwriting recognition should contain the location of the text lines on the scanned page image, together with their machine-readable transcription. Unfortunately, existing electronic editions provided by researchers from the humanities usually do not contain such annotations. They may provide a transcription at page level but lack the information where the individual text lines are located on the page image.

For modern handwriting, subjects may be asked to copy a given text with their own handwriting into prepared forms that facilitate the creation of large research datasets, as for example in the IAMDB [Marti and Bunke (2002)] that contains modern handwriting samples from over 600 writers.

Creating ground truth for historical handwriting is more challenging, as the annotations have to be added to existing manuscripts. It can be done

---

[1]http://www.fki.inf.unibe.ch/databases/iam-historical-document-database

either completely manually or computer-assisted if a handwriting recognition system is available. In either case, it requires a considerable amount of time for manual interaction, especially for ancient scripts and languages that necessitate expert knowledge from the human user.

One of the first datasets that was shared with the research community was the George Washington database containing 20 annotated pages of scanned letters written by George Washington and his associates during wartime. After it has been made available by Rath *et al.* [Rath and Manmatha (2007)], the dataset has been used by a number of research groups for handwriting recognition and keyword spotting. The IAM-HistDB also contains these 20 images with new annotations at line level (see Section 2.3.3).

Several interactive annotation tools have been developed that led to the creation of more datasets. Early systems include DEBORA for annotating Renaissance documents [Bourgeois and Emptoz (2007)] and DMOS for annotating old civil status registers and military forms [Coüasnon *et al.* (2007)]. Several systems have been proposed for annotating old Spanish manuscripts, including STATE [Gordo *et al.* (2008)], CATTI [Romero *et al.* (2007)], and GIDOC [Serrano *et al.* (2010)], which was used to create the publicly available GERMANA[2] database [Pérez *et al.* (2009)].

More recently, the transScriptorium[3] project (2013–2015) and the READ[4] project (2016–2019) with its Transkribus platform had a fundamental impact on the collection and annotation of new datasets. They have not only developed interactive annotation tools and made research datasets publicly available, but also created an active community around the Transkribus platform, which is expected to continue sharing and annotating collections of historical documents.

2.3   The IAM-HistDB

The IAM-HistDB contains three databases with different handwriting styles and languages, namely the Saint Gall database, the Parzival database, and the George Washington database. Together, they provide annotations for over hundred scanned page images to train and evaluate automatic reading systems.

---

[2]https://www.prhlt.upv.es/wp/resource/the-germana-corpus
[3]http://transcriptorium.eu
[4]https://read.transkribus.eu

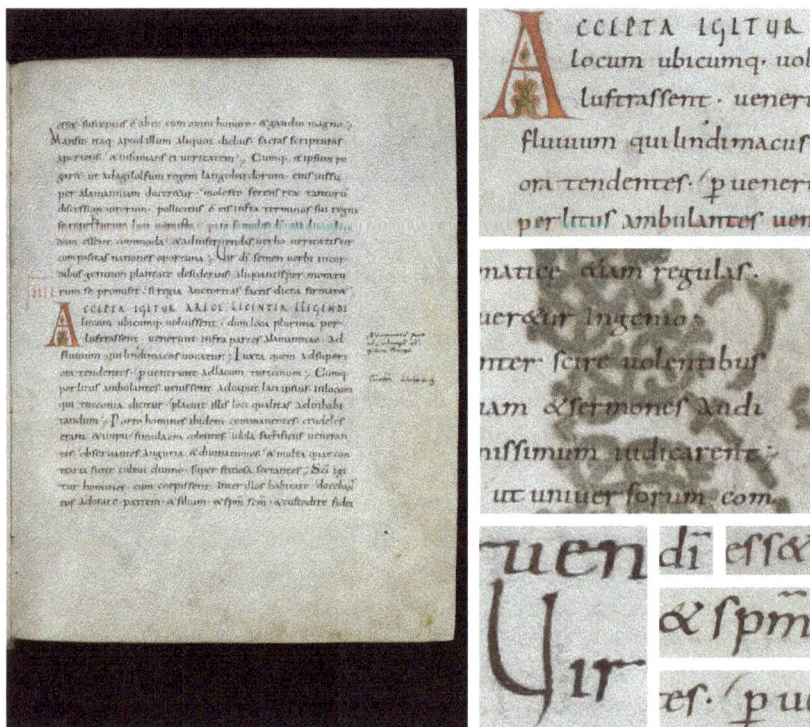

Fig. 2.1: Saint Gall database.

Table 2.1: Saint Gall database statistics.

Saint Gall database	
Century	9th
Language	Latin
Script	Carolingian
Original manuscript	Abbey Library of Saint Gall, Cod. Sang. 562
Physical format	24.0 x 30.0 cm, ink on parchment
Digital format	3328 x 4993 px, color JPEG
Writers	1
Pages	60
Text Lines	1410
Word Instances	11597
Word Classes	4890
Characters	49

2.3.1   *Saint Gall Database*

The Saint Gall database is based on a medieval Latin manuscript from the 9th century written in Carolingian script, which contains the hagiography *Vita sancti Galli* by Walafrid Strabo. The original is held by the Abbey Library of Saint Gall, Switzerland (Cod. Sang. 562), its digital images are available on the e-codices website,[5] a virtual library from the Medieval Institute of the University of Fribourg, Switzerland, and a text edition of the manuscript can be found on the monumenta website[6] based on the Patrologia Latina edition.[7] Figure 2.1 provides visual samples and Table 2.1 summarizes the main characteristics of the database.

Annotations include the text line locations on the page image in form of closed polygons and their corresponding transcription. Besides a diplomatic transcription, i.e. the exact sequence of characters and words visible in the handwriting, the database also provides an aligned version of the text edition from the monumenta website, which often deviates from the handwritten text for better readability, especially with a view to abbreviations, capitalization, and punctuation.

The Saint Gall database has a regular page layout, which contains a single column of 24 straight text lines with ample spacing between the lines. The text foreground is clearly distinguishable from the parchment background. For automated reading, only a relatively small number of 49 characters has to be modeled. Nevertheless, the database poses several typical challenges, including marginal notes, colored initial letters, holes in the parchment, ink bleed-through, lack of spacing between words, frequent word breaks at the line end, and abbreviated words (see Figure 2.1 for visual samples).

The database has been introduced in [Fischer *et al.* (2011)] in the context of transcription alignment. The goal was to automatically align the transcription from the monumenta website with the page image.

2.3.2   *Parzival Database*

The Parzival database is based on a medieval German manuscript from the 13th century written in Gothic script, which contains the epic poem *Parzival* by Wolfram von Eschenbach. The original is held by the Abbey Library of

---

[5]http://www.e-codices.unifr.ch
[6]http://www.monumenta.ch
[7]J.-P. Migne PL114, 1852

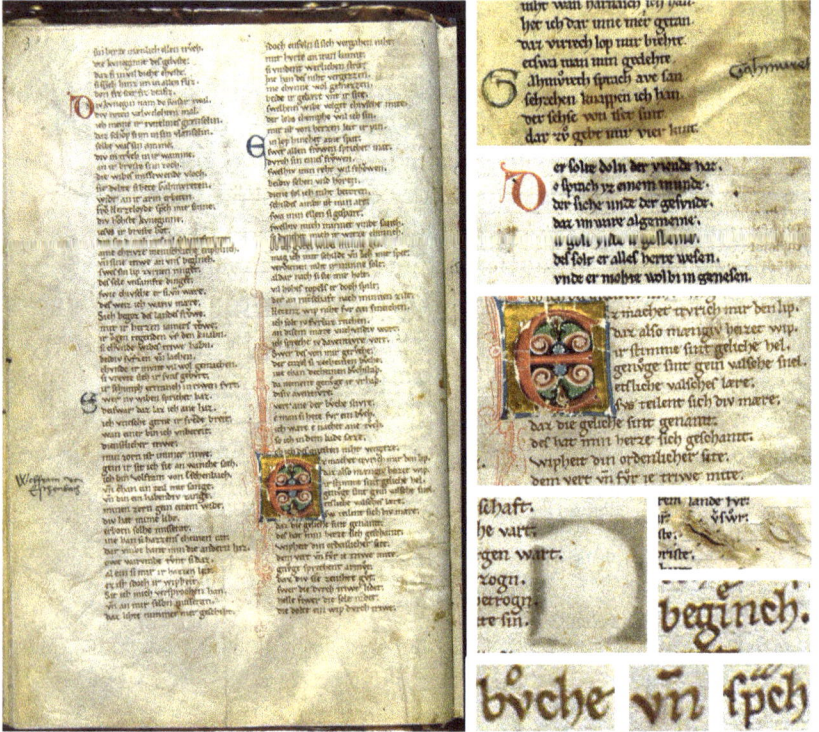

Fig. 2.2: Parzival database.

Table 2.2: Parzival database statistics.

Parzival database	
Century	13th
Language	German
Script	Gothic
Original manuscript	Abbey Library of Saint Gall, Cod. 857
Physical format	21.5 x 31.5 cm, ink on parchment
Digital format	2000 x 3008 px, color JPEG
Writers	3
Pages	47
Text Lines	4477
Word Instances	23478
Word Classes	4934
Characters	93

Saint Gall, Switzerland (Cod. 857) and its digital images together with a transcription were made available on CD-ROM by the German Language Institute of the University of Bern, Switzerland.[8] Figure 2.2 provides visual samples and Table 2.2 summarizes the main characteristics of the database.

Annotations include the transcription for preprocessed line and word images. Preprocessing include binarization, removal of the skew, i.e. the inclination of the text line, and horizontal and vertical scaling. As it was the first database investigated during the HisDoc project, our ground truth creation procedure described in Section 2.4 was not yet in place and we have, unfortunately, not stored the location of the text lines within the page image. The diplomatic transcription includes special characters for abbreviation symbols.

The Parzival database has a two-column layout with pairwise rhyming lines. Around the main text, we find ornaments, colored initial letters, and marginal notes that were added at a later time to the manuscript. The ravages of time have affected the parchment considerably, leading to stains, wrinkles, holes, and faded ink. Some of the torn pages were repaired with visible stitches. For automated reading, a total of 93 characters have to be modeled, including a number of abbreviation symbols. Figure 2.2 provides a visual impression.

The database has been introduced in [Fischer *et al.* (2009)] in the context of handwriting recognition using hidden Markov models (HMM) as well as bi-directional recurrent neural networks with long short-term memory cells (BLSTM). The goal was to transcribe the line and word images.

2.3.3   *George Washington Database*

The George Washington database is based on English letters from the 18th century written in longhand script by George Washington and his associates. The originals are held by the Library of Congress and their digital images have been made available online by the library together with a transcription.[9] Figure 2.3 provides visual samples and Table 2.3 summarizes the main characteristics of the database.

Annotations include the transcription for preprocessed line and word images. Similar to the Parzival database, preprocessing include binarization, removal

---

[8]http://www.parzival.unibe.ch/
[9]George Washington Papers at the Library of Congress from 1741–1799, Series 2, to be found at http://memory.loc.gov/ammem/gwhtml/gwseries2.html

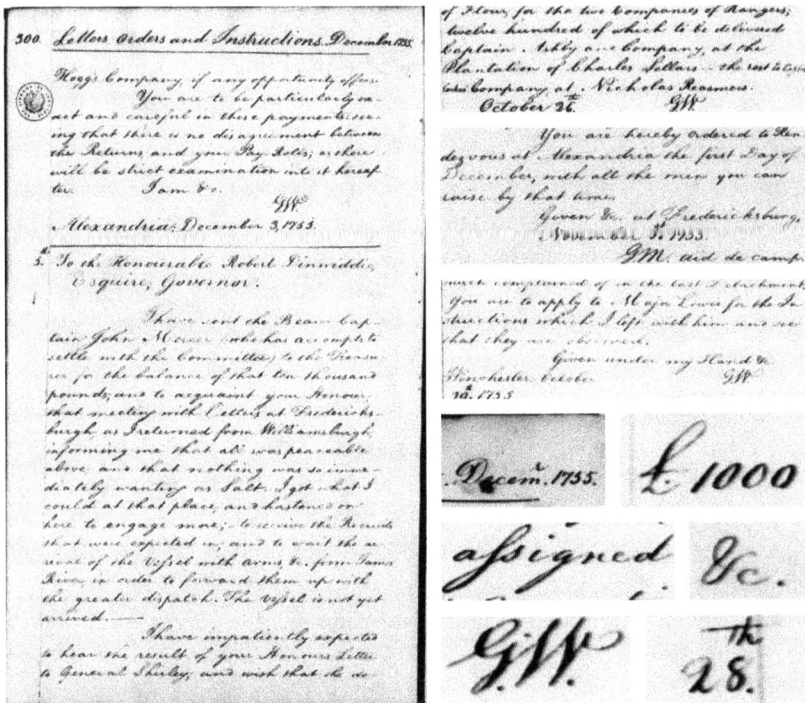

Fig. 2.3: George Washington database.

Table 2.3: George Washington database statistics.

George Washington database	
Century	18th
Language	English
Script	Longhand
Original manuscript	Library of Congress
Physical format	Ink on paper
Digital format	2034 x 3286 px, grayscale JPEG
Writers	2
Pages	20
Text Lines	656
Word Instances	4894
Word Classes	1471
Characters	82

of the skew, and horizontal and vertical scaling. In addition, the slant, i.e. the inclination of the characters, has been removed as well.

The George Washington database has a less regular layout than the medieval manuscripts. Apart from the main text, the letters contain page numbers, rulers, stamps, and signatures. Faded ink and stains render the task of automated reading more difficult. A total of 82 characters have to be modeled, including numbers, currency symbols, double "s" letters, "th" written on top of numbers, the frequently used "etc." symbol, and signatures (see Figure 2.3 for visual samples).

The 20 page images included in the George Washington database have been used in several studies before, e.g., in [Lavrenko *et al.* (2004)] for word recognition. Our database has been introduced in [Fischer *et al.* (2010b)] in the context of keyword spotting. The goal was to retrieve text line images that contain specific search terms provided by the user as free text.

2.4 Semi-Automatic Ground Truth Creation

In this section, we describe the semi-automatic procedure we have developed during the HisDoc project for creating ground truth annotations for automated reading. The aim of this procedure was to find a reasonable balance between the work performed by human users and tasks that can be performed automatically. Also, we wanted laypersons without special knowledge in computer science or linguistics to be able to perform all required manual interactions. The procedure is detailed in [Fischer *et al.* (2010a)]. It consists of five consecutive steps illustrated in Figure 2.4.

Step 1 – Text Selection. The first step is manual and consists in selecting the main text areas on the page image with a polygon.[10] Such areas, typically text columns, are defined as blocks of consecutive text lines. By means of this selection, the main text is separated from margin notes, ornaments, drawings, colored initial letters, and page numbers. The selection is stored in Scalable Vector Graphics (SVG) format.

Step 2 – Foreground Detection. The second step is automatic and aims to separate the text foreground from the page background. We apply a Difference of Gaussian (DoG) filter on grayscale images to locally enhance

---

[10] We used the *Paths* tool of the GIMP software, http://www.gimp.org/.

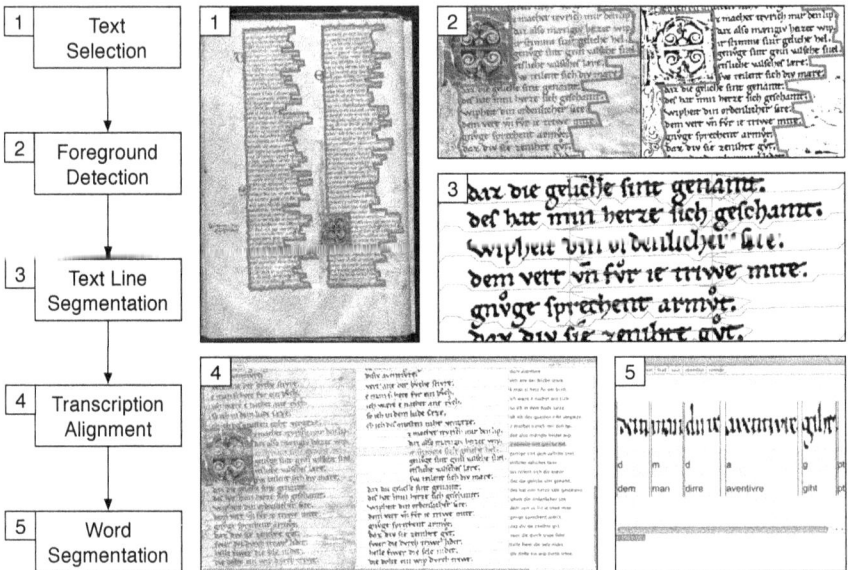

Fig. 2.4: Semi-automatic ground truth creation.

edges, i.e. we subtract two Gaussian blurs with different radii. Afterwards, a global threshold is applied for binarization. The two radii and the threshold are optimized by visual inspection of a few sample pages, in order to exclude ink bleed-through and stains as well as possible. After binarizing the whole page, the main text areas are cut out for further processing, according to the text selection from the previous step. For the IAM-HistDB, this approach led to acceptable results in all cases, despite the fact that the three databases under consideration are quite different.

Step 3 – Text Line Segmentation.   The third step consists of automatic text line segmentation, followed by manual correction. For segmenting the text lines, we use a seam carving approach to cut consecutive lines. First, start and end points of the seams are estimated from horizontal projection profiles. Afterwards, seams are computed from left to right using dynamic programming, avoiding text foreground if possible and staying close to a straight line. For more details on the seam carving algorithm, we refer to [Fischer *et al.* (2010a)]. The resulting seams are inspected and corrected by a human user in a graphical user interface. They can drag with the mouse to adjust the closest seam. Combining the text selection from the first step with the top and bottom seams from the third step, we obtain a polygon around each text line that is stored in SVG format.

Step 4 – Transcription Alignment. The fourth step aims to align the available transcription with the line images. It consists of automatic parsing of the text, followed by manual correction. Parsing is needed to clean the text, standardize its encoding to Unicode, and to split text lines based on heuristics. Manual correction is performed in a text editor, which is integrated with the line segmentation results as illustrated in Figure 2.4. For the IAM-HistDB, the manual interaction ranged from rapid corrections of line breaks to more time-consuming corrections of abbreviations.

Step 5 – Word Segmentation. The fifth and last step consists of automatic word segmentation followed by manual correction. For this purpose a handwriting recognition system based on hidden Markov models (see Chapter 5) is applied in forced alignment mode to compute word boundaries. Afterwards, the boundaries are manually corrected in a graphical user interface. For the IAM-HistDB, the automatic alignment was near-perfect and only few manual corrections were needed.

In summary, the principal ground truth annotations for automated reading consist of polygons around text lines, stored as SVG, together with their diplomatic transcription, stored as plain text in Unicode. These annotations allow to train and evaluate layout analysis systems, which aim to automatically extract line images, and handwriting recognition systems, which aim to transcribe the line images into machine-readable text. For recognition experiments at word-level, we also provide word images, which are annotated with their transcription.

In terms of time consumption, the first bottleneck of the proposed procedure is the manual text selection, which took about 2 minutes per column on average for the IAM-HistDB. The second bottleneck is the manual correction of the text line segmentation together with the manual correction of the transcription alignment, which together took about 3.5 minutes per column if the user was familiar with the task.

2.5 Conclusions

The creation of a comprehensive research database with a variety of different scripts and languages was an important first step in the HisDoc project, as there was almost no data available for training and evaluating handwriting recognition in the context of historical manuscripts at the time. With the Saint Gall, Parzival, and George Washington databases, we have focused on relatively regular layouts and Latin alphabets, in order to facilitate our first attempts towards automated reading.

The proposed semi-automatic procedure for creating ground truth has proven fairly efficient with a bit more than five minutes of manual interaction per page on average. Nevertheless, our experience was that the interaction quickly became repetitive and rather dull. Clearly, there is much room for improvement in that regard, e.g. designing the procedure in a way that the human user focuses on difficult cases, interacts naturally and rapidly with the proposed annotations, and sees how the system gets better at suggesting annotations over time.

References

Bourgeois, F. L. and Emptoz, H. (2007). DEBORA: Digital AccEss to BOoks of the RenAissance, *Int. Journal on Document Analysis and Recognition* **9**, pp. 193–221.

Coüasnon, B., Camillerapp, J., and Leplumey, I. (2007). Access by content to handwritten archive documents: Generic document recognition method and platform for annotations, *Int. Journal on Document Analysis and Recognition* **9**, 2, pp. 223–242.

Fischer, A., Frinken, V., Fornés, A., and Bunke, H. (2011). Transcription alignment of latin manuscripts using hidden Markov models, in *Proc. 1st Int. Workshop on Historical Document Imaging and Processing*, pp. 29–36.

Fischer, A., Indermühle, E., Bunke, H., Viehhauser, G., and Stolz, M. (2010a). Ground truth creation for handwriting recognition in historical documents, in *Proc. 9th Int. Workshop on Document Analysis Systems*, pp. 3–10.

Fischer, A., Keller, A., Frinken, V., and Bunke, H. (2010b). HMM-based word spotting in handwritten documents using subword models, in *Proc. 20th Int. Conf. on Pattern Recognition*, pp. 3416–3419.

Fischer, A., Wüthrich, M., Liwicki, M., Frinken, V., Bunke, H., Viehhauser, G., and Stolz, M. (2009). Automatic transcription of handwritten medieval documents, in *Proc. Int. Conf. on Virtual Systems and Multimedia*, pp. 137–142.

Gordo, A., Llorens, D., Marzal, A., Prat, F., and Vilar, J. (2008). State: A multimodal assisted text-transcription system for ancient documents, in *Proc. 8th Int. Workshop on Document Analysis Systems*, pp. 135–142.

Lavrenko, V., Rath, T. M., and Manmatha, R. (2004). Holistic word recognition for handwritten historical documents, in *Proc. Int. Workshop on Document Image Analysis for Libraries*, pp. 278–287.

Marti, U.-V. and Bunke, H. (2002). The IAM-database: an English sentence database for offline handwriting recognition, *IJDAR* **5**, 1, pp. 39–46.

Pérez, D., Tarazón, L., Serrano, N., Castro, F.-M., Ramos-Terrades, O., and Juan, A. (2009). The GERMANA database, in *Proc. 10th Int. Conf. on Document Analysis and Recognition*, pp. 301–305.

Rath, T. M. and Manmatha, R. (2007). Word spotting for historical documents, *IJDAR* **9**, 2–4, pp. 139–152.

Romero, V., Toselli, A. H., Rodríguez, L., and Vidal, E. (2007). Computer assisted transcription for ancient text images, in *Proc. 4th Int. Conf. on Image Analysis and Recognition*, pp. 1182–1193.

Serrano, N., Tarazón, L., Pérez, D., Ramos-Terrades, O., and Juan, A. (2010). The GIDOC prototype, in *Proc. 10th Int. Workshop on Pattern Recognition in Information Systems*, pp. 82–89.

Chapter 3

DIVA-HisDB
A Precisely Annotated Dataset of
Challenging Medieval Manuscripts

Foteini Simistira Liwicki

DIVA Group, University of Fribourg, Switzerland
EISLAB, Luleå University of Technology, Sweden
foteini.liwicki@ltu.se

3.1 Introduction

In recent years several publicly available databases have been generated in order to assist researchers in the field of Handwriting Recognition (HWR) and Document Image Analysis (DIA) to compare their methods. As research in DIA advances rapidly, the type of tasks become more and more complex. While in the 1990s individual character and word databases were published (CENPARMI [Suen *et al.* (1992)], CEDAR [Hull (1994)]), the difficulty increased to unconstrained text lines (IAM [Marti and Bunke (2002)], George Washington [Rath and Manmatha (2007)]), and, finally, to historical documents with diverse scripts and languages (IAM-HistDB [Fischer *et al.* (2010)], GR-POLYDB [Gatos *et al.* (2015)]). DIVA-HisDB is a publicly available precisely annotated large dataset of challenging medieval manuscripts with comparably complex layout elements, diverse scripts per page, and challenging degradations. The database consists of three medieval manuscripts, 50 pages each, resulting of in total 150 pages. The annotation process was jointly defined with experts from medieval studies and the Ground Truth (GT) was reviewed and refined by an expert as well.

Furthermore, a layout analysis benchmark is specified and results of a state-of-the-art Convolutional Auto-Encoder (Convolutional Auto-Encoder

(CAE)) [Seuret *et al.* (2016)] are presented. The challenging nature of this dataset becomes obvious when considering that the method achieves only a result of around 95 % pixel-level accuracy. This is even further confirmed by showing that other state-of-the-art methods fail on the task of text line segmentation, even when being provided with the text region.

An overview of existing datasets and annotations for document analysis and recognition can be found at [Valveny (2014)]. The U.S. ZIP code data base of CENPARMI (Concordia University) [Suen *et al.* (1992)] contains approximately 17,000 run-length coded binarized digits. Among them are also some samples which are not easy to recognize for humans. The CEDAR database contains digital images of approximately 5,000 city names, 5,000 state names, 10,000 ZIP Codes, and 50,000 alphanumeric characters. The lAM database is a collection of handwritten English sentences from the Lancaster-Oslo/Berge (LOB) corpus and contains 1,066 forms produced by approximately 40 different writers. The George Washington database consists of 20 pages of letters in English, written by George Washington and his associates in the 18th century. The database is available online at the Library of Congress.[1] The most related to DIVA-HisDB databases are the IAM-HistDB (We recently published layout analysis ground truth in [Chen *et al.* (2015)]), containing German medieval manuscripts (13th century)[2] and GRPOLY-DB comprising documents in old Greek Polytonic script.[3] However, the current dataset is larger and contains more complex layout.

3.2   Description

DIVA-HisDB[4] is a collection of three medieval manuscripts (see Figures 3.1 and 3.2) that have been chosen regarding the complexity of their layout, together with partners from e-codices[5] and the Humanities faculty in the University of Fribourg:

- St. Gallen, Stiftsbibliothek, Cod. Sang. 18, codicological unit 4 (CSG18),

- St. Gallen, Stiftsbibliothek, Cod. Sang. 863 (CSG863),

---

[1] http://memory.loc.gov/ammem/gwhtml/gwseries2.html
[2] www.iam.unibe.ch/fki/databases/iam-historical-document-database
[3] http://www.iit.demokritos.gr/ nstaml/GRPOLY-DB
[4] The database will be made publicly available on the project page http://diuf.unifr.ch/hisdoc2
[5] http://www.e-codices.unifr.ch/

- Cologny-Genève, Fondation Martin Bodmer, Cod. Bodmer 55 (CB55).

(a) CSG18, p. 116   (b) CSG863, p. 17   (c) CB55, p. 67v

Fig. 3.1: Samples pages of the three medieval manuscripts in DIVA-HisDB.

(a) CSG18, p. 116

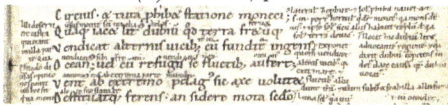

(b) CSG863, p. 17

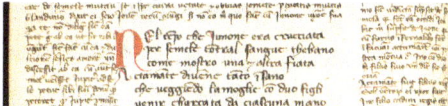

(c) CB55, p. 67v

Fig. 3.2: Details of Figure 3.1.

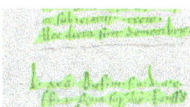

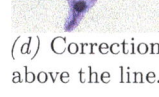

(a) Separation line between marginal glosses.

(b) Corrections above and below the line.

(c) Correction overwriting the text.

(d) Correction above the line.

Fig. 3.3: Annotation examples for separation lines and different type of corrections in DIVA-HisDB (main text body in blue, comments in green).

The three manuscripts are representatives of a specific category of manuscript layout, i.e. complex layout containing a main text body and marginal and/or interlinear glosses, additions, and corrections. This layout category is less numerous than the most common simple layout with a main text body only. Still, a layout analysis tool trained on this more complex layouts will easily be able to deal with simple layouts. In the choice of manuscripts, we focused on the Carolingian period, represented by CSG18 and CSG863, dating from the 11th century, written in Latin language using Carolingian minuscule script and having quite similar layout features. The number of writers in these two manuscripts is unspecified. In order not to be confined to one specific period, we also included CB55, a manuscript from the 14th century that shows a different script (chancery script), language (Italian and Latin), and layout. There is only one writer in this manuscript. This choice allows for training and testing the layout analysis tool in different contexts (same script or cross-script context). The chosen manuscript pages vary from rather simple pages with only a few glosses to complex pages with many glosses, annotations, and decorations. All pages have been digitized with a resolution of 600 dpi and have a size of approximately 20 × 25 cm.

DIVA-HisDB consists of 150 pages in total, 50 pages from each manuscript. For the dataset, as well as for the division into training, validation, and test set we have selected a representative set of pages.

The database consists of 150 pages in total and it is publicly available.[6] In particular:

- 30 pages/manuscript for training, including 10 public-test pages
- 10 pages/manuscript for validation which have been provided as a development set for the competition, and
- 10 pages/manuscript for testing which were previously unpublished.

The images are in JPG format, scanned at 600 dpi, RGB color. The ground truth of the database is available in the following format:

- pixel-label images and
- PAGE XML [Pletschacher and Antonacopoulos (2010)]

The ground truth contains four different annotated classes which might overlap: main-text-body, decorations, comments and background and are encoded by RGB values as follows (the distributions in the individual manuscripts are given in Table 3.1):

---

[6]http://diuf.unifr.ch/hisdoc/diva-hisdb

Table 3.1: Class distribution (in %).

	0	1	2	3
CB55	82.41	8.36	0.55	8.68
CSG18	85.16	6.78	1.47	6.59
CSG63	77.82	6.35	1.83	14.00

Notation 0: background, 1: comments, 2: decorations, 3: text

The three different manuscripts are shortly described in the following.

3.2.1 *CSG18*

This is a composite manuscript; the pages selected for the dataset are part of the codicological unit 4 containing a Psalterium glossatum with comments (see Figures 3.1(a) and 3.2(a)). This manuscript part was written in St. Gall, probably in the second half of the 11th century [Hoffmann (2012)]. In the earlier literature we find divergent datings: in Von Euw [von Euw (2008)], p. 502, dates the Psalterium to the late 10th century, in Scherrer [Scherrer (1875)], p. 6, dates this manuscript part to the 12th century. Note that such uncertainty is quite common in manuscript studies and has to be taken into account when developing automated document classification and dating methods.

The psalms are introduced by a rubric (incipit), their beginning is marked by a red initial and a line written in display script (capitalis rustica); each psalm verse begins with a red majuscule. The comments appear as marginal glosses with interlinear reference marks (a z and other reference marks). There are also interlinear glosses containing explanations and textual variants. The comments and glosses are written in a less calligraphic style than the main text. The manuscript part contains a drawing that is inserted in the main text body (see the description in p. 503 of [von Euw (2008)]), but this page has not been selected for the present dataset.

3.2.2 *CSG863*

This manuscript (see Figures 3.1(b) and 3.2(b)), was written in the second half of the 11th century [Hoffmann (2012)]. Euw [von Euw (2008)], p. 505, presumes the Reichenau as place of origin, while Hoffman [Hoffmann (2012)], p. 207, localizes the manuscript in St. Gall. It contains Lucan's Pharsalia libri decem. Each book begins with a red initial and two lines in display scripts (uncial, capitalis rustica); red incipits and explicits frame the books. There are marginal comments, some with interlinear reference marks, as well as interlinear glosses and corrections. Some pages (see [Bobeth (2013)], p. 169, 249, 253, 378–379, 385–389) contain interlinear musical notation (neumes). Others contain marginal drawings (see the description in [von Euw (2008)], p. 504–505), but they were not selected for the present dataset.

3.2.3   *CB55*

This manuscript (see Figures 3.1(c) and 3.2(c)), known as "Codex Guarneri", was written in the first half of the 14th century in Italy [Allegretti (2003)]. It contains the Inferno and Purgatorio from Dante's Divina commedia. While the manuscript is written in chancery script, it contains marginal glosses in Latin. The chapters are introduced by rubrics and red initials. Each tercet begins with a red-striped majuscule. In the glosses, the Italian reference text is sometimes repeated with a red underline.

3.3   Creation

For annotating the three selected medieval manuscripts we use Graph-Manuscribble [Garz *et al.* (2016)], a semi-automatic tool which is based on document graphs[7] and pen-based scribbling interaction. After an initial annotation and a second correction iteration, all pages have been scrutinized and corrected by an expert. Thereafter, a final validation and correction iteration has been performed verifying that the data is consistent. DIVA-HisDB provides the GT in the PAGE [Pletschacher and Antonacopoulos (2010)] format.

We distinguish between the main text body, the comments (marginal and interlinear glosses, explanations, corrections) and decorations (every character/sign that exceeds the size of a text line and/or is written in red). The main goal of the annotation is the automatic layout analysis and text line segmentation. Therefore these annotation categories are based on spatial and simple visual features like color. Paleographic features like display scripts or black majuscules are not marked as a decoration, since they are too difficult to distinguish for the automatic layout analysis tool in this first step. In future work, when also script analysis will be included, these paleographic features could also be taken into account. We totally disregard

---

[7]The sparse document graph is an automatically derived structural representation of the ink-areas in the document.

elements that don't belong to a text line or are not characters/signs, like separation lines between two marginal glosses (see Figure 3.3(a)). Those elements are very rare.

Since the annotation categories are constituted for a layout analysis purpose, they don't always correspond to the paleographic description of the page. For example, they don't take into account the different time steps of the production/revision of a manuscript. Within the comments' category, we don't distinguish between the original glosses, added by the writer of the main text, and the foliation added in the modern period. Also, if corrections have been made by overwriting the main text, they are not marked as posterior to the original main text (see Figure 3.3(c)); but if the corrections are made above and below the line, e.g., with a sign below the line to mark the affected letters, and the correct letter(s) above the line, they are annotated as comments (see Figures 3.3(b) and 3.3(c)).

Details of the distribution of the annotation categories appear in Table 3.2. For the whole DIVA-HisDB 63.97 % of the total number of regions per anno-tated category are comments, 9.36 % are decorations and 26.67 % consists the main text body. Note that the proportions of the categories differ between the manuscripts. While the amount of textlines and comments is almost the same in CSG863, significantly less comments are present in CSG18. Additionally, by measuring the surface area (number of pixels) for each annotated category, 41.37 % of the total surface area are comments, 1.69 % are decorations and 56.94 % consists the main text body (see Table 3.3).

Table 3.2: DIVA-HisDB: Number of regions per annotated category (com-ments, decorations, main text body).

	CSG18	CSG863	CB55	total/MS	(%)
main text body	1,353	1,538	1,486	4,377	26.67
decorations	672	30	835	1,537	9.36
comments	6,260	1,656	2,584	10,500	63.97
Total	8,258	3,224	4,905	16,414	

3.4 Competition

The objective of the ICDAR 2017 - Competition on Layout Analysis for Challenging Medieval Manuscripts was to allow researchers and practitioners

Table 3.3: DIVA-HisDB: Surface area in pixels per annotated category (comments, decorations, main text body).

	CSG18	CSG863	CB55	surface/MS	(%)
main text body	49,114,900	111,641,860	120,034,717	280,791,477	56.94
decorations	3,945,155	369,512	4,008,359	8,323,026	1.69
comments	60,050,935	19,002,895	124,972,171	204,026,001	41.37
Total	113,110,990	131,014,267	249,015,247	493,140,504	

from academia and industries to compare their performance in layout analysis tasks on a new dataset of challenging medieval manuscripts. This assists computer science society to establish a benchmark on the performance of such methods and the humanists community to easier and quicker study manuscripts. In particular, we formulate three tasks for this competition:

- Task-1: layout analysis
- Task-2: baseline detection
- Task-3: textline segmentation

To allow for a fair competition, a previously unpublished test set is taken for measuring the performance.

Task-1 focuses on the labelling of the pixels. As mentioned above, our ground truth might contain multi-class labeled pixels, belonging to more than one classes except for the background class. For example a pixel can be a part of the main-text-body but at the same time can also be a part of the decoration, for example:

main-text-body + comment:
0b...1000 — 0b...0010 = 0b...1010 = 0x00000A

main-text-body + decoration:
0b...1000 — 0b...0100 = 0b...1100 = 0x00000C

comment + decoration:
0b...0010 — 0b...0100 = 0b...0110 = 0x000006

To avoid unfair penalties for the boundary regions, we add a value for boundary pixels: 0b10...0000=0x800000. This value will be combined with one of the classes, except background. Mislabelling between the foreground and background in the boundary region were not be penalized in the final evaluation.

A boundary comment, for example, is represented as:

> boundary + comment:
> 0b10...0000 — 0b00...0010 = 0b10...0010 = 0x800002

Tasks-2 and Task-3 focus on the segmentation of text blocks into text lines. The text lines have been manually segmented into distinct regions (individual elements in the ground truth XML-file). Thus they can directly be used as ground truth for Task-3. However, we added Task-2 to make our competition and results comparable to other competitions, such as the cBAD.[8]

To generate ground truth for Task-2, we automatically extracted the baselines using the tight polygons from the Task-3 GT. The procedure is as follows:

i) A binary version of the document image is obtained using a global threshold applied on the Difference-of-Gaussian-enhanced document image (as done for the IAM-HistDB [Fischer *et al.* (2010)]).

ii) For each text polygon, get the list of lower contour points of the connected components in the binary image.

iii) Use the least square methods to find a baseline through these points.

iv) Compute the median distance between the points and the line, and discard the points which are farther than 50% of the median distance (outliers).

v) Compute the baseline of the remaining points (inliers).

Eight external research groups registered to participate in the competition and submitted at least one system (see Table 3.4).

Furthermore, a reference system was developed by the organizing lab (University of Fribourg). This ninth submission was not taken into account for determining the winner of the individual tasks.

Beyond the task of the competition - i.e., the accurate layout analysis of the manuscripts - we introduce a new way of technically evaluating the systems: some algorithms were submitted to DivaServices [Würsch *et al.* (2016)] and the evaluation was performed using an evaluation framework incorporating DivaServices.

---

[8]https://scriptnet.iit.demokritos.gr/competitions/5/

Table 3.4: Participating teams.

#	Affiliation	Data	OS	GPU	P*
1	KFUPM (Saudi Arabia)	**	win	no	b
2	BYU (USA)	**	linux	yes	a
3	NCSR "Demokritos" (Greece)	**	linux	no	c
4	MindGarage (Germany)	***	linux	yes	a
5	CASIA, NLPR (China)	**	win	no	b
6	Fraunhofer IAIS (Germany)	**	linux	no	c
7	CVML (Korea)	**	win	no	b
8	CITlab (Germany)	**	linux	no	c
9	DIVA (Switzerland)	**	win	no	a

* Mean of participating:
a) published on DivaServices and open source;
b) published on DivaServices but closed source;
c) not published on DivaServices.
** using only DIVA-HisDB for training
*** using additional training data

3.4.1 *Evaluation and Results*

All evaluation tools are freely available as open source on GitHub and as RESTful API web services on DivaServices. Providing the evaluation methods on DivaServices allows users to run them using our infrastructure and do not need to install anything locally. The executed methods are exactly the same as the ones hosted in their respective GitHub repositories.[9,10] More information about executing methods on DivaServices can be found in [Würsch *et al.* (2017)].

3.4.1.1 *Task-1: Layout Analysis*

The evaluation of the layout analysis at pixel level is based on the Intersection over Union (IU) as proposed in [Marti and Bunke (2001)] as ranking metric. The IU, also known as the Jaccard Index, is defined as:

$$IU = \frac{TP}{TP + FP + FN} \tag{3.1}$$

where TP denotes the True Positives, FP the False Positives and FN the False Negatives.

---

[9]https://github.com/DIVA-DIA/LayoutAnalysisEvaluator
[10]https://github.com/DIVA-DIA/LineSegmentationEvaluator

For each page, the IU is computed class-wise (background, text, comment, decoration) and then averaged. The final evaluation of a system is then obtained by averaging the IU of all pages of the three manuscripts.

In order to provide the user a more exhaustive evaluation of prediction quality, the tool outputs several other standard metrics, including F1-score, precision, and recall — for each class and averaged over the classes. Additionally, a human-friendly visualization of the results is provided in form of a output image obtained by overlapping the evaluated prediction with the original image. This is useful to get a quick estimation of the results and to detect the area of improvement for the evaluated method. More information about this evaluation tool can be found in [Alberti *et al.* (2017)].

The detailed evaluation results for Task-1 are given in Table 3.5. The winner of Task-1 is System-5 with an overall IU 94.90%. To make the results comparable to other competitions, Table 3.6 provides standard evaluation metrics as they are also used in other competitions. Noteworthy, the accuracy and the F1-score are much higher than the IU for all systems. Also note, that the accuracy of most systems is higher than 99%. However, these values do not fully reflect the performance of the systems as they are biased towards the majority class, i.e., if the majority class (text) would represent 99 % of the pixels, the accuracy of a system labelling everything as text would be 99 %.

Table 3.5: IU results for Task-1 (in %).

	CB55	CSG18	CSG863	Overall
System-5	98.35	**93.65**	**92.71**	**94.90**
System-4.1	**98.64**	93.57	89.63	93.95
System-3	96.75	90.69	89.36	92.27
System-2	96.39	87.72	86.42	90.18
System-4.2	93.66	88.37	86.70	89.58
System-6	71.78	74.96	75.46	74.07
System-1	71.50	64.69	59.88	65.35

3.4.1.2 Task-2: Baseline Extraction

The evaluation of the baseline extraction is based on a new performance measure [Grüning *et al.* (2017)] that finds the start and end points of the baseline of each textline and is based on the F-Measure as main metric. In this competition we used the same evaluation tool as the one in ICDAR

Table 3.6: Detailed result statistics for Task-1 (all values are in % and averaged over the manuscripts).

	IU	F1-score	Precision	Recall	Accuracy
System-5	**94.90**	**96.81**	**97.58**	**97.20**	99.57
System-4.1	93.95	96.04	96.55	97.10	**99.60**
System-3	92.27	95.32	95.65	96.09	99.17
System-2	90.18	93.57	93.96	94.87	99.01
System-4.2	89.58	93.86	95.15	93.92	98.34
System-6	74.07	83.32	94.47	84.77	95.12
System-1	65.36	75.50	81.32	75.07	94.70

2017 Competition on Baseline Detection (cBAD) [Diem *et al.* (2017)]. The baseline extraction evaluation tool is open-source and freely available on GitHub.[11] Note that we used a very relaxed threshold (20 pixels difference in y-direction is still considered as being correct) for measuring the precise quality of the detected baseline as our GT has been automatically generated.

Table 3.7 reports the results of the baseline detection task per manuscript and overall. The winner of Task-2 is System-8 with an overall F1-score 98.22%. Noteworthy, System-2 performs slightly better on two manuscripts but considerably worse on CB55.

Table 3.7: F1-score results for Task-2 (in %).

	CB55	CSG18	CSG863	Overall
System-8	**98.96**	98.53	97.16	**98.22**
System-2	95.97	**98.79**	**98.30**	97.68
System-7	95.34	87.34	97.51	93.40

3.4.1.3 *Task-3: Line Segmentation*

The evaluation of the line segmentation task is based on the Intersection over Union (IU) as main metric (see Eq. (3.1)).

Line IU the IU at line level, which evaluates how many of the lines have been correctly detected (see definition of *correct* below). In this

---

[11]https://github.com/Transkribus/TranskribusBaseLineMetricTool

case, TP is the number of correctly detected lines, FP the number of extra lines and FN the number of missed lines.

Pixel IU is the IU at pixel level, which evaluates how well are the line detected. In this case, TP is the number of correctly detected pixels, FP the number of extra pixels and FN the number of missed pixels. In this competition, only the foreground pixels are taken into account, because the exact shape of the polygon does not matter (as long as the included foreground pixels are the same). Two versions of the Pixel IU are reported. The Pixel IU takes all pixels into account, while the Matched Pixel IU only take into account the pixels from the matched lines. The former gives an overall evaluation of the method, while the latter is interesting for assessing the quality of the matched lines.

In order to evaluate a line segmentation prediction, a threshold is used to detect the matching between the prediction polygons and the ground truth polygons. Two polygons are considered as matching, and the line correctly detected, if both the pixel precision and recall of those two polygons is higher than a threshold of 75 %. If the pixel precision is lower than the threshold, then it is a False Positive, and if the Recall is lower than the threshold, then it is a False Negative. Note that it can be both at the same time if the overlap between the two polygons is too small.

The Line IU is computed for each page, as well as the global and matched Pixel IU over the different lines of each page. In the end, three main metrics are reported to assess the line segmentation quality: the mean Line IU, mean global Pixel IU and the mean Matched Pixel IU over all the pages of the three manuscripts.

The line segmentation evaluation tool is open-source and freely available on GitHub.[12] It outputs several other standard metrics as well in order to give more insight on the prediction quality.

The results of Task-3 are provided in Tables 3.8, 3.9 and 3.10. The winner of Task-3 is System-8 with an overall LineIU of 96.99%. We have performed an additional analysis where we applied a line-segmentation algorithm on the corresponding output of Task-1. System-9 performs better than the best individual submission, showing that it is promising to apply pixel-labelling as

---

[12]https:
//github.com/DIVA-DIA/LineSegmentationEvaluator/releases/tag/v1.0.0

Table 3.8: IU Results for Task-3 (in %).

	CB55	CSG18	CSG863	Overall
System-8	**99.33**	**94.90**	**96.75**	**96.99**
System-2	84.29	69.57	90.64	81.50
System-6	5.67	39.17	25.96	23.60
System-9+4.1*	*98.04*	*96.91*	*98.62*	*97.86*

*System-9 using as input the output of System-4.1 for Task-1.

Table 3.9: PIU Results for Task-3 (in %).

	CB55	CSG18	CSG863	Overall
System-8	**93.75**	**94.47**	90.81	**93.01**
System-2	80.23	75.31	**93.68**	83.07
System-6	30.53	54.52	46.09	43.71
System-9+4.1*	*96.67*	*96.93*	*97.54*	*97.05*

PIU denotes Pixel IU
*System-9 using as input the output of System-4.1 for Task-1.

Table 3.10: MPIU Results for Task-3 (in %).

	CB55	CSG18	CSG863	Overall
System-8	**94.02**	**96.24**	92.29	**94.18**
System-2	88.82	92.28	**96.07**	91.27
System-6	81.00	88.93	92.16	88.48
System-9+4.1*	*96.46*	*97.61*	*97.90*	*97.59*

MPIU denotes Matched Pixel IU
*System-9 using as input the output of System-4.1 for Task-1.

a prepossessing step before the line segmentation, resulting in less confusion made by the interlinear glosses.

3.4.2 *Discussion*

In general, the results of the competition show that the tasks of layout analysis and text line segmentation for complex layouts cannot be considered as solved. Although the values of the best systems are always above 90 %, they are far from being perfect.

Furthermore, it is interesting to see that the submitted systems are of diverse nature and have different individual strengths. In all Tasks, the best performing system of CB55 was not the best on the two other manuscripts.[13] A reason for that is that there are only a few interlinear glosses in CB55, which often leads to a confusion of classes. Furthermore, the winning method in Task-1 is based on deep learning, while the winning methods in Task-2 and Task-3 are based on a sequence of other heuristics and algorithms.

The results of Task-2 are higher than those of Task-3. As a result we can conclude that the detection of the baseline is a simpler task yielding better performance for a possible Handwritten Text Recognition (HTR). However, for some applications in the humanities, the exact shapes and boundaries of the text lines are required. Therefore, the results of Task-3, i.e., the IU and the Pixel IU are relevant measures as well. Especially for those values, it is desired that better performance will be achieved.

Task-1 As mentioned above, the values of the IU are constantly lower than those of the accuracy and other standard performance measures. However, they reflect more the real quality of the labelling, as the accuracy is biased towards the majority class (see Table 3.14).

Noteworthy, even when averaging the class-wise performance, the values for precision and recall (individually) are higher than the IU (see Table 3.11, Table 3.12 and Table 3.13). The IU can be seen as a measure which takes into account all mislabellings in one single measure.

We applied an own line segmentation method on the outputs of Task-1. Table 3.8, Table 3.9, Table 3.10 and Table 3.15 report these detailed results. We observe that when using System-9, the scores of the participating systems

Table 3.11: Class-wise IU result statistics for Task-1 (in %).

	0	1	2	3
System-1	95.65	50.16	45.50	70.10
System-6	95.15	61.15	63.10	76.86
System-2	99.48	78.38	89.16	93.69
System-3	99.37	86.03	89.16	94.51
System-4.2	98.25	83.92	85.27	90.87
System-4.1	**99.75**	86.45	**91.38**	**98.22**
System-5	99.73	**90.72**	91.32	97.84

Notation 0: background, 1: comments, 2: decorations, 3: text

---

[13]Considering that System-9 is included in this analysis.

Table 3.12: Class-wise precision result statistics for Task-1 (in %).

	0	1	2	3
System-1	96.06	74.27	68.03	86.93
System-6	98.54	71.04	85.71	82.62
System-2	99.85	81.59	97.06	97.31
System-3	99.67	89.40	96.64	96.91
System-4.2	98.76	90.79	94.68	96.37
System-4.1	**99.87**	89.25	**98.49**	**98.58**
System-5	**99.87**	**94.12**	97.96	98.37

Notation 0. background, 1: comments, 2: decorations, 3: text

Table 3.13: Class-wise recall result statistics for Task-1 (in %).

	0	1	2	3
System-1	99.55	62.71	58.85	78.67
System-6	96.50	79.64	70.64	91.86
System-2	99.62	91.74	91.93	96.13
System-3	99.69	95.07	92.21	97.41
System-4.2	99.47	91.91	90.08	94.08
System-4.1	**99.88**	95.94	92.78	**99.62**
System-5	99.87	**96.27**	**93.16**	99.45

Notation 0: background, 1: comments, 2: decorations, 3: text

Table 3.14: Detailed result statistics for Task-1 (in %).

	IU	F1-score	Precision	Recall	Accuracy
CB55	55.73	69.67	97.38	58.34	90.28
CG18	56.80	70.36	97.89	58.91	91.91
CSG863	54.79	69.04	96.62	58.17	87.52
Overall	55.77	69.69	97.30	58.47	89.90

in Task-3 improved. In particular, the Line IU for System-2 and System-6 increased from 84.29% to 92.54% and from 23.60% to 44%, respectively. This shows that the textline detection task (Task-3) can strongly benefit from the results of the layout analysis task (Task-1).

Another interesting observation is that when using System-9 on the participating systems' of Task-1, the system's order in Task-1 based on the IU was not preserved in Task-3. For example, System-5 (best system in Task-1) performed second in Task-3, and System-4.1 (second in Task-1) performed

Table 3.15: Line IU of System-9+i* for Task-3 (in %).

	CB55	CSG18	CSG863	Overall
System-9+4.1	98.04	**96.91**	98.62	**97.86**
System-9+5	98.35	96.26	98.47	97.69
System-9+4.2	97.46	96.26	96.63	96.78
System-9+3	96.71	89.73	97.11	94.52
System-9+2	**98.36**	79.99	**99.27**	92.54
System-9+1	91.49	19.51	75.92	62.31
System-9+6	15.01	68.05	48.93	44.00

*using as input the output of System-i for Task-1.

Table 3.16: Pixel IU of System-9+i* for Task-3 (in %).

	CB55	CSG18	CSG863	Overall
System-9+4.1	**96.67**	**96.93**	**97.54**	**97.05**
System-9+5	96.33	96.50	97.38	96.74
System-9+4.2	96.39	96.91	96.24	96.51
System-9+3	95.00	91.78	96.01	94.26
System-9+2	94.37	86.86	96.12	92.45
System-9+1	85.55	51.68	79.81	72.35
System-9+6	44.09	75.06	58.36	59.17

*using as input the output of System-i for Task-1.

first in Task-3. A possible reason for this might be because System-4.1 detects better the main-text-body in Task-1 than System-5 (see Table 3.11, Table 3.12 and Table 3.13). Furthermore, we can observe that System-5 detects best the comments, while System-4.1 detects best all other classes.

With this competition we have introduced an extensive benchmark for a challenging dataset for the task of layout analysis. In our ongoing research we are adding more manuscripts to the database and will focus on even more interesting challenges.

References

Alberti, M., Bouillon, M., Liwicki, M., and Ingold, R. (2017). Open Evaluation Tool for Layout Analysis of Document Images, *International Workshop on Open Services and Tools for Document Analysis*.

Allegretti, P. (2003). Catalogo dei codici italiani, Cod. Bodmer 55, in *Corona Nova*, pp. 44–47.

Bobeth, G. (2013). *Antike Verse in mittelalterlicher Vertonung: Neumierungen in Vergil-, Statius-, Lucan-und Terenz-Handschriften* (Bärenreiter).

Chen, K., Seuret, M., Wei, H., Liwicki, M., Hennebert, J., and Ingold, R. (2015). Ground truth model, tool, and dataset for layout analysis of historical documents, in *SPIE/IS&T Electronic Imaging*, pp. 940204–940204.

Diem, M., Kleber, F., Fiel, S., Grüning, T., and Gatos, B. (2017). cBAD: ICDAR2017 Competition on Baseline Detection, in *Proceedings of the 14th International Conference on Document Analysis and Recognition*, pp. 1355–1360.

Fischer, A., Indermühle, E., Bunke, H., Viehhauser, G., and Stolz, M. (2010). Ground truth creation for handwriting recognition in historical documents, in *Proc. 9th Int. Workshop on Document Analysis Systems*, pp. 3–10.

Garz, A., Seuret, M., Simistira, F., Fischer, A., and Ingold, R. (2016). Creating ground truth for historical manuscripts with document graphs and scribbling interaction, in *2016 12th IAPR Workshop on Document Analysis Systems (DAS)* (IEEE), pp. 126–131.

Gatos, B., Stamatopoulos, N., Louloudis, G., Sfikas, G., Retsi nas, G., Papavassiliou, V., Simistira, F., and Katsouros, V. (2015). GRPOLY-DB: An old Greek Polytonic document image database, in *ICDAR, 2015 13th International Conference on*, pp. 646–650.

Grüning, T., Labahn, R., Diem, M., Kleber, F., and Fiel, S. (2017). READ-BAD: A new dataset and evaluation scheme for baseline detection in archival documents, *CoRR* **abs/1705.03311**, http://arxiv.org/abs/1705.03311.

Hoffmann, H. (2012). Schreibschulen und Buchmalerei, *Handschriften und Texte des 9.-11. Jahrhunderts. Hahnsche Buchhandlung.*

Hull, J. J. (1994). A database for handwritten text recognition research, *Pattern Analysis and Machine Intelligence, IEEE Transactions on* **16**, 5, pp. 550–554.

Marti, U.-V. and Bunke, H. (2001). Using a statistical language model to improve the performance of an hmm-based cursive handwriting recognition system, *International journal of Pattern Recognition and Artificial intelligence* **15**, 01, pp. 65–90.

Marti, U.-V. and Bunke, H. (2002). The IAM-database: an English sentence database for offline handwriting recognition, *IJDAR* **5**, 1, pp. 39–46.

Pletschacher, S. and Antonacopoulos, A. (2010). The page (page analysis and ground-truth elements) format framework, in *Pattern Recognition (ICPR), 2010 20th International Conference on* (IEEE), pp. 257–260.

Rath, T. M. and Manmatha, R. (2007). Word spotting for historical documents, *IJDAR* **9**, 2–4, pp. 139–152.

Scherrer, G. (1875). *Verzeichniss der Handschriften der Stiftsbibliothek von St. Gallen* (Buchhandlung des Waisenhauses).

Seuret, M., Ingold, R., and Liwicki, M. (2016). N-light-N: a highly-adaptable Java library for document analysis with convolutional auto-encoders, in *to appear in ICFHR*, pp. 459–464.

Suen, C. Y., Nadal, C., Legault, R., Mai, T. A., and Lam, L. (1992). Computer recognition of unconstrained handwritten numerals, *Proceedings of the IEEE* **80**, 7, pp. 1162–1180.

Valveny, E. (2014). Datasets and annotations for document analysis and recognition, in *Handbook of Document Image Processing and Recognition* (Springer), pp. 983–1009.

von Euw, A. (2008). *Die St. Galler Buchkunst vom 8. bis zum Ende des 11. Jahrhunderts* (Verlag am Klosterhof).

Würsch, M., Ingold, R., and Liwicki, M. (2016). SDK Reinvented: Document Image Analysis Methods as RESTful Web Services, in *International Workshop on Document Analysis Systems*, pp. 90–95.

Würsch, M., Simistira, F., Ingold, R., and Liwicki, M. (2017). Turning Document Image Analysis Methods into Web Services – An Example Using OCRopus, *International Workshop on Open Services and Tools for Document Analysis*.

Chapter 4

Layout Analysis in Handwritten Historical Documents

Mathias Seuret

DIVA Group, University of Fribourg, Switzerland
Pattern Recognition Lab, Friedrich-Alexander-Universität
Erlangen-Nürnberg, Germany
mathias.seuret@fau.de

4.1 Introduction

The analysis of the layout of handwritten documents is an early and crucial step in the typical processing pipeline of these documents. It aims at determining the location and type of content of pages. Two main types of content are usually considered: illustrations, also known as decorations, and text. The text can be of various nature, such as the main text and comments added by readers, while the range of illustrations goes from simple character decorations to high quality drawings.

Analyzing the layout of an ancient handwritten document is a challenging task, as there is very little constrains to how elements can be placed. The preservation quality of the support[1] also differs much from one document to the other. Some of them are so well preserved that they seem to be only years, and not centuries old, while some other suffer heavily from degradations.[2]

---

[1] The material on which the text is written, such as paper or parchment.

[2] A non-exhaustive list of frequent degradations is torn pages, mold, worm holes, abrasion, corrision of the ink, water stains, fingerprints, faded ink, bleed-through ink, and ink stains from the opposite page.

In this chapter, we first present what are the elements targeted by layout analysis methods and some of the challenges provided by the nature of these documents. Then, the typical processing steps of layout analysis methods are presented in a generic way, without providing very specific implementation details. After this, various layout analysis methods, including several ones developed during the HisDoc, Hisdoc 2.0, and HisDoc III projects, are detailed — with some details about the path which led us to the current state of the art. The chapter will be concluded by a brief discussion of some problems on which researchers might have to focus in the next years.

4.2   Segmentation in Regions of Interest

Most layout analysis methods for handwritten documents focus on text data, which means they aim at detecting where the text is in the considered documents.

A typical document contains what can be called the *main* text, that is the text which the author of the document intended to record. We can however already make some distinctions at this level, as the layout of the text is not composed only of locations containing text. Indeed, just as the book that you are holding in your hands, many documents are divided in paragraphs, parts, or titles. Thus, the task of determining if the text at a specific location is a title, a subtitle, or the text body, for example, is included in the layout analysis topic.

Additionally, while ancient texts are nowadays carefully preserved and protected in museum and archives (do not expect to touch them without special training), this was not always the case. For example, scholars who read books frequently took notes on them. These notes are called *glosses*. Extreme use of glosses can be seen in the Diva-HisDB, a dataset presented in [Simistira *et al.* (2016)]. There are two kind of them: marginal and interlinar glosses — their names indeed indicate where they are located. Distinguishing between the main text and the glosses is a layout analysis task as well.

A priori, one could expect that the distinction between these different classes of text (title, main text, glosses, ...) can be done with simple heuristics, as some content is typically larger or colored (titles) or in a different script (glosses). This is however underestimating the variability of conventions and styles which evolved over centuries. This can be illustrated by the following two examples. In many hebrew documents, titles are indicated by skipping one or several lines above them, as discussed in [Seuret *et al.* (2017)], thus there is no style distinction between titles and text body. Also, while it is frequently possible to notice that there are two or more different handwritings in a document, it is not always clear which one corresponds to the main text.[3] Also, some documents, such as marriage records, have their main text written by many scribes over very long periods of time, so the main text might have at least as much script variability as glosses.

Beside localizing the text and detecting which kind of content it corresponds to, it is frequently necessary to segment it to a finer granularity than a *text block*: text lines, words, and characters. Again, in the case of handwritten documents, this segmentation can be challenging. Ascenders and descenders[4] might touch each others, as shown in Fig. 4.1 or overlap. Some writing styles omit space between words,[5] thus word-level segmentation cannot be done without an understanding of the text. Also, in the case of cursive script, it can be considered as impossible to decide exactly where a character ends and the next one starts.

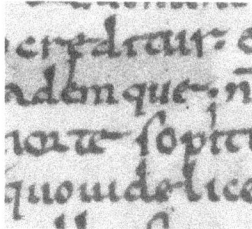

Fig. 4.1: Example of ascenders and descenders touching each others. Close-up from Bern, Burgerbibliothek, Cod. 120.I, f. 2r – Composite manuscript: Ado Viennensis: Chronicon; Aurelius Victor (Pseudo-): Epitome de Caesaribus; Abbo Floriacensis: De gestis Romanorum pontificum, lat. (https://www.e-codices.ch).

We can also note that drawings are frequent in medieval documents. They are used either to embelish the pages, or to act as initial letters for paragraphs or chapters, as shown in Fig. 4.2. The detection of the presence of these drawings — and their localization — is also a part of layout analysis.

---

[3]We could go further and assume that the script corresponding to glosses in a document might be almost identical to the one of the main text of another document!

[4]Descenders are the parts of characters which go below the base line (such as the vertical bar of p or q), and ascenders go above the usual character height (as b or d).

[5]Skipping spaces and punctuation symbols is called *scriptura continua*.

Fig. 4.2: Example of decorated initial letter. Close-up from St. Gallen, Stiftsbibliothek, Cod. Sang. 857, p. 43 – Die St. Galler Nibelungen-handschrift B mit Nibelungenlied und "Klage", "Parzival" und "Wille-halm" von Wolfram von Eschenbach und mit Strickers "Karl der Grosse" (https://www.e-codices.ch).

Thus, handwritten documents can be considered as extremely challenging to process. Nevertheless, due to their huge cultural value, they are definitively worth the effort, and the methods presented later in this chapter prove that while hard, the task is feasible.

4.3   Region Description

In the previous section, we saw some types of elements which are relevant to layout analysis tasks. The reader has probably noticed that how to describe areas of the document was omitted. This section focuses on this aspect.

In printed documents, text lines are more or less straight,[6] rectangular bounding boxes can accurately encompass text lines without containing as well parts of other text lines, such as ascenders or descenders.

This can also be the case for some very regular handwritten documents, as show in Fig. 4.3. In this image, it is easy to draw a rectangle around a text line without touching other text lines. However, the use of bounding boxes has frequently a negative impact on the accuracy of the segmentation, for example on scripts such as the one shown in Fig. 4.4. In this second image, we can see that because ascenders and descenders are very close (sometimes even touching each others), no rectangle can encompass a text line without intersecting other text lines.

---

[6]As the support, such as parchment or paper, can suffer from deformations, text lines are however seldom perfectly straight.

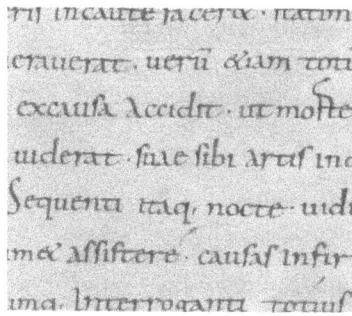

Fig. 4.3: As they are well spaced and horizontal, these text lines can be accurately encompassed by rectangles. St. Gallen, Stiftsbibliothek, Cod. Sang. 562, p. 86 – Vitae sancti Galli et Otmari (https://www.e-codices.ch/).

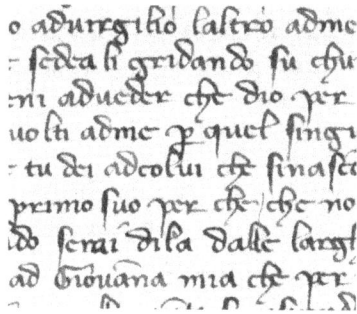

Fig. 4.4: Due to the proximity of ascenders and descenders, polygons are needed for localizing the text lines. Sample from the Diva-HisDB [Simistira *et al.* (2016)]. Cologny, Fondation Martin Bodmer, Cod. Bodmer 55, f. 99v – Dante, Inferno e Purgatorio (Codex Guarneri) (https://www.e-codices.ch/).

While polygons are quite versatile and can surround accurately text as well as drawings, text lines locations can also be approximated with base lines, i.e., lines which follow the bottom of the main part of characters, ignoring descenders.

The advantage of using base lines to localize text lines is that it is significantly easier to produce them manually than to draw accurate polygons. However, the polygonal representation of the text lines contain more information, and allows to easily compute base lines.

In the HisDoc project, we initially used rectilinear polygons, for example in [Baechler and Ingold (2010)], as the early methods were significantly inspired by modern printed documents analysis methods.[7] However, in the case of handwritten text with curvy letters, or text lines which are not straight, such polygons are not optimal and might require a large amount of vertices to approximate diagonals. For this reason, we later switched to unconstrained polygons.

Bounding boxes, polygons, and base lines provide two pieces of information: "what", and "where". It is also possible to indicate only the first one by labeling pixels with regard to the kind of content at their location. Compared to using polygons, this approach has both disadvantages and advantages. For example, if an ascender of a text line touches the line above, then by labeling the pixels of these lines as text, they will be merged as a single entity. However, labeling the pixels can be done by using well understood pattern recognition systems, as it will be shown in Section 4.5.1. Also, once labels are obtained for the pixels of a document image, it is possible to apply further processing steps in order to get polygons out of areas made out of a single class.

Before looking deeper into the layout analysis methods, let us first have, in the next section, an overlook of steps which are frequently parts of the methods.

4.4   Typical Processing Steps

In this section, we will go through some of the usual steps which can be used in layout analysis methods. They form some kind of building blocks which can be used by computer scientists to construct more complex methods or systems.

The choice of which processing steps to use depends both on the goal to reach, and on the specificities of the considered data.

4.4.1   *Binarization*

A binarization operation consists of modifying the values of the pixels of an image in such a way that they are either totally white, or totally black.

---

[7]Such polygons, which have only horizontal and vertical edges, can encompass accurately printed text which has long, vertical ascenders and descenders.

Ideally, it is desired for the binarization to separate the pixels of a document image in a semantical way. The typical goal of a binarization is to distinguish the ink, also called foreground, from the support, also called background. This is illustrated in Figs. 4.5 and 4.6.

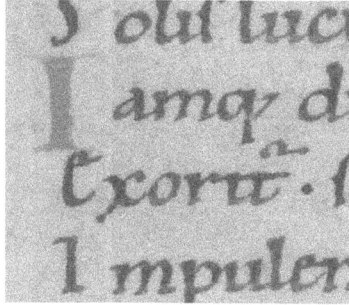

Fig. 4.5: Close-up of a document image. From the Diva-HisDB ([Simistira *et al.* (2016)]). St. Gallen, Stiftsbibliothek, Cod. Sang. 863, p. 11 – Pharsalia libri decem (https://www.e-codices.ch).

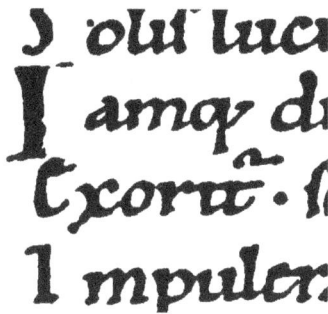

Fig. 4.6: Binarized version of Fig. 4.5. The lighter initial is well detected, excepted for its thinner parts. A stain, near the "o" of the first line, is also considered as foreground.

There are two main approaches for binarizing a document image.

First, a global threshold can be used. This means that all pixels which luminosity are below some threshold are considered as foreground, and the other ones as background.

Second, a threshold can be computed for each individual pixel. This has the advantage that if the luminosity and contrast of the document is not uniform, the binarization is still possible.

The most famous global thresholding method is presented in [Otsu (1979)]. Its principle is to find the threshold separating into two parts the histogram of the image such that the sum of their variances is minimal.

A widely-used local thresholding approach is presented in [Sauvola *et al.* (1997)]. For each pixel, a threshold t is computed using the mean value m and variance v of its neighborhood. The formula is as follows:

$$t = m \cdot \left(1 + k \cdot \left(\frac{v}{r} - 1\right)\right) \tag{4.1}$$

where r is, for normalization purpose, the dynamic range of the variance, and k an user-set parameter. Thus, Sauvola's method has two parameters, i.e., k and the size of the considered neighborhood.

It could be argued that machine learning methods can be used for binarization purpose, and would hence form a third binarization approach. However, they are extremely versatile and can do way more than separating the pixels of an image into two groups, so their usage is discussed in Section 4.4.4.

4.4.2   *Grouping Entities*

Grouping together several elements based on some properties they share is at the core of bottom-up approaches. In this subsection, we will go through some grouping or clustering-based methods which can be used for layout analysis.

Binarization methods have been presented in the previous subsection. As shown in Fig. 4.6, the foreground is composed of black pixels. Groups of pixels touching each others are called connected components, and have been widely used in document image analysis. Connected components are simple to extract, for example by the flood-fill algorithm.[8] The different connected components in the binary image shown in Fig. 4.6 are depicted with different gray levels in Fig. 4.7.

Higher-level elements than pixels can be grouped together. For example, a group of connected components can form a text line, and a group of text lines can be seen as a text area.

---

[8]Most drawing software have it for coloring whole areas in one click — the button usually looks like a bucket of paint.

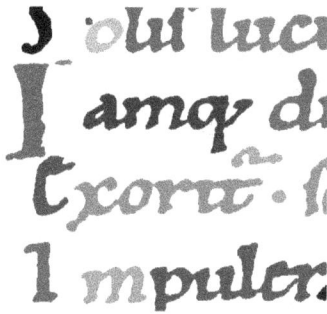

Fig. 4.7: The different connected components in this figure are shown by attributing them random luminosities. While the script is not cursive, letters which touch themselves get merged as a single connected component.

4.4.3 *Cutting*

Cutting is the opposite operation to grouping entities.

The most commonly used cutting operation is the segmentation of a text area in text lines. A widely-used approach is the use of seam-carving. In this method, the localization of the ink corresponding to the text is estimated, for example by binarization, and then cuts separating the text lines as well as possible are computed.

4.4.4 *Labeling Data*

Labeling is the task of attributing a label to an entity, i.e., to describe it. For example, once connected components have been extracted from a document image, they can be labeled as belonging to text, to decorations or being stains.

While this can be done with some simple conditional systems (for example, connected components larger than a threshold could be considered as belonging to decorations), the complexity of ancient manuscripts make such approaches difficult to implement. Also, due to the large variability of style, content, and preservation quality of documents, is likely that a system which performs well on a document will require some tuning by an expert to process another document.

Machine learning methods can be used to solve this issue. They usually work by being shown many examples of what is intended of them. Thus, if results on a new manuscript are less accurate than expected, instead of modifying the method itself, it might be sufficient that a human prepares new training examples with some pages of this manuscript to improve the "knowledge" of the method. Also, the more training data there is, the more likely it is that a machine learning method will be able to process a new manuscript without any adaptation.

4.5   Layout Analysis Methods

In this section, two kinds of layout analysis methods are presented. The first ones labels the pixels with regard to the type of content they have, as described in Section 4.4.4, but do not try to create groups. The second group of methods aim at segmenting the surface of the document in regions of interest, mostly text lines.

4.5.1   *Content Identification*

In the recent years, several pixel labeling methods have been developed by the Diva group.

In [Chen *et al.* (2014)], the pixels of document images are labeled by using a support vector machine ([Chang and Lin (2011)]) which takes as input feature vectors describing the pixels and their neighborhood. The feature vectors are hard-coded, i.e., an expert has to design features which can be helpful for the classification task. The eleven types of features include pixel coordinates, average color of neighborhoods of various sizes, laplacian of the three color channels, and many others, for a total of 111 values. A feature selection method ([Yu and Liu (2003)]) is then applied for determining which of these 111 values are useful for the classification task.

Tests on three different manuscripts led to a selection of different features, which implies that this method, although accurate, required work from an expert for being able to process a new manuscript.

This work has been improved in [Chen *et al.* (2015)] by replacing the hard-coded features by a machine learning approach: the use of autoencoders for automatic feature extraction. An autoencoder is a special neural network which is trained to encode data with a low dimensionality and then reconstruct the input with a good quality.

Autoencoders are used to produce features, as the decoding part is used only at training time. The usual assertion is that the encoding produced by

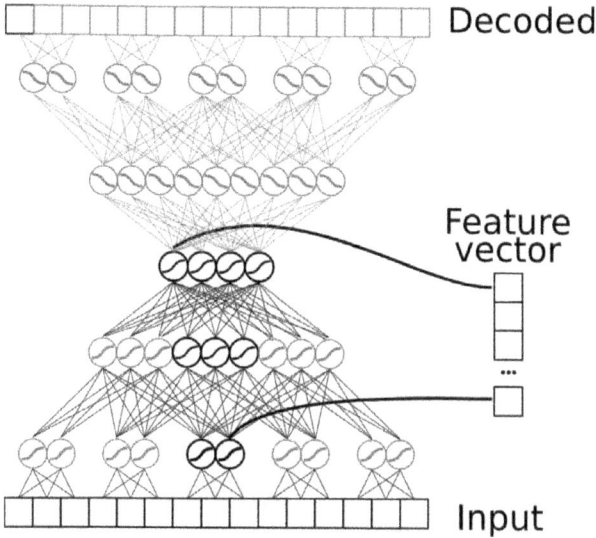

Fig. 4.8: Feature extraction from the center of each convolution of a convolutional autoencoder. The input data passes through the network, losing dimensionality at each layer until a bottleneck is reached, and then the dimensionality increases again, until the input is reconstructed. Typically, only the values at the bottleneck are used, however for layout analysis concatenating the central parts of each encoding layers performs significantly better.

the autoencoder can then be used by a classifier. In [Chen *et al.* (2015)], a stack of convolutional autoencoders is used to produce the feature vectors by concatenating the encodings of the center of each convolution, thus providing feature vectors for target pixels and their neighborhoods at different scales. This is illustrated in Fig. 4.8. While [Wei *et al.* (2015)] showed that the features produced by autoencoders have some redundancy, they still outperform hard-coded features with a much lower effort from the expert.

In [Simistira *et al.* (2016)], the autoencoder was turned into a convolutional neural network by removing its decoding part, and adding a classification layer on top of the last encoding layer. This led to a higher accuracy, while being a method which, once implemented, does not need labour from a machine learning expert to process new documents. Indeed, it is sufficient to present new training data to the network to adapt it for new manuscripts.

In 2017, several methods were proposed for a layout analysis competition using the Diva-HisDB ([Simistira *et al.* (2017)]). The proposed methods for the pixel labeling task were either based on convolutional neural networks, or fully-convolutional neural networks. The first type of neural network classifies the pixel at the center of its input patch, while the second one outputs results for all pixels at once.

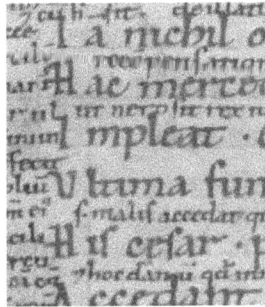

Fig. 4.9: Close-up of a document image. From the Diva-HisDB ([Simistira *et al.* (2016)]). St. Gallen, Stiftsbibliothek, Cod. Sang. 863, p. 5 – Pharsalia libri decem (https://www.e-codices.ch).

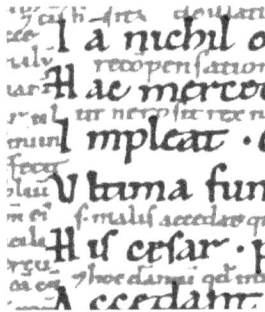

Fig. 4.10: Pixel labeling of Fig. 4.9 obtained with the method presented in [Pondenkandath *et al.* (2017)]. The dark pixels correspond to the main text, and the lighter ones to glosses.

While pixel labeling can be very useful, it does not directly produce groups of pixels, such as text lines. This will be the topic of the next subsection.

4.5.2   Text Line Segmentation

Text line segmentation is one of the most crucial task for the analysis of historical documents. Optical character recognition systems, such as Ocropus ([Breuel (2008)]) or Tesseract ([Smith (2007)]), require text lines as input, thus it is possible to recognize accurately the text only if the text lines have been accurately segmented.

Methods which perform well on printed documents might perform poorly on historical handwritten documents. For example, text lines can be accurately localized in printed documents by using projection profiles. They are the sum, or accumulation, of the foreground pixels present in each row of a document image. As it can be seen in Fig. 4.11, this simple method has problems to cope with handwritten documents, especially in the presence of glosses. For this reason, more advanced methods have been developed to segment the text lines of historical documents.

Fig. 4.11: Comparison of projection profiles on modern printed documents and ancient handwritten documents. In the case of printed content, it is simple to localize the text lines by looking at the projection profile. However, in the case of the handwritten document, the profile is very noisy and would be of little help for segmenting the text lines.

For example, [Garz *et al.* (2012)] propose to compute interest points (based on a method developed by [Lowe (2004)]), and use some heuristics for clustering these points such that the clusters correspond to text lines. This method has the advantage of not requiring to binarize the document — a step often difficult on ancient documents.

Another approach proposed by [Pastor-Pellicer *et al.* (2016)] is to base the segmentation on the detection by a neural network of the main body area of the text, which is defined as the location of the text without ascenders or descenders. For each text line, the contour of its main body area is computed to produce a polygon, and post-processing steps improve the polygon so that it encompasses ascenders and descenders.

Currently, the most successful line segmentation method for historical handwritten documents is seam carving ([Nicolaou and Gatos (2009); Fischer *et al.* (2010); Asi *et al.* (2011)]). It consists in computing cuts, or seams, between each text line of a text area. This implies that there are several requirements.

First, we need to know where where the seams have to start and end, so we need to have an idea of where text lines start and end. This can be done by applying projection profiles at the beginning and end of text areas. It tends to work correctly even if text lines are not straight, however very short text lines, such as the ones appearing frequently at the end of paragraphs, might be missed.

Second, for the seams to avoid as best the text, its position has to be known, or estimated, for example by binarizing the image.

And third, a function for estimating the cost of crossing a pixel with a seam has to be computed. It should have high values for text pixels, and lower values for background pixels.

The main steps of a seam carving applied to a sample image are shown in Fig. 4.12. The first image shows the example on which the method is applied. We can notice that as some descenders go lower than the top part of some ascenders, the text lines cannot be separated perfectly with the straight lines of rectangular bounding boxes.

The second image shows a binarized version of the input image. We can see that the binarization is not perfect, as some thin strokes are lost. However, as the task is not to recognize the text but rather to have an idea of where it is located, it is not an issue.

The third image of Fig. 4.12 shows the cost function attributed to the pixels. In this example, it is based on the distance to the closest foreground pixel

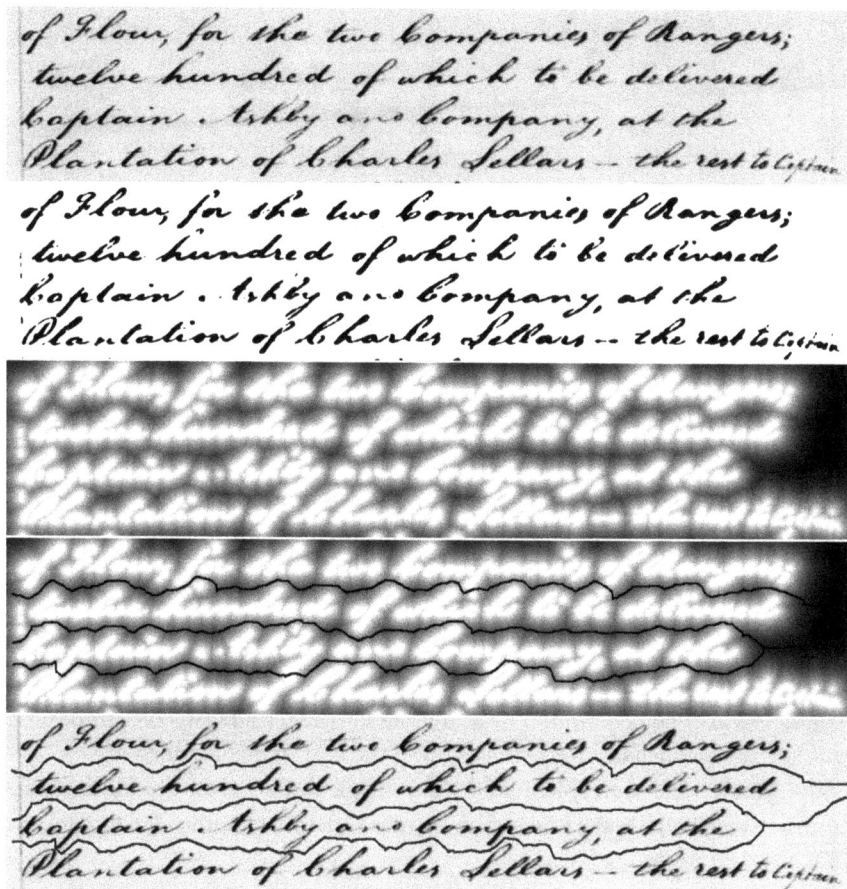

Fig. 4.12: Illustration of some of the seam carving steps: binarization, cost function, seams, and final result.

detected by the binarization. The more white a pixel is, the more expensive it is for a seam to cross it.

To compute the seams, the start and end location of text lines is estimated by making projection profiles, such as the ones shown in Fig. 4.11, at the beginning and end of the binary image. Candidates for beginning locations of seams are the pixels between two sequential starts of text lines. The same applies for the end locations of seams. A matching algorithm can be used to reject some of them if there is not an equal amount of locations detected on both sides of the text area.

Fig. 4.13: Example of a document image with a large amount of marginal and interlinear glosses. The text line segmentation illustrated in Fig. 4.12 would perform poorly on such data. From the Diva-HisDB ([Simistira *et al.* (2016)]). St. Gallen, Stiftsbibliothek, Cod. Sang. 863, p. 4 – Pharsalia libri decem (https://www.e-codices.ch).

The seams are then computed by searching for the path between their desired end locations which minimizes the sum of the cost of pixels which are crossed. Some restrictions are typically added — typical ones are forbidding seams to move backward, or to cross the median line of text lines ([Seuret *et al.* (2017)]).

This rather simple seam carving approach can deal well with clean text such as the one shown in Fig. 4.12, but in the case of an image which has a large amount of glosses, such as the one shown in Fig. 4.13, the segmentation of the main text requires more than a simple seam carving approach.

This is where labeling methods presented in Section 4.5.1 can help. As the main text of the document is composed of well spaced and straight lines, it is clear that it would actually be rather easy to segment if there were no glosses. Thus, if we can distinguish it from the glosses, then we can apply the seam carving only on the main text and the segmentation becomes easy.

The labeling method presented in [Pondenkandath *et al.* (2017)] is very accurate, as it can be seen in Fig. 4.14, and can be exploited by the seam carving method. Thus, instead of using a binarization for deciding which

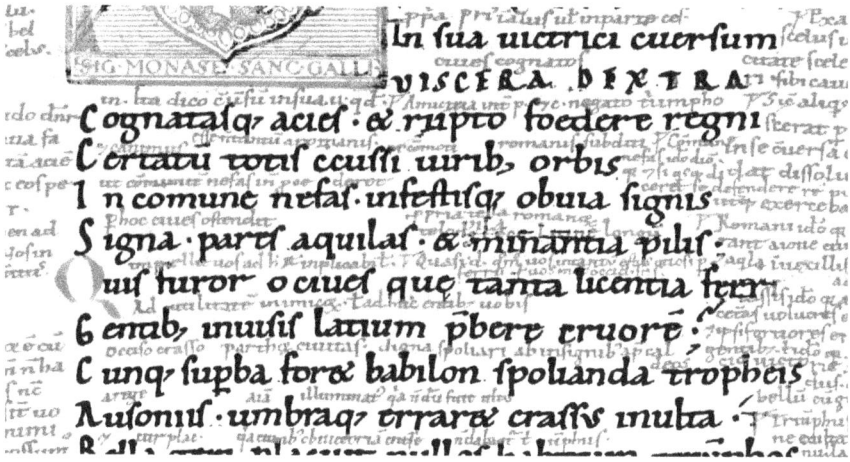

Fig. 4.14: Pixel labeling of the sample of document image shown in Fig. 4.13, produced by the method presented in [Pondenkandath *et al.* (2017)]. Pixels labeled as belonging to the main text are in black, and the rest of the image in lighter gray. The gray content is entirely erased before applying a line segmentation method.

pixels belong to the main text, we can select the pixels labeled as belonging to it.

It is however clear from the figure that if the text lines are simply segmented by seam carving, then they will still contain the glosses. Thus, if we give them to an OCR system, it have recognition problems, as the line images will have some extra-content.

To solve this issue, we can create tight polygons around the main text, thus indicating clearly where it lies. It can be done in a manner inspired by [Garz *et al.* (2016)]. The following processing steps are applied to each text line obtained by seam carving individually. First, the contour points of all main text connected components are listed. Contour points are pixels which are on the border of a component. Then, a graph is built out of them with a Delaunay triangulation ([Delaunay (1934)]), thus connecting all parts of the text line together. Then, Kruskal's minimum spanning tree method ([Kruskal (1956)]) is applied to keep only the minimum amount of edges between connected components. And finally, the polygonalization algorithm available on the DIVAServices[9] is used to create a tight polygon

---

[9] http://divaservices.unifr.ch

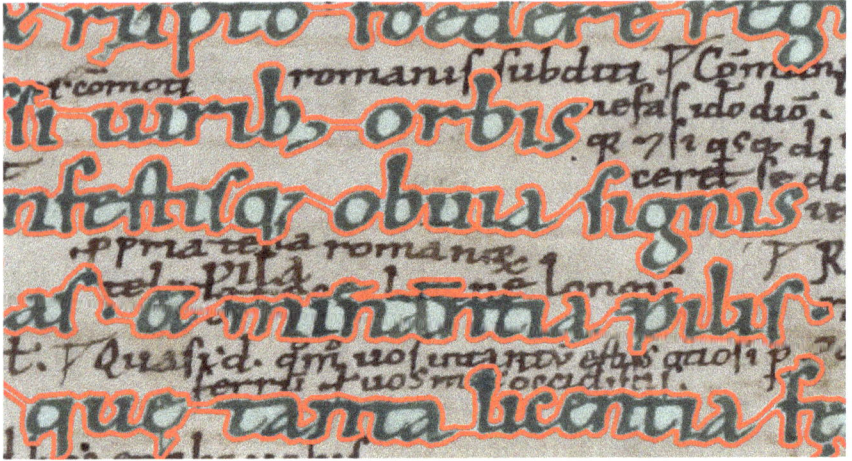

Fig. 4.15: Close-up of tight polygons produced after pixel labeling and seam carving. Note that most of the ink from interlinear glosses is outside of the polygons.

encompassing both the remaining edges and the connected components. The result obtained with this method is illustrated in Fig. 4.15.

4.6 Open Problems

Layout analysis methods can now be successful on difficult historical document images thanks the use of efficient machine learning methods, as shown by results obtained on the Diva-HisDB, a dataset composed of documents with very challenging layouts ([Simistira *et al.* (2017)]).

However, it is not yet solved, as there are still some open issues. Some of them are discussed in the following subsections.

4.6.1 *Semantical Analysis of the Layout*

Current layout analysis methods are based on physical properties of the content: where it is located, and how it looks like. The meaning of the layout is however ignored by the analysis methods. For example, while some methods can detect with a high accuracy if a part of the text has been decorated or highlighted, they do not explain why it is so — it could be because of its importance, or only for esthetical reasons.

The location of the content can also be meaningful. Glosses are not located at random places, but close to the part of the text they refer to. This relationship between glosses and other parts of the content of the document is also a part of the layout. Yet it is, to the authors' best knowledge, not investigated by computer scientists. This might be due to the complexity of the task, as this might require a deep understanding of the document, or to the lack of datasets providing this kind of information.

We can also note that glosses can be of several kinds. For example, they can be corrections of the main text of the document, or additional information or thoughts added by a reader. Thus, classifying text with a higher granularity than "main text or glosses" remains a layout analysis problem to solve.

4.6.2 *Reading Order*

The text of a document is a sequence of paragraphs, lines, and words. It is also a part of layout analysis to determine in which sequence they are supposed to be read. However, this particular problem might have no solution. Indeed, the reading order might depend on the person who reads the text. For example, one scholar could read the main text and then read the glosses, and another scholar could read the glosses at the time they read the main text. Both approaches are perfectly valid, yet they correspond to different sequences.

This implies that to provide a reading order which corresponds to the needs of the user, layout analysis methods would have to learn not only from documents, but also from the preferences of specific users.

4.6.3 *Rare Occurrences*

Layout analysis methods are based on training, validation, and test data. This means that developers use the training data to develop methods and teach machine learning system, use the validation data to compare several variants of the methods and select the best ones, and, finally, use the test data only once to know which accuracy can be expected on unseen data.

This however means that layout analysis methods will deal well only with the kind of layouts and document content used during their development. Rare occurrences are less likely to be present in this data, and therefore are more likely to lead to errors during document image analysis.

Such mistakes can be seen from two points of view. First, as they correspond to elements which occur infrequently, they have a small impact on the overall accuracy, so they can be ignored. Second, as these elements occur infrequently, they might be of high interest for scholars and should therefore not be ignored but detected and investigated.

Fortunately, thanks to the huge efforts made by libraries and archives to digitize their documents, the amount of data available to computer scientists is growing quickly. Thus, we can assume that as time passes, this issue will become occur more rarely.

References

Asi, A., Saabni, R., and El-Sana, J. (2011). Text line segmentation for gray scale historical document images, in *Proceedings of the 2011 workshop on historical document imaging and processing* (ACM), pp. 120–126.

Baechler, M. and Ingold, R. (2010). Medieval Manuscript Layout Model, in *Proceedings of the 10th ACM symposium on Document engineering* (ACM), pp. 275–278.

Breuel, T. M. (2008). The ocropus open source ocr system, in *Electronic Imaging 2008*, pp. 68150F–68150F.

Chang, C.-C. and Lin, C.-J. (2011). LIBSVM: A Library for Support Vector Machines, *ACM transactions on intelligent systems and technology (TIST)* **2**, 3, p. 27.

Chen, K., Seuret, M., Liwicki, M., Hennebert, J., and Ingold, R. (2015). Page segmentation of historical document images with convolutional autoencoders, in *ICDAR, 2015 13th International Conference on*, pp. 1011–1015.

Chen, K., Wei, H., Liwicki, M., Hennebert, J., and Ingold, R. (2014). Robust Text Line Segmentation for Historical Manuscript Images Using Color and Texture, in *2014 22nd International Conference on Pattern Recognition* (IEEE), pp. 2978–2983.

Delaunay, B. (1934). Sur la sphere vide, *Izv. Akad. Nauk SSSR, Otdelenie Matematicheskii i Estestvennyka Nauk* **7**, 793–800, pp. 1–2.

Fischer, A., Indermühle, E., Bunke, H., Viehhauser, G., and Stolz, M. (2010). Ground truth creation for handwriting recognition in historical documents, in *Proc. 9th Int. Workshop on Document Analysis Systems*, pp. 3–10.

Garz, A., Fischer, A., Sablatnig, R., and Bunke, H. (2012). Binarization-free Text Line Segmentation for Historical Documents Based on Interest Point Clustering, in *2012 10th IAPR International Workshop on Document Analysis Systems* (IEEE), pp. 95–99.

Garz, A., Seuret, M., Simistira, F., Fischer, A., and Ingold, R. (2016). Creating ground truth for historical manuscripts with document graphs and scribbling interaction, in *2016 12th IAPR Workshop on Document Analysis Systems (DAS)* (IEEE), pp. 126–131.

Kruskal, J. B. (1956). On the shortest spanning subtree of a graph and the traveling salesman problem, *Proceedings of the American Mathematical society* **7**, 1, pp. 48–50.

Lowe, D. G. (2004). Distinctive image features from scale-invariant keypoints, *International journal of computer vision* **60**, 2, pp. 91–110.

Nicolaou, A. and Gatos, B. (2009). Handwritten text line segmentation by shredding text into its lines, in *2009 10th International Conference on Document Analysis and Recognition* (IEEE), pp. 626–630.

Otsu, N. (1979). A Threshold Selection Method from Gray-level Histograms, *IEEE transactions on systems, man, and cybernetics* **9**, 1, pp. 62–66.

Pastor-Pellicer, J., Afzal, M. Z., Liwicki, M., and Castro-Bleda, M. J. (2016). Complete system for text line extraction using convolutional neural networks and watershed transform, in *2016 12th IAPR Workshop on Document Analysis Systems (DAS)* (IEEE), pp. 30–35.

Pondenkandath, V., Seuret, M., Ingold, R., Afzal, M. Z., and Liwicki, M. (2017). Exploiting State-of-the-art Deep Learning Methods for Document Image Analysis, in *2017 14th IAPR International Conference on Document Analysis and Recognition (ICDAR)*, Vol. 5 (IEEE), pp. 30–35.

Sauvola, J., Seppanen, T., Haapakoski, S., and Pietikainen, M. (1997). Adaptive Document Binarization, in *Proceedings of the Fourth International Conference on Document Analysis and Recognition*, Vol. 1 (IEEE), pp. 147–152.

Seuret, M., Ben Ezra, D. S., and Liwicki, M. (2017). Robust Heartbeat-Based Line Segmentation Methods for Regular Texts and Paratextual Elements, in *Proceedings of the 4th International Workshop on Historical Document Imaging and Processing* (ACM), pp. 71–76.

Simistira, F., Bouillon, M., Seuret, M., Würsch, M., Alberti, M., Ingold, R., and Liwicki, M. (2017). ICDAR2017 Competition on Layout Analysis for Challenging Medieval Manuscripts, in *2017 14th IAPR International Conference on Document Analysis and Recognition (ICDAR)*, Vol. 1 (IEEE), pp. 1361–1370.

Simistira, F., Seuret, M., Eichenberger, N., Garz, A., Liwicki, M., and Ingold, R. (2016). Diva-hisdb: A precisely annotated large dataset of challenging medieval manuscripts, in *Frontiers in Handwriting Recognition (ICFHR), 2016 15th International Conference on* (IEEE), pp. 471–476.

Smith, R. (2007). An Overview of the Tesseract OCR Engine, in *Ninth International Conference on Document Analysis and Recognition (ICDAR 2007)*, Vol. 2 (IEEE), pp. 629–633.

Wei, H., Seuret, M., Chen, K., Fischer, A., Liwicki, M., and Ingold, R. (2015). Selecting Autoencoder Features for Layout Analysis of Historical Documents, in *Proceedings of the 3rd International Workshop on Historical Document Imaging and Processing* (ACM), pp. 55–62.

Yu, L. and Liu, H. (2003). Feature Selection for High-Dimensional Data: A Fast Correlation-based Filter Solution, in *Proceedings of the 20th international conference on machine learning (ICML-03)*, pp. 856–863.

Chapter 5

Automatic Handwriting Recognition in Historical Documents

Andreas Fischer

DIVA Group, University of Fribourg, Switzerland
iCoSys Institute, University of Applied Sciences and Arts
Western Switzerland
andreas.fischer@unifr.ch

5.1 Introduction

Automated reading of handwriting is an intriguing and largely unsolved problem in computer science [Lorette (1999)]. Despite decades of continuous progress, the goal to match or even surpass the astounding capabilities of humans to read handwritten text is still far from being reached [Bunke and Varga (2007)]. One of the main reasons is that automatic systems still lack semantic understanding that is often needed to decipher difficult cases, such as handwritten notes taken years ago with crossed out text and abbreviated words. This is especially true for ancient manuscripts, where the transcription of a phrase may only be found through expert knowledge in paleography, linguistics, and history.

Standard recognition techniques for optical character recognition (OCR) that are based on character segmentation, followed by character recognition, typically fail in the case of handwriting. When facing variable character shapes and touching characters, recognition is needed to perform segmentation and, *vice versa*, segmentation is needed to perform recognition. This conundrum, also known as Sayre's paradox [Sayre (1973)], requires special recognition techniques that perform segmentation and recognition at the same time.

A well-established approach to handwriting recognition is based on Hidden Markov Models (HMM) [Ploetz and Fink (2009)], inspired by their success for modeling sequences in speech recognition [Rabiner (1989)]. In the past decade, recurrent neural networks have also been applied with great success to the task of handwriting recognition, especially when using long short-term memory cells (LSTM) [Graves *et al.* (2009)]. Both HMM and LSTM are able to perform segmentation-free recognition, i.e. they do not require annotated start and end positions of characters and words within text line images. Instead, it is sufficient to know the transcription of the text lines, which greatly reduces the effort for human annotators when preparing the training data. An example is illustrated in Figure 5.1.

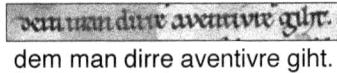

dem man dirre aventivre giht.

Fig. 5.1: Learning sample for handwriting recognition.

Besides the training of appearance models, HMM as well as LSTM allow to integrate language models during recognition [Marti and Bunke (2001); Zamora-Martínez *et al.* (2014)], which are trained on electronic text corpora and guide the recognition towards the most plausible recognition alternative in the underlying language.

In the HisDoc project, we have adopted the strategy to work with text line images and character models. For the layout analysis module (see Chapter 4), extracting text line images is a feasible goal since they can often be found with high accuracy based on their regular structure without recognizing individual characters or words. For the text recognition module, modeling characters has several advantages when compared with modeling words. Most importantly, word models would require human annotators to provide several learning samples for each word class. Character models are shared across different words and can be combined for modeling any word, even if it is not listed in a dictionary. From the beginning of the project, both HMM and LSTM have been investigated for character modeling in historical manuscripts [Fischer *et al.* (2009)].

In the following, we present the HisDoc handwriting recognition system in more detail. Section 5.2 describes image preprocessing and feature extraction, Section 5.3 elaborates character modeling with HMM and LSTM, Section 5.4 presents experimental results for automatic transcription, and Section 5.5

describes several extensions that have been proposed during the HisDoc project. Concluding remarks are provided in Section 5.6.

5.2 Image Preprocessing and Feature Extraction

Handwriting may differ greatly in style, size, and orientation, even when focusing on the main text of a single historical manuscript. Also, the page background can change significantly from one page to another. Image preprocessing aims to remove some of these variations to support handwriting recognition. However, if the preprocessing fails, unwanted distortions may be introduced that render recognition more difficult. Hence, a balance has to be found how much preprocessing, if any, should be applied to the original text line images.

In the HisDoc system, we first perform a binarization in order to separate the ink foreground from the page background. The binarization method consists of a local edge enhancement with a Difference of Gaussians filter, followed by a global threshold. Text lines are then extracted from the binarized page image according to their enclosing polygons. Afterwards, a series of transformations are applied to the text line images as suggested in [Marti and Bunke (2001)]. First, a rotation is applied to correct the skew, i.e. the inclination of the text line. It is estimated using a linear regression on the lower contour. Second, a shearing operation is applied to remove the slant, i.e. the inclination of the letters. It is estimated on long vertical segments of the handwriting. Third, vertical scaling is applied to obtain three writing regions of equal height, i.e. the descenders, the lowercase letters, and the ascenders. Here, the height of the lowercase letters is estimated using a linear regression on the upper contour. Finally, horizontal scaling is used to standardize the width of the characters. To that end, the number of black-white transitions on the middle line from left to right is normalized. Figure 5.2 provides examples for the three datasets of the IAM-HistDB (see Chapter 2), highlighting the baseline and the height of the lowercase letters with dashed lines.

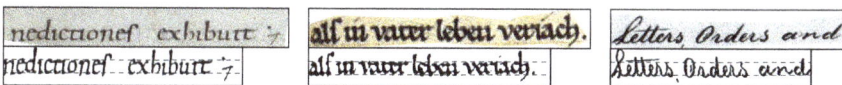

Fig. 5.2: Text line image normalization.

After image preprocessing, a sliding window is moved in reading direction from left to right over the normalized text line image as illustrated in Figure 5.3. The aim of this sliding window approach is to segment the handwriting into smaller parts that can then be connected to characters and words during recognition. Each window is described with n real-valued features, leading to a representation of the text line with a feature vector sequence

$$x = x_1, \ldots, x_N, \quad x_i \in \mathbb{R}^n. \tag{5.1}$$

Fig. 5.3: Feature extraction with sliding window.

Feature extraction can help to focus the recognition system on a few important properties of the handwriting, thus reducing the complexity of the character models. However, it can also lead to the loss of important information present in the original image. Similar to image preprocessing, a balance has to be found how much data reduction, if any, should be applied.

In the HisDoc system, we have mainly used the nine geometric features proposed in [Marti and Bunke (2001)]. They are based on a narrow sliding window with a size of one image column. Three global features include the fraction of black pixels, the center of gravity, and the second order moment. Six local features include the position of the upper and lower contours, the gradient of the contours, the fraction of black pixels between the contours, and the number of black-white transitions.

5.3 Character Modeling

When pursuing the sliding window approach, handwriting recognition can be stated as a sequence-to-sequence problem. The goal is to extract a character sequence $c_1, \ldots, c_M$ from the feature vector sequence $x_1, \ldots, x_N$ where the number of characters is less than or equal to the number of feature vectors ($M \leq N$).

We have investigated two types of machine learning models for this task, which are described briefly in the following. HMM are generative models that aim to estimate the probability density function of the features in order to deduce the most probable character sequence. LSTM are discriminative models that aim to directly estimate the posterior probabilities of the characters for each feature vector. Both models rely on efficient dynamic programming algorithms for aligning the character sequence with the feature vector sequence during training and recognition.

5.3.1 HMM Character Models

For HMM-based recognition, character models with linear topology are considered as illustrated in Figure 5.4. The different states represent the beginning, middle, and end parts of the character along the feature vector sequence. The model starts in the first state (initial probability $\pi_1 = 1.0$), where it either stays with probability a_{11} or changes to the second state with probability a_{12} (transition probabilities $a_{11} + a_{12} = 1.0$). Similarly, the model either rests in a state or changes to the next one until the final state is reached. At each state s_i, the probability density function of the n real-valued features is modeled with $p(x|s_i)$, $x \in \mathbb{R}^n$. For handwriting, the character shapes and the connection between two characters can be highly variable, leading to complex probability density functions. We model them with a mixture of Gaussians, using diagonal covariance matrices in order to reduce the number of trainable model parameters.

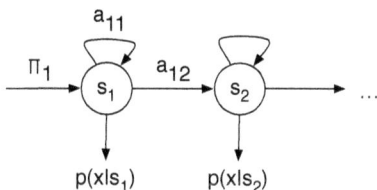

Fig. 5.4: HMM character model with linear topology.

During training, the HMM character models are concatenated according to the text line transcription. Their model parameters are optimized with the Baum-Welch algorithm [Rabiner (1989)], which uses dynamic programming to take all possible state transitions into account. During recognition, as illustrated in Figure 5.5, HMM character models are concatenated to words from a dictionary and the text line is interpreted as a sequence of words, which are separated by the whitespace character "sp". The most likely sequence of state transitions is found with the Viterbi algorithm [Rabiner

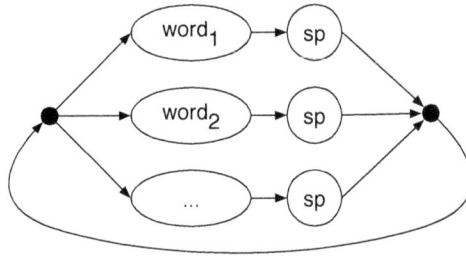

Fig. 5.5: Text line recognition model.

(1989)], which also uses dynamic programming to efficiently explore all possible state transitions.

Although the use of a word dictionary makes it impossible for the system to recognize out-of-vocabulary words, it is considered a best practice for handwriting recognition. Taking into account a relatively low character recognition accuracy when compared with printed text, using a dictionary allows to recover from character recognition errors and ensures that only valid words are transcribed. Furthermore, it allows to integrate language models at word level, which estimate the *a priori* probability of word sequences. In the HisDoc system, we rely on statistical n-gram language models with Kneser-Ney smoothing in order to account for unseen word combinations [Kneser and Ney (1995)].

Formally, following Bayes' rule, the HMM-based approach finds the best word sequence w^* with respect to

$$w^* = \arg \max_{w \in \mathcal{W}} p(w|x) = \arg \max_{w \in \mathcal{W}} p(x|w)p(w) \qquad (5.2)$$

where $\mathcal{W}$ is the set of all valid word sequences. The posterior probability $p(w|x)$ is maximized indirectly by means of the HMM likelihood $p(x|w)$ and the language model prior $p(w)$. In practice, likelihood and prior are balanced with a grammar scale factor, and a word insertion penalty is used to control the number of recognized words [Marti and Bunke (2001)].

5.3.2   *LSTM Character Models*

For LSTM-based recognition, we consider a two-state character model suggested in the context of connectionist temporal classification (CTC) [Graves *et al.* (2009)]. The model is either in the character state "c" or in the no-character state "ϵ". In both states, the output neuron of a recurrent

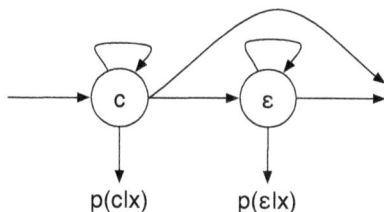

Fig. 5.6: LSTM character model.

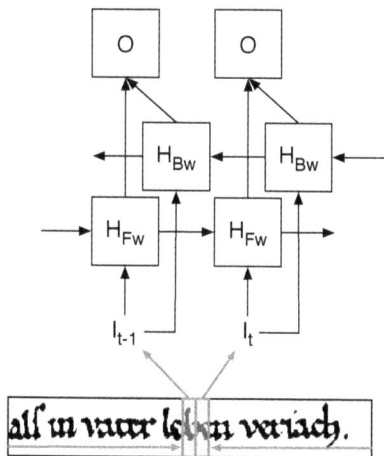

Fig. 5.7: Bidirectional LSTM network.

neural network estimates directly the state posteriors $p(c|x)$ and $p(\epsilon|x)$, respectively, for the feature vector $x \in \mathbb{R}^n$. The model is allowed to switch directly from one character to the next, or to a no-character state in between.

Figure 5.7 illustrates the bidirectional, recurrent neural network that is used in the HisDoc system. At each position of the sliding window, the feature vector is provided as input to two hidden layers of the neural network, one for the forward direction and one for the backward direction. The hidden layers also receive input from the previous time step (forward direction) and the next time step (backward direction), respectively. Both hidden layers are connected to the same output layer, which contains one output neuron per character, plus an additional neuron for the no-character state.

Instead of standard perceptrons, long short-term memory cells (LSTM) [Hochreiter and Schmidhuber (1997)] are used in the recurrent hidden layers. Overcoming the vanishing gradient problem, they are able to keep information over a relatively large number of time steps, controlling the flow of information with special input, output, and forget gates. The gates are perceptrons that are either open or closed according to their activation function, i.e. the network is able to learn when to accept new input, when to produce an output, and when to reset the memory.

Similar to HMM, the LSTM character models are concatenated according to the text line transcription during training. The loss function is computed at each time step with the CTC [Alex Graves *et al.* (2006)] algorithm, which uses dynamic programming to consider all possible state transitions. The weights of the neural network are then optimized by means of backpropagation through time.

Recognition is also performed similar to HMM. The characters are concatenated to words of a dictionary, followed by space (see Figure 5.5), and the optimal sequence of words is found by means of dynamic programming based on their posterior probabilities. In addition to the LSTM-based appearance models, language model probabilities can be taken into account as well. For more details on the bidirectional LSTM architecture, we refer the reader to [Graves *et al.* (2009); Fischer *et al.* (2009)].

5.4   Automatic Transcription

The HisDoc handwriting recognition systems, both HMM-based and LSTM-based, have been experimentally evaluated on the three datasets of the IAM-HistDB (see Chapter 2), namely the Saint Gall, Parzival, and George Washington datasets.

Table 5.1 summarizes the experimental setup for each of the datasets. Several hundred text lines are used for training the machine learning systems, validating their meta-parameters, and testing their final performance. The number of character models that have to be trained, including special characters, varies from 49 (Saint Gall) to 93 (Parzival). Because it is difficult to compare recognition systems with different out-of-vocabulary conditions, we have adopted a common evaluation protocol with closed vocabulary, i.e. all words from the entire dataset are included in the recognition dictionary.

Two recognition tasks are considered: single word recognition and text line recognition. The former is based on a human-corrected segmentation of the text lines into isolated words. Each word of the dictionary is assumed

Table 5.1: Datasets used for evaluating automatic transcription. Number of text lines in the training, validation, and test sets, number of characters in the alphabet, and number distinct words in the dictionary.

Dataset	Text Lines			Alphabet	Dictionary
	Train	Valid	Test		
Saint Gall	468	235	707	49	5762
Parzival	2237	912	1328	93	4934
George Washington	325	168	163	82	1471

to have the same *a priori* probability to be present in the isolated word image. The latter takes complete text lines into account and performs the recognition with the help of a word bigram language model. The language model is trained and optimized on the transcriptions of the training and validation sets. It predicts the probability of the next word based on its immediate predecessor during recognition.

The implementation of the HisDoc system is based on the HTK toolkit[1] for HMM-based recognition and on an early version of the RNNLIB library[2] for LSTM-based recognition. Language models are based on the SRILM toolkit[3] in both cases. For text line recognition with LSTM character models and word bigram language models, we have implemented our own decoder based on beam search and token passing [Fischer (2012)], which is capable to efficiently cope with very large dictionaries containing hundreds of thousands of words.

Several meta-parameters of the machine learning systems are optimized with respect to the recognition accuracy achieved on the validation set. For HMM-based recognition, parameters include the number of states and the number of Gaussian mixtures for the character models, as well as the grammar scale factor and the word insertion penalty for the language model integration. For LSTM-based recognition, most parameters are fixed with respect to suggestions in [Graves *et al.* (2009)] and some preliminary experiments, including a learning rate of 10^{-4}, a momentum of 0.9, and 100 LSTM cells both in the forward and backward hidden layers. Furthermore, the language

---

[1] http://htk.eng.cam.ac.uk
[2] http://sourceforge.net/projects/rnnl/
[3] http://www.speech.sri.com/projects/srilm/

model integration requires no parameter optimization, i.e. a grammar scale factor of 1 and a word insertion penalty of 0 are used. The validation set is only used for selecting the best out of ten random initialized networks, which is then evaluated on the test set.

Table 5.2 presents the word recognition accuracy achieved for automatic transcription on the independent test set. In the case of single word recognition it corresponds directly with the percentage of correctly recognized words. In the case of text line recognition it is calculated as

$$Acc = \frac{N - S - D - I}{N} \tag{5.3}$$

with respect to the total number of words N in the ground truth transcription, the number of word substitution errors S, word deletion errors D, and word insertion errors I. The different types of errors are identified using the string edit distance, also known as Levenshtein distance, between the output of the recognition system and the ground truth transcription.

Table 5.2: Word recognition accuracy in percentage for automatic transcription of single word images and text line images, respectively.

Dataset	System	Single words	Text lines
Saint Gall	HMM	93.6	89.4
	LSTM	96.0	93.8
Parzival	HMM	85.9	84.5
	LSTM	91.1	93.3
George Washington	HMM	69.5	75.9
	LSTM	80.3	81.9

Overall, the HisDoc system achieves promising word accuracies over 80% on the George Washington dataset and over 90% on the Saint Gall and Parzival datasets. In our experiments, LSTM-based handwriting recognition systematically outperformed HHM-based recognition in all cases when using the same nine geometric features (see Section 5.2), highlighting the great potential of LSTM memory cells for modeling and recognizing complex sequential data.

When comparing single word recognition with text line recognition, we can observe that they achieve similar accuracies. This encourages the recognition at text line level, as they are often easier to extract from the page image than individual words.

The lower performance on the George Washington dataset can be explained by the fact that only 325 text lines are available for training a total amount of 82 character models. Furthermore, the George Washington dataset contains cursive handwriting with complex connections between the characters. More transcribed text line images for training are expected to further improve the results.

Note that the recognition accuracies reported in Table 5.2 should be interpreted as upper bounds. In a real-world scenario, any error during the text line extraction step (see Chapter 6) and any out-of-vocabulary word that is not present in the dictionary may lead to additional errors in the automatic transcription.

5.5 Extensions

One of the main constraints of automatic transcription based on machine learning is the relatively large number of training samples that human annotators have to provide. During the HisDoc project, we have developed two extensions of the handwriting recognition systems that specifically target this constraint, namely keyword spotting and transcription alignment.

Keyword spotting has been proposed early on in the literature [Manmatha *et al.* (1996)] as a means to identify specific search terms in handwritten historical documents, rather than performing a full transcription. In the query-by-example approach, only a single example image of the keyword is needed to retrieve similar images from a document collection. In the query-by-string approach, the user enters a search term with the keyboard and a weakly trained model is used for retrieval. We have contributed to the latter approach by introducing an HMM-based [Fischer *et al.* (2010, 2012)] and an LSTM-based [Frinken *et al.* (2012)] keyword spotting system that operate at the sub-word level, i.e. they are based on trained character models similar to automatic transcription. When compared with keyword spotting approaches at the word level [Rodriguez and Perronnin (2009)], they have the advantage that character models can be trained across different words and thus it is not necessary to collect examples of the search term beforehand. For more details on keyword spotting, we refer to Chapter 6.

Transcription alignment aims to match existing transcriptions with their corresponding images, which is not only useful for the end user when searching and browsing historical documents but also for automatically generating learning samples for handwriting recognition systems. Although many text editions of historical manuscripts have been made available by researchers in the humanities, most of them are not aligned at the text line level, i.e. it is not known where a specific text line is located in the image. In the case of diplomatic transcriptions, the characters in the transcription perfectly match the characters visible in the image and the problem of transcription alignment is reduced to finding the start and end positions of the individual words [Kornfield *et al.* (2004)]. However, the transcription can also deviate from the image, for example when abbreviations are written out in full or when the order of the words is changed for better readability. During the HisDoc project, we have addressed this problem with alignment systems based on character models and demonstrated their effectiveness even when the character models are only weakly trained [Fischer *et al.* (2011a,b)].

5.6   Conclusions

Although the accuracies achieved for handwritten text recognition in historical documents are still far from being perfect, the results obtained with the HisDoc system on the IAM-HistDB are promising. When recognizing text line images with LSTM character models, a training set of hundreds of transcribed text lines, a closed vocabulary, and word bigram language models estimated on the manuscript itself, we report a word accuracy of 93.8% on the Saint Gall dataset, 93.3% on the Parzival dataset, and 81.9% on the George Washington dataset.

The reported results should be interpreted as an upper bound of the performance that can be expected in practice, as they do not take errors into account stemming from text line extraction and out-of-vocabulary words. However, there are also possibilities to increase the performance when taking external resources into account, such as character models that are trained on similar handwritings and language models that are estimated on large electronic text corpora written in the language of the manuscript at hand.

Technically, handwriting recognition has further evolved in the past decade. For Latin manuscripts, working at text line level and performing the recognition with LSTM character models has remained the state of the art [Puigcerver (2017)]. One of the major improvements we have observed is related to image preprocessing and feature extraction (see Section 5.2). The current trend is to replace handcrafted features with features that are learned by deep convolutional neural networks from the data [Toledo *et al.* (2017)], leading to significant improvements of the overall recognition accuracy.

Considering the remaining errors, the results of automatic transcription are not directly usable for generating digital editions of historical documents. However, they offer the possibility to index the documents and make them searchable by content, allowing paleographers, historians, linguists, as well as other experts and the general public alike, to explore large collections of handwritten historical documents via text search.

References

Alex Graves, Santiago Fernández, Faustino Gomez, and Jürgen Schmidhuber (2006). Connectionist temporal classification: Labelling unsegmented sequential data with recurrent neural networks, in *23rd Int. Conf. on Machine Learning*, pp. 369–376.

Bunke, H. and Varga, T. (2007). Off-line Roman cursive handwriting recognition, in B. Chaudhuri (ed.), *Digital Document Processing* (Springer), pp. 165–173.

Fischer, A. (2012). *Handwriting Recognition in Historical Documents*, Ph.D. thesis, University of Bern, Switzerland.

Fischer, A., Frinken, V., Fornés, A., and Bunke, H. (2011a). Transcription alignment of latin manuscripts using hidden Markov models, in *Proc. 1st Int. Workshop on Historical Document Imaging and Processing*, pp. 29–36.

Fischer, A., Indermühle, E., Frinken, V., and Bunke, H. (2011b). HMM-based alignment of inaccurate transcriptions for historical documents, in *Proc. 11th Int. Conf. on Document Analysis and Recognition*, pp. 53–57.

Fischer, A., Keller, A., Frinken, V., and Bunke, H. (2010). HMM-based word spotting in handwritten documents using subword models, in *Proc. 20th Int. Conf. on Pattern Recognition*, pp. 3416–3419.

Fischer, A., Keller, A., Frinken, V., and Bunke, H. (2012). Lexicon-free handwritten word spotting using character HMMs, *Pattern Recognition Letters* **33**, 7, pp. 934–942.

Fischer, A., Wüthrich, M., Liwicki, M., Frinken, V., Bunke, H., Viehhauser, G., and Stolz, M. (2009). Automatic transcription of handwritten medieval documents, in *Proc. Int. Conf. on Virtual Systems and Multimedia*, pp. 137–142.

Frinken, V., Fischer, A., Manmatha, R., and Bunke, H. (2012). A novel word spotting method based on recurrent neural networks, *IEEE Trans. on Pattern Analysis and Machine Intelligence* **34**, 2, pp. 211–224.

Graves, A., Liwicki, M., Fernandez, S., Bertolami, R., Bunke, H., and Schmidhuber, J. (2009). A novel connectionist system for improved unconstrained handwriting recognition, *IEEE Trans. PAMI* **31**, 5, pp. 855–868.

Hochreiter, S. and Schmidhuber, J. (1997). Long short-term memory, *Neural Computation* **9**, 8, pp. 1735—1780.

Kneser, R. and Ney, H. (1995). Improved backing-off for m-gram language modeling, in *Proc. Int. Conf. on Acoustics, Speech, and Signal Processing*, pp. 181–184.

Kornfield, E. M., Manmatha, R., and Allan, J. (2004). Text alignment with handwritten documents, in *Proc. 1st Int. Workshop on Document Image Analysis for Libraries*, pp. 195–209.

Lorette, G. (1999). Handwriting recognition or reading? What is the situation at the dawn of the 3rd millenium? *Int. Journal on Document Analysis and Recognition* **2**, 1, pp. 2–12.

Manmatha, R., Han, C., and Riseman, E. (1996). Word spotting: A new approach to indexing handwriting, in *Proc. Int. Conf. on Computer Vision and Pattern Recognition*, pp. 631—637.

Marti, U.-V. and Bunke, H. (2001). Using a statistical language model to improve the performance of an hmm-based cursive handwriting recognition system, *International journal of Pattern Recognition and Artificial intelligence* **15**, 01, pp. 65–90.

Ploetz, T. and Fink, G. A. (2009). Markov models for offline handwriting recognition: A survey, *Int. Journal on Document Analysis and Recognition* **12**, 4, pp. 269–298.

Puigcerver, J. (2017). Are multidimensional recurrent layers really necessary for handwritten text recognition? in *Proc. 14th Int. Conf. on Document Analysis and Recognition*, pp. 67–72.

Rabiner, L. R. (1989). A tutorial on hidden Markov models and selected applications in speech recognition, *Proceedings of the IEEE* **77**, 2, pp. 257–285.

Rodriguez, J. and Perronnin, F. (2009). Handwritten word-spotting using hidden Markov models and universal vocabularies, *Pattern Recognition* **42**, 9, pp. 2106–2116.

Sayre, K. M. (1973). Machine recognition of handwritten words: A project report, *Pattern Recognition* **5**, 3, pp. 213–228.

Toledo, J. I., Dey, S., Fornés, A., and Lladós, J. (2017). Handwriting recognition by attribute embedding and recurrent neural networks, in *Document Analysis and Recognition (ICDAR), 2017 14th IAPR International Conference on*, Vol. 1 (IEEE), pp. 1038–1043.

Zamora-Martínez, F., Frinken, V., Espana-Boquera, S., Castro-Bleda, M. J., Fischer, A., and Bunke, H. (2014). Neural network language models for off-line handwriting recognition, *Pattern Recognition* **47**, 4, pp. 1642–1652.

Chapter 6

Handwritten Keyword Spotting in Historical Documents

Volkmar Frinken and Shriphani Palakodety

Onu Technology, San Jose, USA
volkmar@onai.com, spalakod@onai.com

Handwritten keyword spotting in historical documents bridges the gap between scanned documents, whose content remains inaccessible, and well processed documents on which a recognition systems can be successfully employed. In this chapter we provide an overview of state-of-the-art research into keyword spotting for handwritten documents first and then introduce a recurrent neural network-based method that is well suited for historical documents. We explain in detail the motivation, internal mechanism, its strengths and its limitations. We conclude the chapter with an overview of the most important historical databases used for keyword spotting.

6.1   Introduction

Historical documents and corpora are of immense value in several fields. Collecting and curating these corpora is a labor-intensive task. Several such corpora spanning centuries of human history have been curated over the past few years. While significant efforts have been made to digitize these documents, proper transcriptions are often not available. The digitized documents are usually saved as images and are thus not properly accessible.

Processing historical documents and making them accessible presents certain unique challenges that traditional systems for handwriting recognition are not tuned for. For instance, paper and ink quality degrade over time, handwritten text is often not well separated, characters are decorated with beautiful ligatures, and the text is often packed with unique abbreviations and symbols.

As an alternative to full text recognition, keyword spotting offers a good compromise. Keyword spotting is the task of retrieving positions in a document that correspond to a search query, often just a word or a phrase. Keyword spotting requires less reliable data, returns a ranked list of positions in the document where a keyword is found. The output of a keyword spotting system allows us to index, search, and analyze these historical documents - making them far more accessible than just an image scan.

This chapter is organized as follows. In Section 6.2, an overview of the field of handwriting keyword spotting is provided. This is followed by the detailed description of particular approach based on neural networks in Section 6.3. We reflect on the limitations and look at further research directions in Section 6.4. Section 6.5 introduces frequently used databases and current research directions, and conclusions are drawn in Section 6.6.

6.2 Related Work

The best and most reliable keyword spotting system would simply be the use of a fully developed handwriting recognition system with language model integration that produces a set of recognition hypotheses, i.e. as a top-N list or a recognition lattice. With such a system, a user could simply execute a text query against the recognition output. Unfortunately, this is not always possible. Instead, keyword spotting is used whenever one or several resources for such a system are lacking. This could be the lack of sufficient training data, a language model, maybe even the complete set of characters and abbreviations occurring in the text, or simply insufficient CPU capacity to execute a complex system when large data collections need to be searched quickly. Thus, one way to classify different keyword spotting systems would be regarding the scenario in which they are useful or the lacking resources. However, this does not capture well the diverse techniques that have been developed and their relations.

Instead, we propose two align keyword spotting approaches along three axes; the way documents are represented (as raw pixels, extracted statistical features, or extracted structures), the way the search query is represented (as an example picked by the user, as string, or a more complex embedding), and

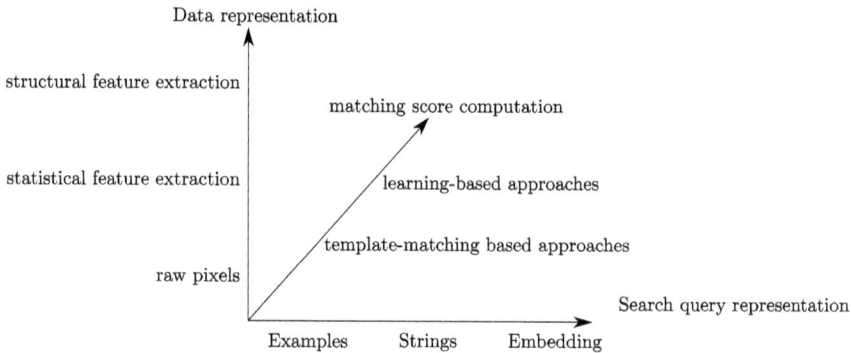

Fig. 6.1: A rough overview of the taxonomy of keyword spotting approaches.

the way the spotting is performed (computing a distance measure to a set of template or via a learned model), as shown in Fig. 6.1, whereas different keyword spotting taxonomies can be found in the literature, the most frequent approaches to sort keyword spotting publications are classifying them into *Query-by-Example* and *Query-by-String* approaches [Stauffer (2018)]. We argue that embedding-based query representations are a true extension of this binary split, as we will explain below. For extensive reviews of various keyword spotting approaches, we refer to [Giotis *et al.* (2017); Stauffer (2018)].

6.2.1 *Example-Based Search Queries*

The diverse nature of resource limitations result in a diverse set of keyword spotting approaches. In the most restrictive case, when only digitized images are available, Query-by-Example (QbE) approaches are used. The user selects one — or a few — snippets of the text that serve as templates against which the rest of the document is compared. In some publications, the text is assumed to already be segmented into words or candidate regions. In this case, the problem can be reduced to a distance measure between two images each containing a single word, e.g. via comparing contour sequences [Rath and Manmatha (2003, 2007); Terasawa and Tanaka (2009)] or flexible sequence matching [Mondal *et al.* (2016)]. Other approaches transform the respective words into graphs and measure their distance based on some graph distance metrics [Stauffer *et al.* (2018); Wang *et al.* (2014)].

Alternatively, text lines or entire document pages can be scanned for regions similar to example queries. Successful approaches include shape-based matching [Leydier *et al.* (2009)], comparison of larger zoning features [Gatos *et al.* (2011)], or key-points, such as SIFT [Konidaris *et al.* (2016); Rusinol *et al.* (2011)]. Recently, CNN that extract and compare visual descriptors have been shown to be successful as well [Rusinol *et al.* (2015)].

6.2.2 *String-Based Search Queries*

A more flexible alternative to QbE is to allow the search query to be any arbitrary string, called Query-by-String (QbS). This cannot be done in a language agnostic fashion, since the system needs to know how to compare arbitrary strings with candidate regions. Frequently used approaches include the segmentation of the document into text lines, which are then matched with character models composed from the search string. Extensive research has been done using hidden Markov models for different kind of feature representation, such as pseudo-2D HMM [Edwards *et al.* (2014)], extracted statistical features [Rodriguez and Perronnin (2009); Fischer *et al.* (2012)] and deep learning pre-processed features [Wicht *et al.* (2016)]. The related state-of-the-art keyword spotting approach that will be explained in more detail later in this chapter is based on recurrent neural networks [Frinken *et al.* (2012)].

6.2.3 *Embedding-Based Search Queries*

A relatively recent keyword spotting research direction is to embed the query and the search document in a space in which a distance function is defined. This embedding (a real-valued vector) thus allows a unified representation for both strings and images (examples). As a result, query embeddings allow querying both using strings and example-images [Almazán *et al.* (2014)]. Furthermore, any input data domain for which a mapping can be constructed could be utilized (sound, graphs, etc.). Thus, embedding-based search queries can be seen as a true extension over the commonly used *Query-by-Example/Query-by-String* split, even though many authors label their work as *Query-by-String* [Wilkinson and Brun (2016); Almazán *et al.* (2014); Rothacker *et al.* (2017); Sudholt and Fink (2016); Ghosh and Valveny (2017)].

The embedding function for strings can be done via Latent Semantic Analysis [Aldavert *et al.* (2013)], representing words as character index matrices [Gómez *et al.* (2017); Wilkinson and Brun (2016); Wilkinson *et al.* (2017)], or *Pyramidal Histogram of Characters* (PHOC). The latter is a

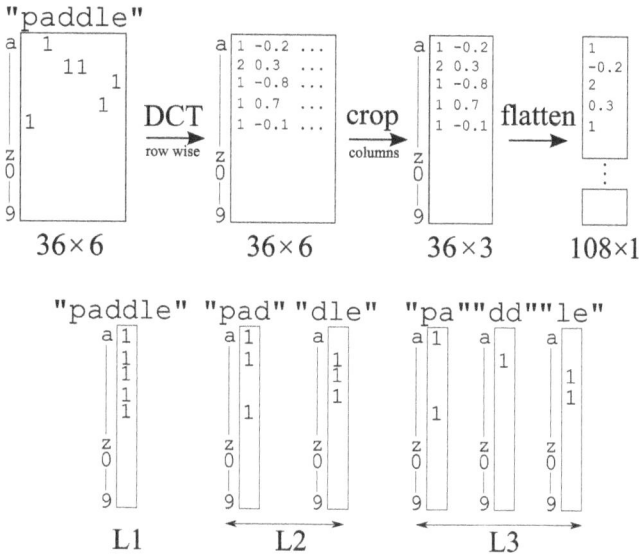

Fig. 6.2: Two embeddings for the string `paddle`. The top show shows a discrete cosine transformation (DCT) of the character index matrix, the bottom row shows the corresponding PHOC embedding (image from [Wilkinson *et al.* (2017)]).

representation of a character string of arbitrary length as a fixed length vector. The character histograms of the entire string is concatenated to the histograms of the first half of the string and the second half. This is done recursively up to a pre-defined level [Almazán *et al.* (2014); Rothacker *et al.* (2017); Sudholt and Fink (2016); Ghosh and Valveny (2017)]. An example of these two embeddings is shown in Fig. 6.2. CNNs for word string embeddings are researched in [Sudholt and Fink (2018)].

Researched distances in the embedded space include the simple dot product as an approximation of a Gaussian kernel in an SVM-based approach [Almazán *et al.* (2014)], Levenshtein distance [Gómez *et al.* (2017)], or learned distances via an CNN output activation in an simultaneous embedding of query and data [Wilkinson and Brun (2016)].

6.3   LSTM NN-Based Keyword Spotting

In this section we will discuss one particularly successful approach from [Frinken *et al.* (2012)] based on bidirectional long short-term memory

(LSTM) neural networks. The approach addresses line-based keyword spotting, i.e. text lines are ranked according to a the likelihood of the search term appearing in said lines. Automatic line segmentation techniques are an active research area [Diem *et al.* (2017)] and state-of-the-art approaches are significantly more robust than word-level segmentation. Line-based keyword spotting is thus a good starting point for a historical document analysis system — on one hand high quality system components exist and are easy to assemble. On the other hand, text lines serve as a reasonably fine-grained sub-unit of a document since the user can easily see where a queried phrase appears in a text line.

6.3.1 *Document Representation*

The LSTM model presented in this section draws from techniques discussed previously in this book. In particular, layout analysis, and text line extraction allow us to perform the first pre-processing step — breaking up a document into a sequence of lines.

The next step requires us to represent text lines as vector sequences. We briefly cover the approach discussed in [Marti and Bunke (2001)]. A broader overview of other popular text line representations can be found in [Frinken and Bunke (2014)].

The extracted text lines are first binarized. Then, skew, slant, and writing width are estimated using pixel distributions. The text line is normalized using image rotation, shear, and horizontal resizing. In the final normalization step, the x-height of the line is identified and non-linear vertical resizing is performed to normalize the text height.

To create the sequence of vectors, 9 statistical features are extracted from each vertical pixel column via a sliding window. The 0th, 1st, 2nd moment of the pixels, the number of black/white transitions within the pixel column, the position and inclination of the top and bottom contour, as well as the distance between the contours. Finally, to account for the fact that keyword spotting is done with a neural networks, the input features are normalized to their *standard score*, i.e. $x'_i = \frac{x_i - \hat{x}_i}{\sigma_i}$, where $\hat{x}_i$ and σx_i are the mean and standard deviation of the ith index across the entire database.

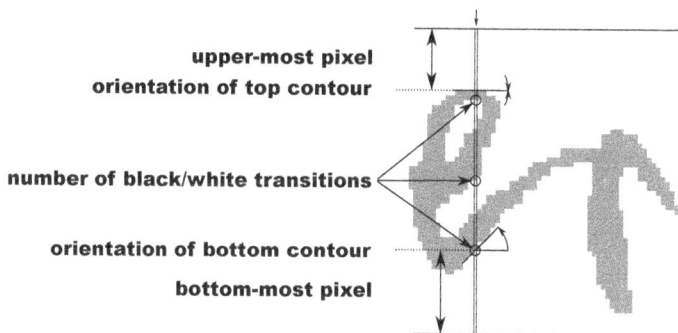

upper-most pixel
orientation of top contour

number of black/white transitions

orientation of bottom contour
bottom-most pixel

Fig. 6.3: At each position of the sliding window a feature vector x_i is computed based on the local pixels within that window.

6.3.2 LSTM Neural Networks

In the Section 6.3.1, we introduced a representation of the document as a collection of lines where each line is represented using a sequence of feature vectors. Based on this, we construct the LSTM model to label document regions based on the presence or absence of a keyword.

Text line sequences can be of arbitrary length containing arbitrarily many words. Hence resizing, cropping, or padding the input to fit into a fixed size is not easily achievable. Instead, we employ a recurrent neural network that consumes one feature vector in each time-step and produces a hidden state and an output vector.

For a context-dependent recognition, the neural network requires recurrent connections that update the hidden state after each input element. However, simple recurrent connections turn out to be unfeasible, due to the so-called *vanishing gradient problem* [Hochreiter (1991)]. The repeated multiplication of a value with the same weight in the recurrent connection leads to an exponential blow-up or decay of the values along the forward and backward passes. One way around this problem is to structure the network as a 2nd order network, in which recurrent weights are dynamically adjusted.

In Long Short-Term Memory networks, this is realized through multiplication nodes that act as gates. Each cell of the hidden layer contains (i) a core in a summation node, that aggregates the previous hidden state and the newly received information; (ii) an input gate, that controls how much new information is added to the cell; (iii) a forget gate that controls how much information is passed on from the previous time step to the core; and (iv) an output gate that controls how much information is emitted to the network (see Fig. 6.4). These gates resemble the set and reset operation of a binary flip-flop circuit. However, all internal operations are differentiable. The network can learn to open the gate based on some conditions, e.g. the beginning of a word, and emit information based on other conditions at an arbitrary distance. Hence, LSTM cells are capable of learning long term dependencies within sequences.

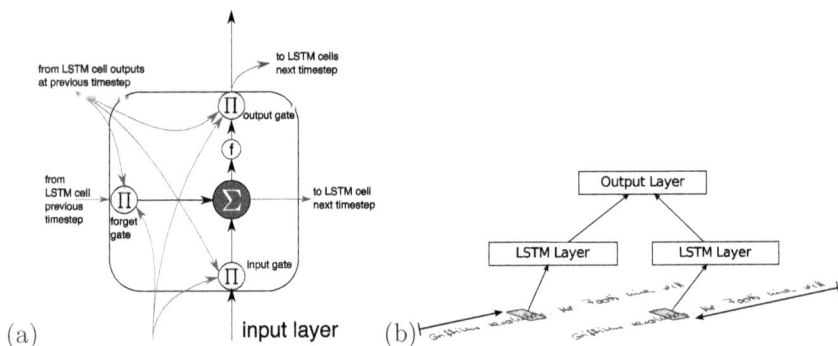

Fig. 6.4: The overall architecture of a BLSTM neural network for handwritten text lines. In (a) a LSTM cell is shown with the three gates that control the information flow in and out of the cell. In (b) the bidirectional sum before merging values in the softmax output layer is depicted.

As it turns out, character shapes depend on the context on both sides — the preceding and succeeding characters both influence the appearance. Thus, we process the sequence in both directions, forward and backward, and sum up the individual activations at each time step before passing the information into the softmax output layer (see Fig. 6.4), producing output sequence y. With this, we can train a network to produce a context-dependent sequence of output activations for arbitrarily long input sequence.

6.3.3 *Connectionist Temporal Classification*

Next, we focus our attention to the Connectionist Temporal Classification (CTC) output layer. To train a keyword independent network, each grapheme of the training data (characters, numbers, marks, etc.) should be represented with an output node on its own, whereas the output activation can be interpreted as the probability of that grapheme occurring at that position.

Unfortunately, for words which contain successively repeating characters (like `latter` for instance), this presents a few challenges. If the output nodes simply predict character probabilities, a longer written character would appear the same as a doubled character, making it hard to disambiguate between say `latter` and `later` (for instance). Thus, we add a further ε output node and encode words as state machines that require a ε observation between two instances of the same character, and ε observation between any other character transition. The example query `abb` becomes $a^{i_1}\varepsilon^{i_2}b^{i_3}\varepsilon^{i_4}b^{i_5}$, with $i_1, i_3, i_4, i_5 \geq 1$ and $i_2 \geq 0$. The character transitions as state machine can be seen on the left side of Fig. 6.5.

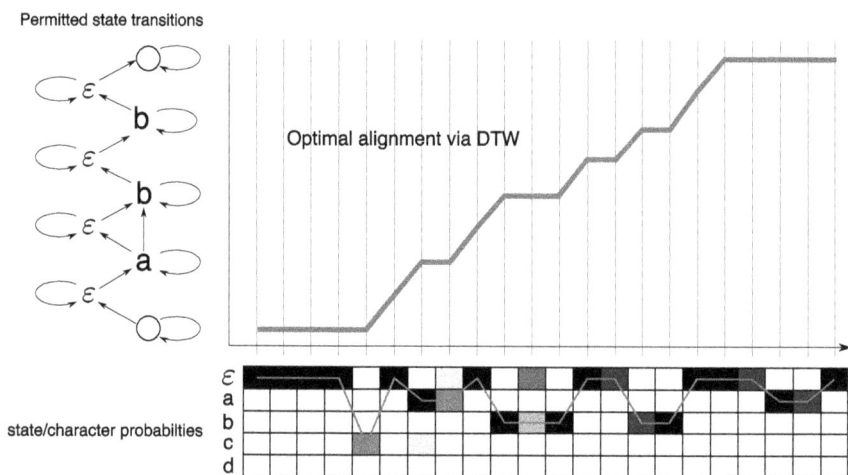

Fig. 6.5: Dynamic time warping can be used to map a state machine of possible character transitions to a sequence of posterior character probabilities. The product of the posteriors along the path, however, does not have a useful statistical meaning and decreases exponentially with the length of the text line.

For training, the forward-backward algorithm is used to align the target grapheme sequence with the sequence of output probabilities. The algorithm returns the posteriors for each grapheme at each time step, which is then compared to the network output activations to compute the gradient.

Without a language model to constrain the space of recognizable words or text lines, dynamic time warping (DTW) can be employed to find the most likely sequence of output activations. The output is reduced by ignoring repeated symbols and deleting the ε symbol (in that order). The two sequences $aaa\varepsilon\varepsilon bb\varepsilon\varepsilon bb$ and $a\varepsilon\varepsilon\varepsilon\varepsilon b\varepsilon bbbb$ would both first be reduced to $a\varepsilon b\varepsilon b$ then recognized as *abb*.

Given this initial mechanism, we can use DTW to detect keywords. With DTW, a *keyword state machine* that loops over a filler model [Fischer *et al.* (2012)], then alternate grapheme/ε symbols, and then the filler model can be mapped to a sequence of output activations in a way that maximizes the product of all posteriors along the path, as shown in Fig. 6.5.

6.3.4   *Extending CTC for Efficient Keyword Spotting*

While the previously mentioned approach of finding the best mapping between a keyword works to some degree, it has considerable downsides. Its matching score is the product of the one single path though the entire sequence that maximizes the product of posteriors. This, however, means, that also observation probabilities outside the keyword impact the score. Additionally, the text line length has an adverse effect on the score as well. Since all output activations are in $[0, 1]$, the product decreases exponentially with the number of factors producing very low scores for longer lines.

To solve this problem, the output activations are extended by a further node, called '*any*' node and denoted with the symbol $*$. The sequence of output activations is denoted with y^* Per definition, the activation of the $*$-node is always 1. If now, the filler model is replaced with the $*$-node in the *keyword state machine*, a few observations can be made. First, the $*$-node activation is the sum of all other output probabilities, hence the DTW algorithm is not sensitive to the context of the text outside the keyword any more. Secondly, arbitrarily many $*$-node activations can be multiplied to a matching score, without changing the score. Hence, the text line length does not decrease the matching score. An example of how the DTW algorithm maps the modified *keyword state machine* to a sequence of output activations is shown in Fig. 6.6.

A third observation one can make is that matching score calculated as a DTW product still decreases exponentially with the length of the keyword observation, which seems problematic as well. Hence, we normalize the score via

$$\text{matchingScore}(w) = \frac{\log\left(\text{DTWProduct}\left(\text{SM}\left(w, y^*\right)\right)\right)}{|\text{keyword observation}|} \quad,$$

Permitted state transitions

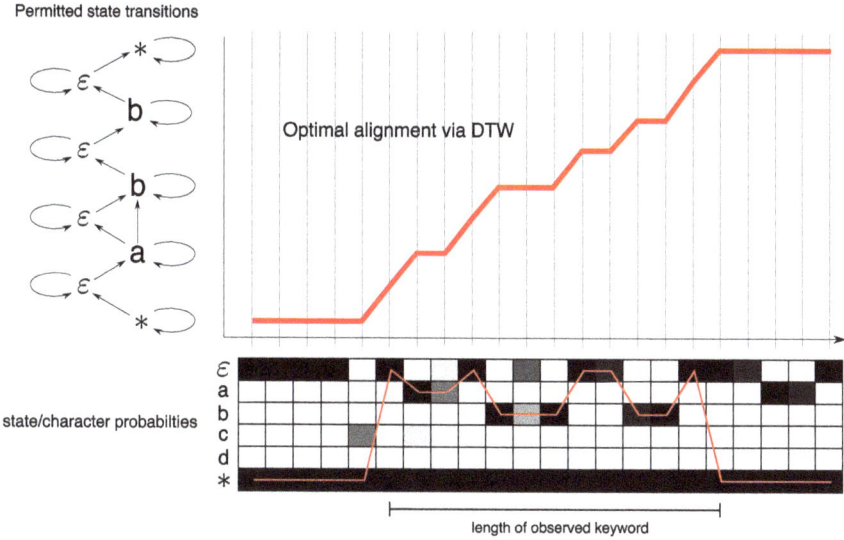

Fig. 6.6: Augmented with a *-node whose activation is constant 1, DTW can be used to find the keyword at its most likely position and the product of the values along the path is independent of the length of the text line.

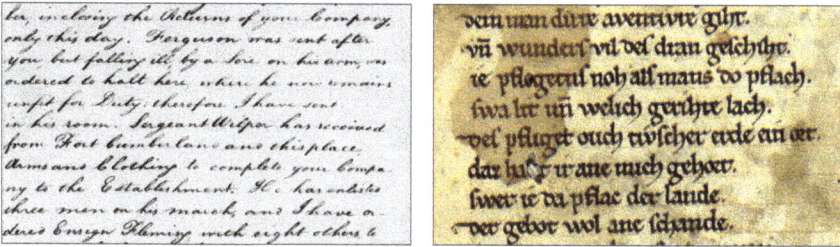

Fig. 6.7: A sample of the GW dataset (left) and PARCIVAL dataset right.

where SM is the modified *keyword state machine* and $DTWProduct$ the product of the DTW-mapping of the state machine to the sequence of output activations.

6.3.5 *Experimental Evaluation*

To evaluate LSTM-based keyword spotting experimentally, we trained and tested this approach on two different historical datasets.

The GW Data set [Fischer *et al.* (2012)] consists of 20 pages of letters, orders, and instructions of George Washington from 1755. The pages originate from a large collection with a variety of images, the quality of which ranges from clean to very difficult to read. The selected pages we use are relatively clean. The text is part of a larger corpus, written not only by George Washington but also by some of his associates. It exhibits some variations in writing style. However, the writing on the pages we consider is fairly consistent. We consider 20 pages (4,894 words on 675 text lines). 10 pages are used for training, 5 pages for validation, and 5 for testing.

The second experiment was done on the PARCIVAL dataset [Fischer *et al.* (2012)], a 47 page long excerpt of a handwritten historical manuscript in Medieval German, written in the 13th century, consisting of 4,477 text lines with 23,478 words. We selected 2,237 lines of transcribed text as training set, and used 912 additional lines as a validation set. The test set contained 1,329 lines. The text is written in middle high German. Samples of both datasets are shown in Fig. 6.7.

For both experiments, we trained 10 neural networks, using simple back-propagation with a fixed learning late (10^{-4}) and stopped training when no further improvement of the CTC loss could be detected on the validation set. We selected all words occurring in the training set to perform the word spotting, build the *keyword state machine* and used DTW to compute the matching score. We ranked all text lines of all keywords according to their normalized matching score and applied a global threshold to compute recall and precision values.

The applied threshold of a system regulates it sensitivity. With a lower threshold, the results are noisier but the system misses less true positives. For various thresholds, we computed the number of *true positives* (TP), *true negatives* (TN), *false positives* (FP), and *false negatives* (FN). These number were then used to plot a precision-recall scatter plot for each neural network. Precision is defined as number of relevant objects found by the algorithm divided by the number of all objects found $\frac{TP}{TP+FP}$, while recall is defined as the number of relevant objects found divided by the number of all relevant objects in the test set $\frac{TP}{TP+FN}$. A precision-recall plot therefore gives us an idea about the noise in the returned results, given the percentage of how many true elements are found. We considered for each system every single likelihood it returned as a possible threshold. Note that such a threshold is used as a global threshold to accept or reject lines (threshold based). Due to the high number of tested thresholds, the points in the scatter plot can be considered as continuous curves.

The precision-recall plots of the spotting performance over all keywords are shown in Fig. 6.8 and the average precision, equivalent to the area under the curve of the precision-recall plot, is given in Table 6.1 for the set of the 10 networks. It can be seen that the performance is highly dataset dependent. The absolute performance on the PARCIVAL dataset is significantly higher than on the GW dataset. Not only is the PARCIVAL dataset larger than GW, it displays a highly regular writing style that renders the spotting task faily easy. In fact, we can observe that at a recall rate of 90%, LSTM-based keyword spotting still retrieves relevant text lines with a precision of > 90%.

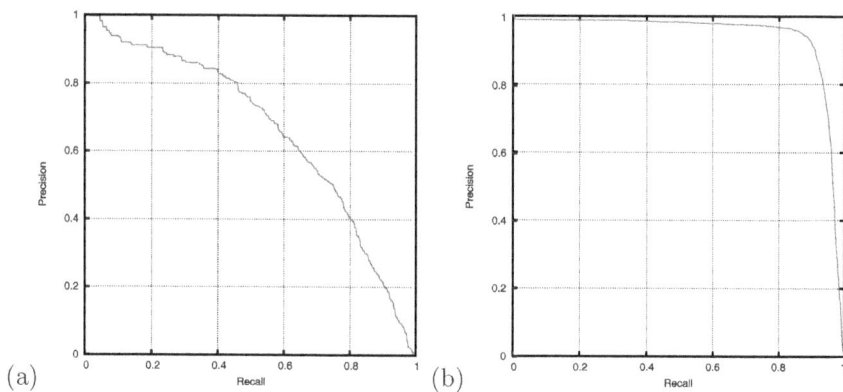

(a)   (b)

Fig. 6.8: Precision-recall plot for the keyword spotting task on the GW dataset (a) and the PARCIVAL dataset (b).

Table 6.1: Average precision using all keywords.

NN setup	GW	PARCIVAL
Average of 10 NN	0.71	0.92
Best NN on validation set	0.84	0.94

6.4   Remarks and Further Research

LSTM-based keyword spotting approaches significantly outperform previously popular techniques, such as HMM-based keyword spotting or dynamic time warping on many different historical and contemporary data sets

[Frinken *et al.* (2012); Jain *et al.* (2011); Toselli *et al.* (2016)]. While this approach shows impressive results, it also has limitations, based on the required data pre-processing needed for training and usage. The neural network employed in both experiments has 200 hidden nodes (100 each for the forward and backward text line processing), resulting in over 10^5 weights that require on the order of 10^4 annotated text lines for training.

Following are two promising ways to alleviate this problem, transfer learning and semi-supervised learning. In transfer learning, a neural network is initially trained on one dataset and then later fine-tuned on a different dataset. It can be shown that this improves recognition accuracy, resp. decreases the need of training data for the target data set [Pratt (1997)]. In the context of LSTM-based keyword spotting for historical documents, we can train the network on modern, synthetic, or otherwise well known and transcribed corpora first. Then we retrain the network on the historic dataset under consideration. This has shown to be advantageous, even if the set of graphemes in the target dataset is different [Frinken *et al.* (2010)].

A second strategy is semi-supervised learning [Chapelle *et al.* (2006)]. Instead of using only labeled data for training, unlabeled data can be incorporated into the training as well. Unlabeled data can be gathered very efficiently in great numbers and can be used to estimate the prior data probability. A simple, yet widely applicable technique to indirectly incorporate this information is *self-training*. In short, an initial system is used to recognize the set of unlabeled data which is then used to augment the original training set to train a stronger system. Again, in the context of LSTM-based keyword spotting for historical documents, it means that we can start with a small set of labeled text lines and use the rest of the dataset as unlabeled data. Then, a set of arbitrary keywords can be spotted on the unlabeled data and the locations with the highest matching score are then cut out and added to the training set. In [Frinken *et al.* (2014)], the authors train an initial keyword spotting system on the first 10 pages of the PARCIVAL dataset mentioned above and show a significant performance increase through self-training with most confidently spotting keyword.

Finally it should be noted that the presented LSTM-based keyword spotting requires the data to be segmented into text lines and those text lines to be normalized to a certain degree. Thus, text in lines that are difficult or impossible to segment might be missed, such as annotations between lines or words containing ornamented characters. In such cases, segmentation-independent spotting methods might be considered instead [Almazán *et al.* (2014); Konidaris *et al.* (2016); Rusinol *et al.* (2011); Rothacker *et al.* (2017)].

6.5   Common Databases

This section provides a selection of some of the most important resources for historical document analysis with a focus on Latin scripts. The listed databases are frequently used for keyword spotting approaches and other related tasks, such as handwriting recognition (cf. Chapter 6 in this book).

The list of databases, provided in Fig. 6.9, display a rich variety in languages, writing styles, time epochs, and database sizes. GW [Rath and Manmatha (2003)] was among the first historical databases used for keyword spotting and was even considered the standard benchmark for the task [Sudholt and Fink (2018)]. PARCIVAL is the only selected database written in blackletter script, all others are cursive scripts. ESPOSALLES incorporates the largest timespan, stretching from 1451 to 1905. Alvermann Konzilsprotokolle and Botany In British India are two collections prepared in the Europe project *Recognition and Enrichment of Archival Documents* (READ) and became popular through their use in the ICFHR 2016 Handwritten Keyword Spotting Competition [Pratikakis *et al.* (2016)]. The RODRIGO database with manuscripts written in 1545, has a transitional writing style with clear Gothic in old Castilian. Finally, the GERMANA database is selected as a good example of a multilingual corpus containing text from five different European languages.

6.6   Conclusion

Human created data is messy, complicated and often very context-dependent, and up until now we have only scratched the surface automatic historical document processing. Unsolved problems include text embedded in figures, abbreviations that can only be recognized in context, words overlaying one another and general document degradation. Large amounts of dormant content, important for the common heritage of mankind still awaits more powerful spotting and recognition methods in the future.

Modern machine learning techniques require lots of training data, which might not always be available in this field. Furthermore, historical document exhibit an incredible variety of different styles. The various scenarios in which some keyword spotting approaches are appropriate and others are not,

Database	Resolution	Pages	Language	Preprocessing
GW	line word	20	18th century English	Binarized, Normalized lines and words
PARCIVAL	page line word	47	Middle High German	Binarized, Normalized lines and words
ESPOSALLES	line	29	Catalan, Spanish	lines split
AK	word	105	German	word bounding boxes
BOT	word	170	English	word bounding boxes
RODRIGO	line	853	Spanish (old Castilian)	lines split
GERMANA	line	764	multilingual (Spanish, Catalan, French, Latin, Italian German)	lines split

Fig. 6.9: A list of popular historical databases. (GW): The George Washington Papers at the Library of Congress [Fischer *et al.* (2012)]; (PARCIVAL): excerpts from Parcival manuscript from the Abbey Library of Saint Gall [Fischer *et al.* (2012)]; (ESPOSALLES): Marriage License Records of the Cathedral of Barcelona [Romero *et al.* (2013)]; (Alvermann Konzilsprotokolle): Minutes from the University of Greifswald [Pratikakis *et al.* (2016)]; (BOT): also *Botany In British India*, an article on hemp cultivation in India from the India Office Records at the British Library [Pratikakis *et al.* (2016)]; (RODRIGO): An old Spanish translation of an earlier work on the history of Spain, by the Archbishop of Toledo, Don Rodrigo Jiménez de Rada[Serrano *et al.* (2010)]; (GERMANA): Notes and documents related to Doña Germana de Foix, last Queen of Aragón [Pérez *et al.* (2009)].

the limitation of historical data, and the rapid development of computer vision, machine learning, and language modeling creates a unique setup with frequent publications of new, exiting techniques and interesting ideas.

References

Aldavert, D., Rusinol, M., Toledo, R., and Lladós, J. (2013). Integrating visual and textual cues for query-by-string word spotting, in *Int'l Conf. on Document Analysis and Recognition*.

Almazán, J., Gordo, A., Fornés, A., and Valveny, E. (2014). Segmentation-free word spotting with exemplar svms, *Pattern Recognition* **47**, 12, pp. 3967–3978.

Almazán, J., Gordo, A., Fornés, A., and Valveny, E. (2014). Word spotting and recognition with embedded attributes, *IEEE transactions on pattern analysis and machine intelligence* **36**, 12, pp. 2552–2566.

Chapelle, O., Schölkopf, B., and Zien, A. (2006). *Semi-supervised learning* (MIT Press).

Diem, M., Kleber, F., Fiel, S., Grüning, T., and Gatos, B. (2017). cBAD: ICDAR2017 Competition on Baseline Detection, in *Proceedings of the 14th International Conference on Document Analysis and Recognition*, pp. 1355–1360.

Edwards, J., Teh, Y. W., Forsyth, D., Bock, R., Maire, M., and Vesom, G. (2014). Making latin manuscripts searchable using ghmm's, in *Int'l Conf. on Neural Information Processing Systems*, pp. 385–392.

Fischer, A., Keller, A., Frinken, V., and Bunke, H. (2012). Lexicon-free handwritten word spotting using character HMMs, *Pattern Recognition Letters* **33**, 7, pp. 934–942.

Frinken, V. and Bunke, H. (2014). *Handbook of Document Image Processing and Recognition*, chap. Continuous Handwritten Script Recognition (Springer-Verlag London).

Frinken, V., Fischer, A., Baumgartner, M., and Bunke, H. (2014). Keyword spotting for self-training of BLSTM NN based handwriting recognition systems, *Pattern Recognition* **47**, 3, pp. 1073–1082.

Frinken, V., Fischer, A., Bunke, H., and Manmatha, R. (2010). Adapting BLSTM neural network based keyword spotting trained on modern data to historical documents, in *Int'l Conf. on Frontiers in Handwriting Recognition*.

Frinken, V., Fischer, A., Manmatha, R., and Bunke, H. (2012). A novel word spotting method based on recurrent neural networks, *IEEE Trans. on Pattern Analysis and Machine Intelligence* **34**, 2, pp. 211–224.

Gatos, B., Kesidis, A. L., and Papandreou, A. (2011). Adaptive zoning features for character and word recognition, in *2011 International Conference on Document Analysis and Recognition* (IEEE), pp. 1160–1164.

Ghosh, S. and Valveny, E. (2017). R-PHOC: Segmentation-free word spotting using cnn, in *Int'l Conf. on Document Analysis and Recognition*, pp. 801–806.

Giotis, A. P., Sfikas, G., Gatos, B., and Nikou, C. (2017). A survey of document image word spotting techniques, *Pattern Recognition* **68**, pp. 310–332.

Gómez, L., nol, M. R., and Karatzas, D. (2017). LSDE: Levenshtein space deep embedding for query-by-string word spotting, in *Int'l Conf. on Document Analysis and Recognition*.

Hochreiter, S. (1991). *Untersuchungen zu dynamischen neuronalen Netzen*, Master's thesis, TU Munich.

Jain, R., Frinken, V., Jawahar, C. V., and Manmatha, R. (2011). BLSTM Neural Network based word retrieval for Hindi documents, in *Int'l Conf. on Document Analysis and Recognition*, pp. 83–87.

Konidaris, T., Kesidis, A. L., and Gatos, B. (2016). A segmentation-free word spotting method for historical printed documents, *IEEE Transactions on pattern analysis and machine intelligence (TPAMI)* **19**, 4, pp. 963–976.

Leydier, Y., Ouji, A., LeDourgoio, F , and Emptoz, H. (2009). Towards an omnilingual word retrieval system for ancient manuscripts, *Pattern Recognition* **42**, 9, pp. 2089–2105.

Marti, U.-V. and Bunke, H. (2001). Using a statistical language model to improve the performance of an hmm-based cursive handwriting recognition system, *International journal of Pattern Recognition and Artificial intelligence* **15**, 01, pp. 65–90.

Mondal, T., Ragot, N., Ramel, J.-Y., and Pal, U. (2016). Flexible sequence matching technique, *Pattern Recognition* **60**, C, pp. 596–612.

Pérez, D., Tarazón, L., Serrano, N., Castro, F.-M., Ramos-Terrades, O., and Juan, A. (2009). The GERMANA database, in *Proc. 10th Int. Conf. on Document Analysis and Recognition*, pp. 301–305.

Pratikakis, I., Zagoris, K., Gatos, B., Puigcerver, J., Toselli, A. H., and Vidal, E. (2016). Icfhr2016 handwritten keyword spotting competition (h-kws 2016), in *2016 15th International Conference on Frontiers in Handwriting Recognition (ICFHR)* (IEEE), pp. 613–618.

Pratt, L. Y. (1997). Discriminability-based transfer between neural networks, in *NIPS Conf: Advances in neural information processing systems*, pp. 204–211.

Rath, T. M. and Manmatha, R. (2003). Word image matching using dynamic time warping, in *IEEE Conference on Computer Vision and Pattern Recognition, Proceedings*, Vol. 2 (IEEE).

Rath, T. M. and Manmatha, R. (2007). Word spotting for historical documents, *IJDAR* **9**, 2–4, pp. 139–152.

Rodriguez, J. and Perronnin, F. (2009). Handwritten word-spotting using hidden Markov models and universal vocabularies, *Pattern Recognition* **42**, 9, pp. 2106–2116.

Romero, V., FornéS, A., Serrano, N., SáNchez, J. A., Toselli, A. H., Frinken, V., Vidal, E., and LladóS, J. (2013). The esposalles database: An ancient marriage license corpus for off-line handwriting recognition, *Pattern Recognition* **46**, 6, pp. 1658–1669.

Rothacker, L., Sudholt, S., Rusakov, E., Kasperidus, M., and Fink, G. A. (2017). Word hypotheses for segmentation-free word spotting in historic document images, in *Int'l Conf. on Document Analysis and Recognition*.

Rusinol, M., Aldavert, D., Toledo, R., and Lladós, J. (2011). Browsing heterogeneous document collections by a segmentation-free word spotting method, in 63–67 (ed.), *Int'l Conf. on Document Analysis and Recognition*.

Rusinol, M., Aldavert, D., Toledo, R., and Lladós, J. (2015). Efficient segmentation-free keyword spotting in historical document collections, *Pattern Recognition* **48**, 2, pp. 545–555.

Serrano, N., Castro, F., and Juan, A. (2010). The rodrigo database, in *Proceedings of the Seventh International Conference on Language Resources and Evaluation (LREC'10)*, pp. 2709–2712.

Stauffer, M. (2018). *Graph-based Keyword Spotting in Handwritten Historical Documents*, Ph.D. thesis, University of Pretoria, South Africa.

Stauffer, M., Fischer, A., and Riesen, K. (2018). Keyword spotting in historical handwritten documents based on graph matching, *Pattern Recognition* **81**, pp. 240–253.

Sudholt, S. and Fink, G. A. (2016). Phocnet: A deep convolutional neural network for word spotting in handwritten documents, in *Frontiers in Handwriting Recognition (ICFHR), 2016 15th International Conference on* (IEEE), pp. 277–282.

Sudholt, S. and Fink, G. A. (2018). Attribute CNNs for word spotting in handwritten documents, *Int'l J. on Document Analysis and Recognition* **21**, 3, pp. 199–218.

Terasawa, K. and Tanaka, Y. (2009). Slit style hog feature for document image word spotting, in *ICDAR'09*, pp. 116–120.

Toselli, A. H., Vidal, E., Romero, V., and Frinken, V. (2016). HMM word graph based keyword spotting in handwritten document images, *Information Sciences* **370–371**, pp. 497–518.

Wang, P., Eglin, V., Garcia, C., Largeron, C., Lladós, J., and Fornés, A. (2014). A coarse-to-fine word spotting approach for historical handwritten documents based on graph embedding and graph edit distance, in *ICPR*, pp. 3074–3079.

Wicht, B., Fischer, A., and Hennebert, J. (2016). Deep learning features for handwritten keyword spotting, in *Int'l Conf. on Pattern Recognition*.

Wilkinson, T. and Brun, A. (2016). Semantic and verbatim word spotting using deep neural networks, in *Int'l Conf. on Frontiers in Handwriting Recognition*.

Wilkinson, T., Lindström, J., and Brun, A. (2017). Neural Ctrl-F: Segmentation-free query-by-string word spotting in handwritten manuscript collections, in *IEEE International Conference on Computer Vision*, pp. 4433–4442.

Chapter 7

DIVAServices - Transforming Document Analysis Methods into Web Services

Marcel Gygli

DIVA Group, University of Fribourg, Switzerland
Institute for Interactive Technologies, University of Applied Sciences and
Arts Northwestern Switzerland
marcel.gygli@fhnw.ch

7.1 Abstract

Document Image Analysis (DIA) as a field is evolving rapidly: the amount of data to be processed is rapidly growing and new approaches, ideas, and methods are published frequently. However, for many of these publications there is no technical implementation of the proposed methods available, making it hard to either reproduce the results, use them for comparison on new data, or as part of new methods. With DIVAServices we are building a platform that allows to address parts of these issues. The platform allows researchers to publish the technical implementation of their research as a Web Services. All of these Web Services use a standardized interface such that interacting with each individual method is not confusing. This allows other researchers from within, but also outside the field of document analysis, to incorporate them into their own research. DIVAServices aims at building a complete ecosystem, supporting method providers, and users, in all interactions with the platform. We provide several different tools, e.g., for testing methods, for publishing methods, or for managing data. Using this platform, new research in DIA can integrate methods and results from other researchers in a much easier way.

7.2   Introduction

Document Image Analysis (DIA) has come a long way. But the goals mostly have not changed over time: Extracting as much knowledge and information as possible from scanned modern or historical documents. The technology for DIA has massively evolved over the last couple of decades. Today we can train end employ end-to-end system for various complex use cases, like text recognition [Wang *et al.* (2012)]. What has not changed over the years is the complexity necessary for using such published methods in ones own research or simply trying it out on your own data. Published research papers often contain not enough information that would allow for reprogramming the method in order to reproduce the results or using it for further research. There is a slow but growing trend towards releasing source code related to publications online on sites such as Github.[1] This is a good first step, but does not solve all of the problems mentioned above. Getting a method run from source code still requires an effort (e.g., compiling the code, getting all required libraries, and others).

With DIVAServices we tackle some of these issues by providing a RESTful Web Service [Richardson (2007)] platform supporting researchers and outside users alike. The framework exposes access to individual DIA methods through a unified REST Application Programming Interface (API). Each method is accessible through a unique endpoint (HTTP address) and can be executed by issuing a POST request to it, providing necessary parameter and data information. We decided for a Web Service architecture because of its recent popularity within the Document Image Analysis field [Neudecker *et al.* (2011); Sánchez *et al.* (2013); Wang *et al.* (2012)] but also in other fields [Goujon *et al.* (2010)].

In this chapter we provide a complete overview of the DIVAServices platform, providing a complete overview of the architecture.

The remainder of this chapter is structured as follows: In the following section we discuss related work and what inspired our work. Section 7.4 provides a thorough explanation of the complete DIVAServices back-end infrastructure. This is followed by explanation how to interact with the methods and data provided through DIVAServices in Section 7.5 We show some of the tools we built around the core framework in Section 7.7. This is followed by a set of examples showcasing how methods provided on

---

[1]see: https://www.github.com

DIVAServices can be integrated into applications and ongoing research. We close this chapter with concluding thoughts and pointers for future work.

7.3   Related Work

For the purpose of this book chapter we focus our related work section on frameworks and applications that are very similar to DIVAServices. For a more thorough review of related work we refer the reader to our previously published articles on DIVAServices [Würsch *et al.* (2018); Würsch *et al.* (2016)] We first review similar approaches from within the DIA community and then broaden the view to other fields as well to see how they tackle this similar problem.

7.3.1   *Web Services in Document Image Analysis*

Web Services in the DIA community have gained some traction over recent years. One of the first publications introducing Web Services as a tool for DIA research is presented in [Lopresti and Lamiroy (2011)]. Lopresti and Lamiroy introduce Document Analysis Research Engine (DARE), this imaginary service lives in the cloud and can support a researcher in Document Analysis in all stages of research. From preparing the data, to running experiments, and evaluation the results against human performance as well as other available methods. Lopresti and Lamiroy in [Lamiroy and Lopresti (2011)] provide a reference implementation of DARE that they call Document Analysis and Exploitation (DAE). This implementation, using the Simple Object Access Protocol (SOAP) Web Service methodology, provides access to datasets and methods.

Within the IMPACT project [Neudecker *et al.* (2011)] a Web Service framework was designed and built with a heavy focus on scalability. After the end of the project the outcomes were merged into *The Impact Centre of Competence in Digitisation.*[2] This not for profit organisation access to 41 different methods as RESTful Web Services. Full access to these Web Services is only available to paying members. Furthermore, there is no documented way for outsiders to provide access to their own methods on this platform.

A more recent Web Service project within the DIA community started in project tranScriptorium [Sánchez *et al.* (2013)] and is continued in the project

---

[2]see: https://www.digitisation.eu

READ. Transkribus[3] is one of the most comprehensive client applications to perform transcription of documents supported by semi-automatic methods. The more powerful methods, such as Handwritten Text Recognition (HTR) are hosted on a High-Performance Computing (HPC) center and accessed through a RESTful Web Service interface. These Web Services can be used by anyone (upon registration), but there is no way for outsiders to provide their own methods within this framework.

7.3.2   *Web Services in Other Fields*

In other fields Web Services have already become a de facto standard from various operations. One of the best examples is in Bioinformatics, where the European Bioinformatics Institute (EMBL-EBI) provides access to a wide array of methods, and data [Chojnacki *et al.* (2017)]. According to their latest statistics[4] they can provide access to 120 Petabytes of data and handles an average of 12.6 million jobs per month. This clearly shows that such an infrastructure, supported and managed by a complete research community can have a large impact in simplifying access to tools and services for all.

DIVAServices is inspired by all of the abovementioned works but aims at offering a unique set of tools and services. One of the big differences to all related projects is that DIVAServices is fully committed to the idea of open research. Therefore all source code for the core framework as well as all tools and services built by us are released under an open source license. Furthermore we put a big focus on making it as simple as possible for researchers to provide their own methods on our platform for others to use.

7.4   DIVAServices - The RESTful Web Service Framework

As mentioned above, DIVAServices at its core is a RESTful Web Service framework. This means the interaction is performed over standard HTTP requests (in our case mainly GET and POST requests). In the case of DIVAServices we differ a bit from traditional RESTful design, as a *resource* in our case is a provided method, and therefore API endpoints are flexible and evolve over time.

---

[3]see: https://transkribus.eu
[4]see: https://www.ebi.ac.uk/about/our-impact

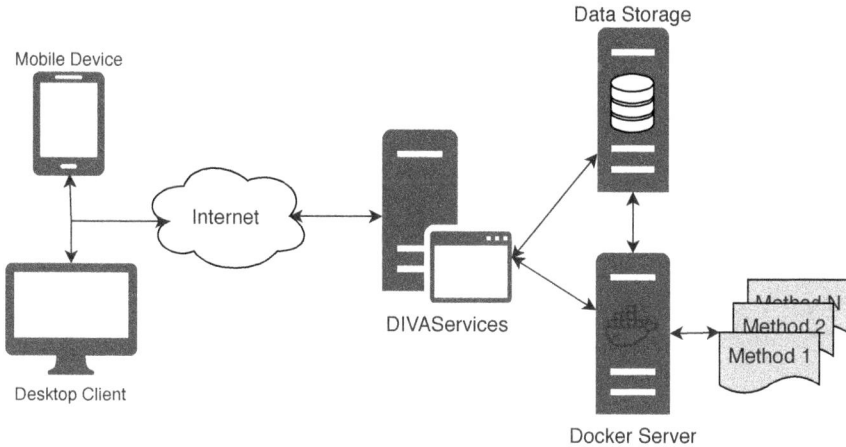

Fig. 7.1: The core architecture of DIVAServices consisting of three parts: DIVAServices, the internet facing part that processes all incoming requests, a data storage where all data is stored, and a Docker instance where all method are installed and executed. (Figure taken from [Würsch *et al.* (2018)].)

Figure 7.1 provides an overview of the DIVAServices architecture. The core architecture is comprised of three parts: DIVAServices the is the internet facing part that processes all incoming requests and performs the necessary tasks (e.g., saving data, or executing a method). The *Data Storage* is a regular file server and stores all data that has been made available to the service. Finally, a *Docker* [Boettiger (2015)] instance that hosts all available methods as singular docker images. With Docker we make use of a tool that allows us to support almost any command line executable, in any programming language, that can be executed in a Unix environment. Additionally, we can ensure encapsulating of the individual methods, and do not run into the classical dependency hell. Every method gets its own environment, with the required dependencies, that is completely independent from all other installed methods.

7.5 Core Interactions with DivaServices

Interaction with DIVAServices is always performed using standard HTTP requests and all information is encoded using the Java Script Object Notation

(JSON). POST requests can be used to upload data or execute a method, and GET requests for gathering information about available data and methods. These requests can either be performed using REST clients (e.g., Insomnia[5] or Postman[6]) and most programming languages support interacting with RESTful Web Services either with built-in support or through libraries.

In the following parts we give an overview of the different important parts of interacting with DIVAServices. Namely accessing information about which methods are available and how they work, uploading data to the service, and executing a method. For detailed instructions we refer the reader to our Tutorials that are available online.[7]

7.5.1 *Accessing Method Information*

Before a method can be executed, the user needs to know what methods are available and what parameters need to be provided for each method. A list of all available methods is available at the root API endpoint.[8] A partial excerpt of the JSON response for such a GET request is provided in Listing 7.1. For each method a *url* is provided, leading to the method information. This information is structured into three parts: *general*, *input*, and *output*.

- The *general* part contains standard information about who built the method, what it can be used for etc.
- In *input* the list of parameters is provided that are necessary for this method to run. Table 7.1 exemplifies how two different input types can be further specified through options. An exhaustive description of all available input types and how to specify them is available in our online documentation.[9]
- *output* provides the list of outputs that are generated by this specific method. Currently DIVAServices supports two different types of outputs: *file*, the output a single file, and *folder* a list of multiple files all stored in one folder.

---

[5]see: http://insomnia.rest
[6]see: https://www.getpostman.com/
[7]see: https://lunactic.github.io/DIVAServicesweb
[8]see: http://divaservices.unifr.ch/api/v2
[9]see: http://bit.ly/divaservices_inputs

Listing 7.1: JSON response when fetching the list of all available methods on DIVAServices. Each entry consists of a *name*, a short *description*, a *type*, and a *url* under which the method is available.

```
[
    {
        "name": "Otsu Binarization",
        "description": "Otsu Binarization",
        "type": "binarization",
        "url": "http://divaservices.unifr.ch/api/v2/binarization/otsubinarization/1"
    },
    ...
]
```

Table 7.1: Available options for two different input types *number*, and *file*. An exhaustive list of all available input types and how to use them is available online.[9]

Type	Field	Description	Type
	required	parameter is mandatory	boolean
	default	default value	number
number	min	Minimal value	number
	max	Maximal value	number
	steps	step size	number
	required	parameter is mandatory	boolean
file	**mimeTypes:default**	default mime-type that can be used for this method	string
	mimeTypes:allowed	a list of all allowed mime-types for this method	list of strings

7.5.2 *Providing Data*

Having all the information of a method allows for its execution. The last step before running a method is uploading the data that should to the DIVAServices platform. This can be performed using a POST request to the */collections* endpoint to create a new collection. A description of the format of this POST request and how to give your collection a specific name is available online as well.[10] All files within a collection have an *identifier* that have the following structure: %collection_name%/%file_name%.%ext%. These *identifiers* are important as they will be used to reference data items when running a method.

---

[10]see: https://lunactic.github.io/DIVAServicesweb/articles/data-management/

7.5.3   Execution of a Method

A method is executed by issuing a POST request to the methods API endpoint, containing all parameter and data information in the request body. In Listing 7.2 an example request is provided that could be used to execute an interest point detection method. Parameters required by the method are provided in the *parameters* object of the request, and the data that should be used is provided in the *data* array. In order to reference data the *identifier* as described above has to be used. Matching is performed based on the *name* property of the inputs in the method definition.

Listing 7.2: Example request for executing a method on DivaServices. All regular input parameters are set in the *parameters* object, while data elements are provided in the *data* array.

```
{
    "parameters":{
        "threshold":0.000001,
        "maxFeaturesPerScale":-1,
        "numOctaves":3,
        "numScales":100,
        "blurSigma":1,
        "detector":"Harris"
    },
    "data":[
        {
            "inputImage": "testCollection/ubb-A-II-0004_0002r.jpg"
        }
    ]
}
```

Listing 7.3: Example request for executing a method on DivaServices All regular input parameters are set in the *parameters* object, while data elements are provided in the *data* array.

```
{
    "results": [
        {
            "resultLink": "http://divaservices.unifr.ch/api/v2/results/rowdyinfantilecur
                ↪ /data_0/data_0.json"
        }
    ],
    "resultCollection": "testCollection_otsubinarization_2018_7_10_12_27_14",
    "resultCollectionLink": "http://134.21.72.182:8080/collections/
        ↪ testCollection_otsubinarization_2018_7_10_12_27_14",
    "status": "done"
}
```

Such a request will start the execution of the method on the platform. This execution is performed asynchronously, meaning the calling client receives an immediate result which contains a URL the client can poll to retrieve the final results once they are available. Listing 7.3 shows an example of such a result. *resultCollection* references to a collection that is automatically created containing all created results for direct reuse on DIVAServices without the need of having to download and re-upload the result files.

With all of this information it is possible to run experiments on DIVAServices.

7.6 Example Use of DivaServices

In this section we want to provide a complete example of how to run an experiment with DIVAServices. The goal of our exemplary workflow is to extract printed text from a color input image using a combination of

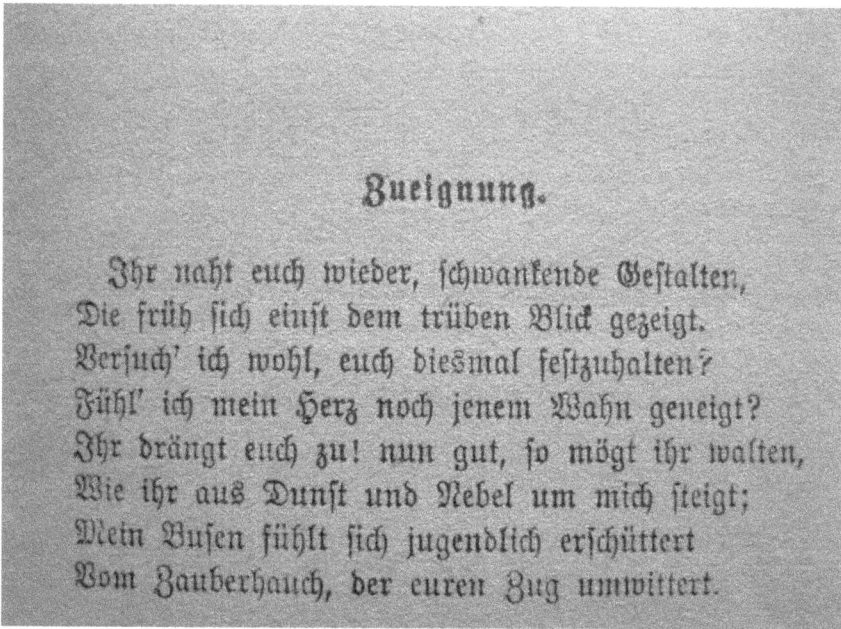

Fig. 7.2: The original input image for the workflow. The page contains the first page of Goethes Faust. For the purpose of this chapter, the image has been adapted to grayscale. (Figure taken from: Wikimedia.[11])

---

[11]see: https://commons.wikimedia.org/wiki/File:
Goethe_Faust_Opening_Fraktur_20052706.jpg

methods. The source image is shown in Figure 7.2 containing the first page of Goethes Faust set in Fraktura. In order to perform OCR on this image the following steps are applied: The image first is binarized, then individual text lines are extracted, and finally OCR on these text line images is applied using a pretrained model for recognizing text written in Fraktura. A working prototype of this workflow is implemented as a website using JavaScript and available online.[12] We will discuss the most important aspects of the process, showing source code snippets that would allow for reproducing the experiment.

7.6.1 *Upload the Original Image*

In a first step we have to upload the source image to DIVAServices. As described above in the previous chapter this is performed using a POST request to the */collections* endpoint. To have the possibility to allow the upload of images that are not accessible over a public URL we encode the source image in base64 and send this information in the POST request. Listing 7.4 shows how this request will look like, and Listing 7.5 shows how this upload can be performed using JavaScript. This will create a new collection with a random name, and add the file to it with the original file name provided by the user.

In order to binarize this image we need to remember the generated name of the collection (in the code this is performed in the last step) as well as the file name, as this generates the *identifier* needed to reference the image.

Listing 7.4: JSON body for providing the original source image to DIVAServices.

```
{
    "files": [
        {
            "type": "base64",
            "value": \%base64_encoded_string\%,
            "name": "original_image.jpg"
        }
    ]
}
```

---

[12]see: https://github.com/lunactic/DAS_2018_Tutorial/

```
function uploadImage () {
    var data = JSON.stringify ({
        "files": [
            {
                "type": "base64",
                "value": currentImage,
                "name": currentFile.name
            }
        ]
    });
    fetch("http://divaservices.unifr.ch/api/v2/collections", {
        method: "POST",
        body: data,
        headers: new Headers({ 'content-type': 'application/json' })
    }).then(function (res) {
        return res.json();
    }).then(async function (data) {
        collection = data.collection;
    })
}
```

Listing 7.5: My Javascript Example.

7.6.2 *Binarize the Image*

For this workflow we will use Otsu's [Otsu (1979)] binarization algorithm, but the provided source code shows how easy it would be to exchange this with any of the other available methods on DIVAServices. The execution is started by issuing a POST request to the URL of the specific method containing a JSON body similar to the one already shown in Listing 7.2. The source code needed for performing this binarization is shown in Listing 7.6. The result of this step is shown in Figure 7.3. A collection containing this image is automatically created and using this we can automatically create the *identifier* we will need for the text line segmentation step.

```
var data = JSON.stringify ({
    "paramteres":{},
    "data": [
        {
            "inputImage": identifier
        }
    ]
});
fetch("http://divaservices.unifr.ch/api/v2/binarization/
    otsubinarization/1",{
    method: "POST",
    body: data,
    headers: new Headers({ 'content-type': 'application/json' })
}).then(function (res) {
    return res.json();
}).then(async function (data) {
    //Poll for the result
    try {
        var result = await getResult(data.results[0].resultLink);
```

```
} catch (error) {
    return reject(error);
}
var resultCollection = data.resultCollection
identifier = resultCollection + "/" + result.output[0].file.
    options.filename
resolve();
});
```

Listing 7.6: My Javascript Example.

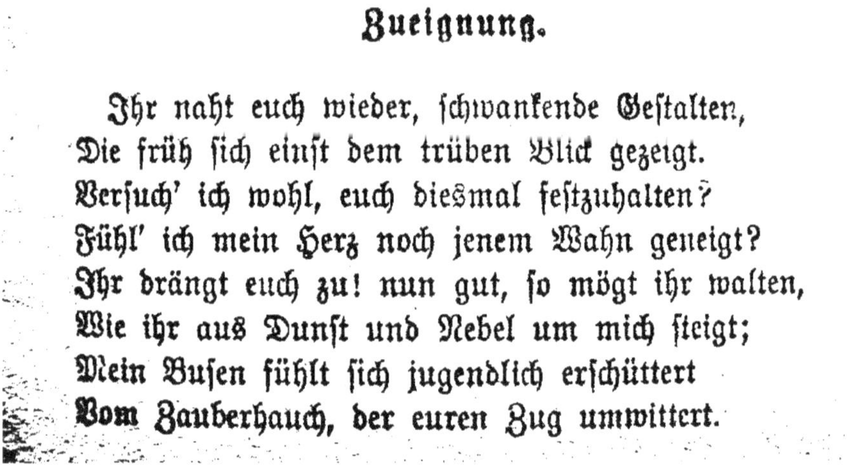

Zueignung.

Ihr naht euch wieder, schwankende Gestalten,
Die früh sich einst dem trüben Blick gezeigt.
Versuch' ich wohl, euch diesmal festzuhalten?
Fühl' ich mein Herz noch jenem Wahn geneigt?
Ihr drängt euch zu! nun gut, so mögt ihr walten,
Wie ihr aus Dunst und Nebel um mich steigt;
Mein Busen fühlt sich jugendlich erschüttert
Vom Zauberhauch, der euren Zug umwittert.

Fig. 7.3: The original image after applying the binarization algorithm. This image shows that there could be better binarization options available that would lead to a cleaner result. With DivaServices exchanging one binarization method with another one is very simple and shown in the online source code.

7.6.3 *Extracting Text Lines*

Using the *identifier* generated at the end of the binarization step we can reference the generated binary image when performing text line segmentation. In this example we will use the segmentation provided by OCRopus as it will generate text line images already in the form needed by its own OCR engine which is used in the final step. This method requires no parameters so the execution is very similar to the binarization and we will omit from showing the JavaScript source code here. The method produces two different results: Individual text line images, as well as a color-coded segmentation image where each foreground pixel belonging to a line is marked with a specific color. In Figure 7.4 we show an adapted version of the colored text line image. The default coloring is changed for better visualization. Figure 7.5 similarly shows the text line image of a single extracted text line that is extracted.

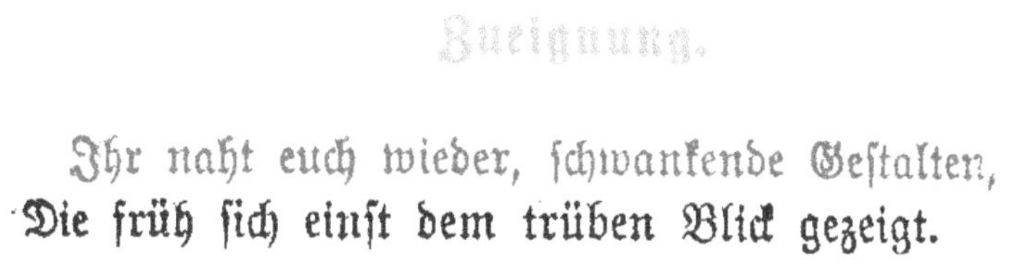

Zueignung.

Ihr naht euch wieder, schwankende Gestalten,
Die früh sich einst dem trüben Blick gezeigt.

Fig. 7.4: The extracted textlines using the text line segmentation method from OCRopus. The output coloring was changed here for better visualization.

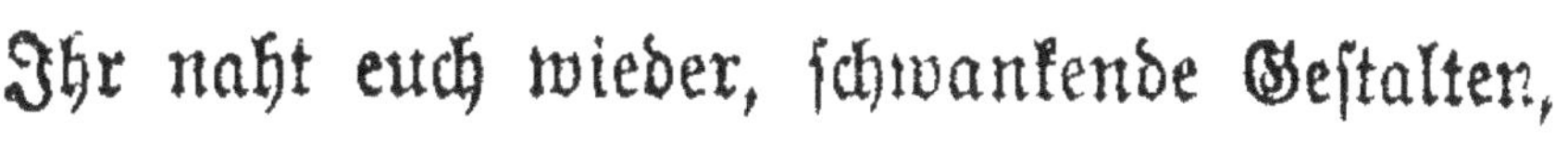

Ihr naht euch wieder, schwankende Gestalten,

Fig. 7.5: Single extracted text line image.

As described above a collection containing all these images is automatically created on DivaServices that can be used in order to perform OCR.

7.6.4 *Performing OCR*

The last step in this workflow is to perform the actual character recognition. For this we will apply the OCR module from OCRopus. As inputs this method requires a trained model as well as the extracted text lines from the previous step. For the model we use a pretrained one that is available online[13] and store it on DivaServices such that we can reference it using an *identifier* as well.

With all this we can start the execution of the method again by issuing a POST request providing all necessary information (the *identifier* of the model, as well as the name of the automatically created collection). This process will return a list of text files, each containing the recognition result of a specific textline. In Figure 7.6 we show the generated transcription aligned with the original input image. This transcription shows, that with the pretrained Fraktura model the recognizer is able to correctly transcribe the special characters appearing in Fraktura ligature (e.g., the long s).

---

[13]see: https://github.com/jze/ocropus-model_fraktur

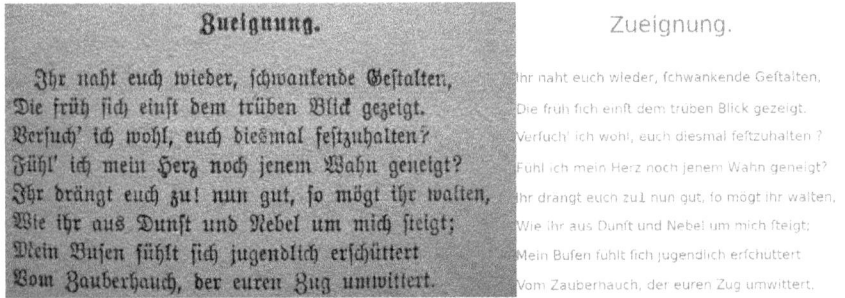

Fig. 7.6: The generated transcription, manually aligned with the original input image for visualization purposes. The text recognition is performed at line level.

This example shows that using DIVAServices a programmer is able to quickly build a workflow, combining multiple methods, that are provided by the system. The provided solution requires less than 300 lines of code, require no external libraries, and can be executed in any regular internet browser.

7.7   The Ecosystem of DivaServices

The core platform of DIVAServices simply provides access to DIA methods over a RESTful Web Service interface. Browsing such an interface and gathering information for a human is not very easy as the only response is provided in JSON. So since the inception of DIVAServices it was clear that there is a need for systems that should be built around the core platform to make interaction with it easier.

In [Würsch *et al.* (2018)] we argue that tools and services in the ecosystem for a platform like DIVAServices should address the following points:

- **Data-Management**: Provide access to and browse data that is available on the platform. Allow for the search of existing datasets.
- **Experimentation**: Tools that enable users to run quick experiments on the existing methods in order probe the capabilities of these methods.
- **Method-Management**: Allowing third-parties to provide methods and manage those. Such tools should also provide insights into how these methods perform (e.g., how often they are used, on what data, etc.).

- **APIs / Libraries**: Providing good tooling in different programming languages is important. These libraries should help developers in interacting with the platform, e.g., in the process of creating complex workflows.

In this section we want to show two examples of tools that we built alongside DIVAServices targeting the Experimentation and Data-Management point from above. DIVAServices-Spotlight, a web application that allows user to experiment with the existing methods, and DIVAccess, a web application that allows users to browse the existing data on DIVAServices.

7.7.1 Diva*Services-Spotlight*

DIVAServices-Spotlight [Würsch *et al.* (2016b,a)][14] is a web application that allows users perform experiments with the existing methods. Users can upload their own images, apply they different methods on them get access to the results. We aimed at building the user interface in an intuitive way that also allows it to be used by non domain experts, especially scholars in the Digital Humanities who often can greatly benefit from the offered methods. The idea is that users can use DIVAServices-Spotlight to find the correct methods they want to use given their use case, before taking the time and implement it in a similar fashion as explained in Section 7.6.

In Figure 7.7 we show an excerpt from the web application showing parts of the result page. The user applied an music object detection method [Pacha *et al.* (2018)] on an image containing hand drawn music scores. Once the result is made available to the user he will be able to see the original input image on the left, as well as a visualization of the results on the right. The two windows are synchronized such that the user can move, and zoom the image and investigate the results closely while referencing back to the original input.

Currently, DIVAServices-Spotlight does not support all the features that the platform offers. Mainly it can not work with methods that require more than one file as input. Furthermore, the application currently does not check if a certain input works on a given method, this can sometimes lead to methods not working on certain inputs and returning errors. It should also be noted that DIVAServices-Spotlight should not be used as a productive application in an active research environment but for the sole purpose of

---

[14]see http://divaservices.unifr.ch/spotlight

Input   Output

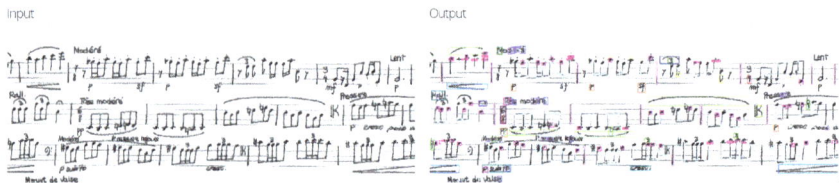

Fig. 7.7: Input and Output visualization on Spotlight. The displayed method here performs object detection on music scores and was provided to DIVAServices by the authors of the paper [Pacha *et al.* (2018)].

running small scale experiments. For all other purposes we strongly advise to build applications targeting the specific use case and directly interacting with DIVAServices through the REST API as shown in Section 7.6.

7.7.2 Diva*Services-WebInterface*

DIVAServices-WebInterface[15] provides access to all the data that is available on DIVAServices. It allows user to browse and search for existing collection, and view all the individual files that are stored within each collection. This should help users in finding data that might be of use to them for their specific use cases, e.g., as training data for a machine learning approach. Figure 7.8 provides an example of the browsing of files in a collection. If the collection contains only image files the user is presented with a preview of each of these files.

Fig. 7.8: Browsing files in a collection with DIVAccess. For images, the user is directly presented with a preview of it.

Additionally, like DIVAServices-Spotlight, DIVAServices-WebInterface allows users to run small experiments using the existing methods. In this regards it solves some of the issues, that DIVAServices-Spotlight has (e.g., it is possible to use methods with multiple file inputs), but it is also targeted more towards developers and less towards a non expert user group.

---

[15]see: http://divaservices.unifr.ch/data

7.7.3   Diva*Services-Management*

In order to address the Method-Management, we built DIVAServices-Management,[16] a tool for anyone to semi-automatically provide methods to the DIVAServices platform. As shown in Figure 7.9 the overview page lists the methods installed by this specific user and how often they have been used.

Fig. 7.9:   Overview of methods provided by a specific user. The user can see how often each of his provided methods has been used, and whether or not they have produced any error messages.

The application provides a wizard that guides users when providing new methods. In this wizards the user is asked to provide all the information necessary to add the method onto the platform (needed inputs, generated outputs, and the Docker image to be used).

The features of this application could still be greatly expanded. For method providers it would be interesting to see on what kind of data their methods were used on, what kind of results were produced but also if users are pleased with the results.

7.8   Conclusion and Future Work

In this Chapter we provide a thorough introduction into the DIVAServices platform. A platform that provides access to state-of-the-art DIA methods as RESTful Web Services. At the time of writing the platform offers access to 31 different methods, provided by various institutions.

In our continuous effort to promote open research all source code created by the authors of this chapter that are related to DIVAServices are released under a GNU Lesser General Public License, version 2.1 (LGPL) license. This allows others to see examples on how to interact with the platform, the approaches we used when building it in a hope that others will follow similar.

---

[16]see http://divaservices.unifr.ch/management

Going forward we have plans to enrich the main DIVAServices platform, as well as the ecosystem with more tools and features. One of the main tools we plan to build in the future is an API for developers that help them building workflows directly in a programming language without the need to chain the methods themselves. This API would hide the inner workings of interacting with DIVAServices and aid software developers when building applications that want to make use of methods provided through the platform.

Also we are constantly in the process of expanding the list of methods that are available on DIVAServices to provide as much state-of-the-art methods as possible.

References

Boettiger, C. (2015). An introduction to Docker for reproducible research, *ACM SIGOPS Operating Systems Review* **49**, 1, pp. 71–79, doi:10.1145/2723872. 2723882.

Chojnacki, S., Cowley, A., Lee, J., Foix, A., and Lopez, R. (2017). Programmatic access to bioinformatics tools from EMBL-EBI update: 2017, *Nucleic Acids Research* **45**, W1, pp. W550–W553, doi:10.1093/nar/gkx273.

Goujon, M., McWilliam, H., Li, W., Valentin, F., Squizzato, S., Paern, J., and Lopez, R. (2010). A new bioinformatics analysis tools framework at EMBL-EBI, *Nucleic Acids Research* **38**, SUPPL. 2, doi:10.1093/nar/gkq313.

Lamiroy, B. and Lopresti, D. (2011). An open architecture for end-to-end document analysis benchmarking, in *Proceedings of the International Conference on Document Analysis and Recognition, ICDAR*, ISBN 9780769545202, pp. 42–47, doi:10.1109/ICDAR.2011.18.

Lopresti, D. and Lamiroy, B. (2011). Document analysis research in the year 2021, in *Modern Approaches in Applied Intelligence, LNCS*, Vol. 6703 (Springer), pp. 264–274.

Neudecker, C., Schlarb, S., Dogan, Z. M., Missier, P., Sufi, S., Williams, A., and Wolstencroft, K. (2011). An experimental workflow development platform for historical document digitisation and analysis, in *Proceedings of the 2011 Workshop on Historical Document Imaging and Processing - HIP '11*, p. 161.

Otsu, N. (1979). A Threshold Selection Method from Gray-level Histograms, *IEEE transactions on systems, man, and cybernetics* **9**, 1, pp. 62–66.

Pacha, A., Hajič, J., and Calvo-Zaragoza, J. (2018). A Baseline for General Music Object Detection with Deep Learning, *Applied Sciences* **8**, 9, p. 1488, doi:10.3390/app8091488, http://www.mdpi.com/2076-3417/8/9/1488.

Richardson, L. (2007). *RESTful Web Services* (O'Reilly), ISBN 978-0-596-52926-0, doi:0596554605.

Sánchez, J. A., Schofield, P., Depuydt, K., Gatos, B., Davis, R. M., and Mühlberger, G. (2013). tranScriptorium: an European Project on Handwritten Text

Recognition, in *DocEng'13, September 2013, Florence, Italy* (ACM Press), ISBN 9781450317894, pp. 227–228.

Wang, T., Wu, D., Coates, A., and Ng, A. (2012). End-to-end text recognition with convolutional neural networks, in *Proceedings - International Conference on Pattern Recognition*, ISBN 9784990644109.

Würsch, M., Bärtschi, M., Ingold, R., and Liwick, M. (2016a). DIVAServices-Spotlight – Experimenting with Document Image Analysis Methods in the Web, in *Digital Humanities* (Krakow, Poland).

Würsch, M., Ingold, R., and Liwicki, M. (2016b). DivaServices—A RESTful web service for Document Image Analysis methods, *Digital Scholarship in the Humanities* **32**, suppl_1, pp. i150–i156.

Würsch, M., Ingold, R., and Liwicki, M. (2016). SDK Reinvented: Document Image Analysis Methods as RESTful Web Services, in *International Workshop on Document Analysis Systems*, pp. 90–95.

Würsch, M., Liwicki, M., and Ingold, R. (2018). Web Services in Document Image Analysis - Recent Developments and the Importance of Building an Ecosystem, in *13th IAPR Workshop on Document Analysis Systems* (Vienna, Austria), p. accepted.

Chapter 8

GraphManuscribble: Interactive Annotation of Historical Manuscripts

Angelika Garz

DIVA Group, University of Fribourg, Switzerland
angelika.garz@gmail.com

8.1 Introduction

Give a person a page of a manuscript, and they will instantly and intuitively be capable of recognising its fundamental structures, regions, and objects; we can identify handwritten words, form text lines, and recognize embellishments and decorations in historical documents without difficulty regardless of the language or script it is written in. Whether that is an ancient European script, Arabian, Cyrillic, illegible cursive handwriting, or exotic layouts such as the spiraling texts in Babylonian Aramaic Magic Bowls, intricate curving lines, or more elusive layouts such as writing embedded in works of art such as paintings. To us, a manuscript is composed of meaningful structures, regions, and objects that we can interpret; and we can agree on the regions and their semantic meaning on a high level, establish connections and relations between parts, and understand boundaries and belonging, without needing to read or understand the content.

Yet automatically processing these documents, handwritten documents with complex layouts in particular, remains a difficult task that has not been solved. To overcome this difficulty, semi-automatic methods that integrate the human user into the process are needed. We propose a semi-automatic document image annotation system called *GraphManuscribble* developed for directly interacting with a digital facsimile of a manuscript; particularly to segment, extract, or mark its contents. It exploits the new human-computer interaction patterns evolving around touch-screen devices that are operated with a stylus, such as Microsoft Surface, and builds upon document graphs that capture the structure of a manuscript similar to human perception.

We humans are excellent in perceiving objects — when looking at the world, we perceive a complex scene composed of many groups of object, themselves comprising smaller parts. Yet, as the famous saying '*the whole is something else than the sum of its parts*' [Koffka (1935)] says, we can isolate it from other objects and background, complete a figure that is occluded or fill a gap; we also tend to group objects that are similar with respect to a certain aspect, or we group them to a bigger object, and also we perceive objects as belonging together if they are close.

This ability of so-called perceptual grouping is to '*solve the problem of 'what goes with what' and the differentiation of figure from ground*' [Han et al. (1999)]. It has been studied in Gestalt psychology, which states that '*form emerges as result of the relationship [and complex interactions] between the parts*' [Brock (2006)]. Gestalt psychology has identified several properties of human perception that allow us to distinguish and define a collection of patterns and to make a grouping with respect to a similarity criterion [Breidbach and Jost (2006)]: proximity, similarity, closure, symmetry, continuity, familiarity, 'common fate' (parallelism), and 'Good Gestalt' (c.f. Fig. 8.1 for an illustration). Pattern recognition and computer vision researchers have drawn inspiration from those factors for grouping algorithms.

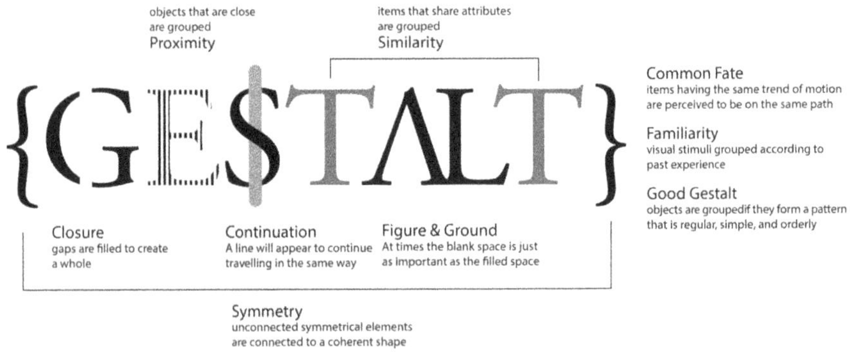

Fig. 8.1: Gestalt principles illustrated. Figure adapted from original source: http://yusylvia.wordpress.com.

In this chapter, we explore how to harness the concepts of Gestalt psychology for the purpose of semi-automatically annotating and segmenting historical manuscripts in a way that is intuitive and comprehensible to a user on the one hand, and efficient and effective on the other. In order to mimic the perceptual grouping described previously in our document images, we adopt graphs [Conte *et al.* (2004); Vento (2013); Kandel *et al.* (2007)]. Graphs are mathematical structures that model (pairwise) relations between objects; we employ them to represent document structures such as layout elements, their parts, and their respective relationships. Graph edges put into relation parts (nodes) with one another, group, and organize them (topology). Given an appropriate definition of topology, i.e., selection of parts and their relations, graph-based grouping can achieve a structure on the document page that is similar to human perception.

The essence of the semi-automatic document image annotation system *GraphManuscribble* we present in this chapter is captured in the metaphor of a propagating highlighter pen: using a pen input device a user scribbles directly onto a document image in order to select or annotate manuscript parts, and harnessing a graph that captures the structure of the document in a way that strongly resembles the user's own perception and expectations, the highlighting is propagated through the document following this structure.

Employing the graph that captures the document's structure facilitates a way of natural human-machine interaction: graphs allow for imprecise interactions on the user's part since the user simply marks interesting areas, the annotation is propagated through the document's structure owing to the graph. We suggest a swift and natural user interaction pattern to interact with the graph, which we call 'scribbling'. Scribbling is universal: our toddlers as soon as they get pen or paint into their fingers — often to the despair of their parents —, pupils to pass time in the classroom, adults when talking on the phone or in a meeting. Scribbling is skill that we learn easily and with little effort — it does not require prior knowledge or schooling — and we enjoy it as a pastime. Thus, we have decided to make use of this natural skill. Technically speaking, the user inserts and deletes graph edges in order to create text lines and decoration elements. Finally, while the user exerts imprecise interactions in a manner natural to them, the accurate operations such as the precise region segmentation are automatically retrieved from the graph. The layout elements segmented by the user are then represented as non-convex polygons, which can efficiently be extracted from the graph. Although the proposed system is not limited to segmenting a page but could also be used for any kind of physical annotation, we will concentrate on that aspect in this chapter.

A sample image patch annotated with scribbles using the proposed tool, and a segmentation derived from this annotation represented as a coloured polygon are shown in Fig. 8.2. Videos illustrating the interaction to obtain this segmentation.[1] and further supplementary material are provided on the project homepage.[2]

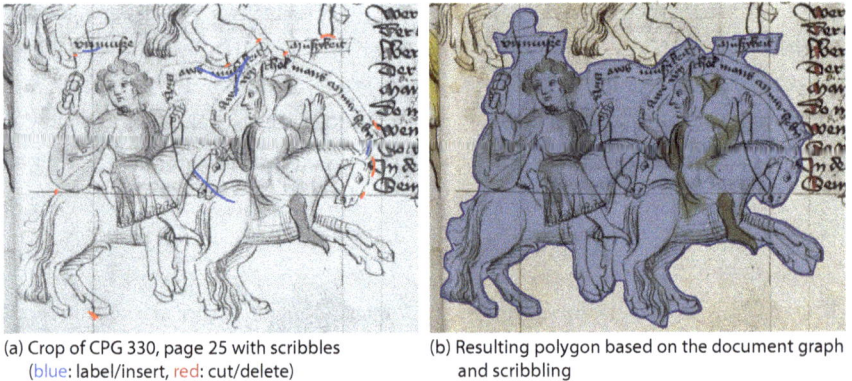

(a) Crop of CPG 330, page 25 with scribbles
(blue: label/insert, red: cut/delete)

(b) Resulting polygon based on the document graph
and scribbling

Fig. 8.2: Central idea of the proposed system: when using a document graph to represent the foreground structures of a document with only a few scribbles we can segment layout elements. The polygon used to represent the segmentation is derived from the labelled and segmented underlying graph. Image source DOI:10.11588/diglit.141#0025.

In the following, we discuss related work in Section 8.2, provide details on the underlying document graphs in Section 8.3, and present the scribbling interaction in Section 8.4. Conclusions and an outlook to future work are provided in Section 8.5.

Note that the contents of this chapter closely correspond to specific sections of the author's PhD thesis [Garz (2017)]. We refer the reader to the thesis for a more comprehensive introduction into the topic.

---

[1]https://youtu.be/gMTQWxwZy9E
[2]http://diuf.unifr.ch/hisdoc/graphmanuscribble

8.2   Related Work

Integrating users into the segmentation process has been studied, e.g., to generate ground truth for training and evaluating machine learning algorithms or to provide semi-automatic systems for scholars. In this summary, we will focus on the annotation of the physical layout which is most relevant with respect to the proposed tool, and will omit the aspect of logical labelling; see Table 8.1 for an overview of the tools surveyed in this section.

8.2.1   *Document Segmentation and Annotation Systems*

Amongst other characteristics, we can group annotation systems into those representing entities by rectangular or polygonal regions, and those aiming at accurate pixel annotation. An example of the latter is WebGT [Biller *et al.* (2013)] for web-based ground truth creation with the idea of simultaneously serving to humanists and computer scientists to allow collective annotation of historical documents. The system follows a bottom-up approach, where the user starts on character level and builds a hierarchy. Although pixels are labelled with a semi-automatic approach relying on connected components with local thresholding, the entities are presented to the user as bounding boxes. Since bounding boxes are likely to overlap it remains unclear how users verify their selection with respect to specific pixels. WebGT draws on mouse gestures and keyboard shortcuts as interaction patterns.

PixLabeler [Saund *et al.* (2009)] is a ground truthing tool for modern printed documents with pixel labelling. They rely on binarized images. Pixels are selected by either rectangle, lasso, polygon, or a brush. Rectangle or lasso are drawn by dragging the mouse, and polygons by clicking to create their vertices. With the brush, foreground pixels are selected when the brush is dragged over them. Automatic labelling is limited to detection of connected components, vertical and horizontal lines.

The APEP-te platform [Karatzas *et al.* (2014)] is a set of tools for document processing, specifically ground truthing and evaluation. It is based on Clavelli et al. 's framework [Clavelli *et al.* (2010)] and has been used for the ICDAR 2011 and 2013 Robust Reading competitions [Karatzas *et al.* (2011); Shahab *et al.* (2011); Karatzas *et al.* (2013)]. Similar to WebGT, the system follows a bottom-up approach starting from pixel-labelling and then grouping those to larger entities. User interaction is mostly based on the mouse, and pixel labelling is done '*in various ways, from individual pixel labelling to adjustable flood fill operations*' [Karatzas *et al.* (2014)].

Table 8.1: Related work in interactive semi-automatic annotation tools. The table is sorted chronologically, giving the name of the tool and the paper, the year, the goal the tool has been developed for, the data considered (e.g., historical manuscripts, modern printed documents), the goal of the annotation, the representation of the annotation, automatic methods supporting the user, the interaction patterns used, and finally the input devices (I) considered (m and k stand for mouse and keyboard, respectively).

Paper	Goal	Data	Annot.	Repr.	Automatic	Interaction	I
Pink Panther: [Yanikoglu and Vincent (1998)]	ground truth, benchmarking	modern print	polygon labelling	polygons, rectangles	-	click polygon vertices	m
TrueViz: [Kanungo et al. (2000); Lee and Kanungo (2003)]	visualization of ground truth, edit meta data for OCR	modern print	-	bounding boxes, polygons	-	click	m, k
OCROpus: [Breuel (2008)]	document analysis system, focus on OCR	print	-	polygons	fully automatic	parameter tuning	m, k
LabelMe: [Russell et al. (2008)]	annotation, ground truth	natural images	polygon labelling	polygons, bounding boxes	-	click	m
PixLabeler: [Saund et al. (2009)]	ground truth	modern print	pixel labelling	color-coded pixels	detect connected components, vertical & horizontal lines	draw rectangle, lasso, polygon, paint brush	m
GEDI: [Doermann et al. (2010)]	document image annotation	modern print	polygons, rectangles	polygons, rectangles	transcription text line alignment	click polygon vertices	m, k
IAM-HistDB tool: [Fischer et al. (2010)]	ground truth	historical handwritten	rectangles	polygons	segmentation, then corrected by the user	click & drag polygon vertices	m
Aletheia: [Clausner et al. (2011)]	comprehensive document annotation system	historical handwritten to modern print	polygons	polygons	several	draw rectangle, lasso, polygon, paint brush, separating lines, etc	m, k
WebGT: [Biller et al. (2013)]	ground truth	historical Arabic manuscripts	pixel labelling	bounding boxes	detect connected components with adaptive threshold	click on connected components, draw separate lines	m, k
APEP-te platform: [Karatzas et al. (2014)]	ground truth, evaluation	modern and historical print	pixel labelling	color-coded pixels, rectangles	several	*'individual pixel labelling to adjustable flood fill operations'* [Karatzas et al. (2014)]	m, k
[Kassis and El-Sana (2016)]	page segmentation in text blocks	Arabic handwritten	pixel labelling	pixel labelling	Gabor filters, Grab Cut [Rother et al. (2004)]	scribble	m

Fig. 8.3: Image patch (a), with different segmentations (c.1–c.6), and a heat map (b) representing the average labelling, where blue is labeled background and red is labeled foreground in 100 % of the cases, respectively. Figure adapted from [Barney Smith (2010)].

Although pixel-labelling can be seen as a very versatile way of annotating a manuscript, it is limited in other aspects. Albeit each pixel can be annotated with several labels and also belonging can be encoded, each such coding remains a binary decision, and pixel-labels are an inefficient data storage and can be tedious for processing. Also, changing pixel labels is a potentially dull job for a human. The aspect of binary decisions particularly comes forth when considering that users put to the task of pixel-accurate segmentation often cannot actually agree on which pixels belong to an object and which are background, as borders are fuzzy and smooth when zooming in enough [Barney Smith (2010)]. An analysis of ground truth for binarization [Barney Smith (2010)] showed that the variability in the pixel labelling done by different participants is significant (c.f. Fig. 8.3). This gives rise to several questions: *How accurate does a labelling really need to be? Respectively, how accurate can it be? When do we force a binary decision without the need? Or when does such a boundary become a philosophical rather than academic question?* Also, different applications or tasks at hand might ask for a different granularity or tightness of labels.

Polygonal representations, on the contrary, can answer several of these questions — they are readily understood by users, are efficient to store, and can be adjusted with little effort if done well. Operations that modify polygons are well-defined topological algorithms, such as joining or intersecting polygons, or simplifying a detailed to a more coarse representation. Furthermore, the advantage of pixel-based methods being a '*more universal measure for assessing labeling quality, either on a pixel count basis or in terms of groupings of labeled pixels into connected components or larger structures*' [Saund *et al.* (2009)] can be countered on the basis that also with polygons such a foreground pixel-based measure is possible when using a binarized image in conjunction with the polygon annotation [Fischer *et al.* (2014); Garz *et al.* (2013); Yanikoglu and Vincent (1998)].

There is an abundance of tools for modern printed documents, some of which we list in the following. Pink Panther [Yanikoglu and Vincent (1998)] is one of the early tools; it combines ground truthing and automatic page segmentation benchmarking. Labelling is done with rectangles and polygons using mouse clicks; relationships between labels can be established. GEDI [Doermann *et al.* (2010)] is a system for document image annotation relying on rectangles and polygons using mouse clicks; it also comprises a comprehensive set of ground truthing tools. GEDI's particular highlight is text annotation which allows a transcription to be aligned with the image. Aletheia [Clausner *et al.* (2011)] is arguably the most comprehensive system for annotating modern and historical printed documents alike. It supports both, top-down and bottom-up approaches. When employing a top-down approach, the user selects composite structures such as text blocks, and refines the selection with split and shrink tools; grouping is supported for bottom-up. Regions are annotated with rectangles and polygons using mouse interaction. Other examples include TrueViz [Kanungo *et al.* (2000); Lee and Kanungo (2003)] for ground truth and meta data editing, and OCRopus [Breuel (2008)], an open-source document analysis, segmentation, Optical Character Recognition (OCR), and language modelling system.

A well-known online annotation tool in Computer Vision is LabelMe [Russell *et al.* (2008)] developed for collaboratively annotating large datasets of natural images. The main interest was object detection and classification. Users draw polygons by clicking along the boundary of an object.

In the domain of historical documents, examples include DMOS for civil status registers and military forms [Coüasnon *et al.* (2007)], DEBORA for Renaissance documents [Bourgeois and Emptoz (2007)], CATTI [Romero *et al.* (2007)] and STATE [Gordo *et al.* (2008)] for old Spanish manuscripts, PhaseGT [Nafchi *et al.* (2013)] for binarization of historical document images, and the IAM-HistDB system [Fischer *et al.* (2010)] for old German manuscripts. Of this collection, the IAM-HistDB tool is maybe the tool most relevant to this chapter, although it was mainly developed for text line annotation. The tool is a semi-automatic system where a user first draws a polygon around the text area, and then corrects the polygons created by a seam-carving algorithm that separates two lines. Correcting the polygons is done by dragging their vertices with a mouse.

Recently, Kassis and El-Sana [Kassis and El-Sana (2016)] proposed a system based on Gabor-filter processing and scribbling; the segmentation is performed on pixel level. The authors employ Gabor filters in order to capture the texture of document regions, and then segment a page based on the filtering result, user scribbles, and Grab Cut [Rother *et al.* (2004)]. They claim that their approach requires less effort from the user than our proposed system; however, their comparison is not entirely sound since their segmentation is very coarse: they only segment text blocks, not text lines.

8.2.2 *Human-Computer Interaction in Image Segmentation*

A common thread through the annotation tools summarized before is their interaction pattern: users create polygons or bounding boxes with mouse clicks; a few support '*brushing*' foreground pixels of binarized documents.

Methods relying on interaction patterns most closely related to the scribbling interaction proposed in this chapter originate in computer vision (c.f. Table 8.2 for an overview). Different interaction patterns have been adopted for image segmentation methods, most of which rely on pixel data. They are similar our proposed system with respect to coarse user interaction and automatically refined segmentation.

Amongst them are notably Adobe's *Magic Wand*[3] and *Quick Selection*[4] tools, the *Intelligent Scissors* [Mortensen and Barrett (1998)] (aka magnetic lasso), and GrabCut [Rother *et al.* (2004)]. The document annotation system APEP-te's [Karatzas *et al.* (2014)] flood-filling of foreground pixels can also be related to the *propagating highlighter* property of our proposal. Generally, we observe a growing trend towards human-machine interaction patterns that make use of both, touch-sensitive screens and pen-input devices, to permit a direct natural interaction with documents displayed on the screen [Toselli *et al.* (2010)].

---

[3]Adobe Systems Incorporated (2016). Adobe Photoshop User Guide.
[4]Adobe Systems Incorporated (2007). Adobe Photoshop CS3 Product Overview.

Table 8.2: Related work in human computer interaction for segmentation. The table gives the respective approaches and the interaction pattern employed.

Paper	Year	Method	Interaction
Adobe Magic Wand	-	select regions within a intensity and color threshold	click onto region with mouse
Adobe Quick Selection	2007	select regions with similar pixel intensities, color, and texture	click and drag with mouse
Snakes/Active Contours [Kass et al. (1988)]	1988	energy minimizing deformable spline	click control points with mouse
Intelligent Scissors/Magnetic Lasso [Mortensen and Barrett (1998)]	1998	minimum cost path using pixel intensities, colour	trace the boundary with the mouse
GrabCut [Rother et al. (2004)]	2004	Graph Cut [Greig et al. (1989)] with priors	draw a bounding box, scribble to select fore and background

Adobe's *Magic Wand* tool starts from a user-specified point in an image and selects connected pixels that lie within a color range from that pixel (c.f. Fig. 8.4(a)). The tolerance level is user-defined and sometimes tedious to determine. First introduced in Photoshop CS3 in 2007, the *Quick Selection* tool is similar to the Magic Wand but more powerful. It is a brush that selects pixels based on their intensity, color, and texture; its selection is limited by the edges of objects (c.f. Fig. 8.4(b)).

The *Intelligent Scissors* [Mortensen and Barrett (1998)] allow the user to roughly trace an object's boundary with the mouse and using contrast information the best segmentation path along the boundary is found (c.f. Fig. 8.4(c)[5]). A related approach for automatic refinement of magnetic lasso selection are *Snakes* or *Active Contours* [Kass et al. (1988)] (c.f. Fig. 8.4(d)). Snakes can be understood as deformable splines that are matched to an image with energy minimization. The user gives a control points, and the snake deforms such that it fits the nearest salient contour.

Grab Cut [Rother et al. (2004)] where the user draws a bounding box and an iterative graph cut [Greig et al. (1989)] based on Gaussian mixture models performs the segmentation (c.f. Fig. 8.4(c.1–c.2)).

The methods summarized above rely on pixel data; that is gradients in pixel intensities, color or texture differences. For documents with their rather

---

[5]In Fig. 8.4 Photoshop CS6's *Magnetic Lasso* was used.

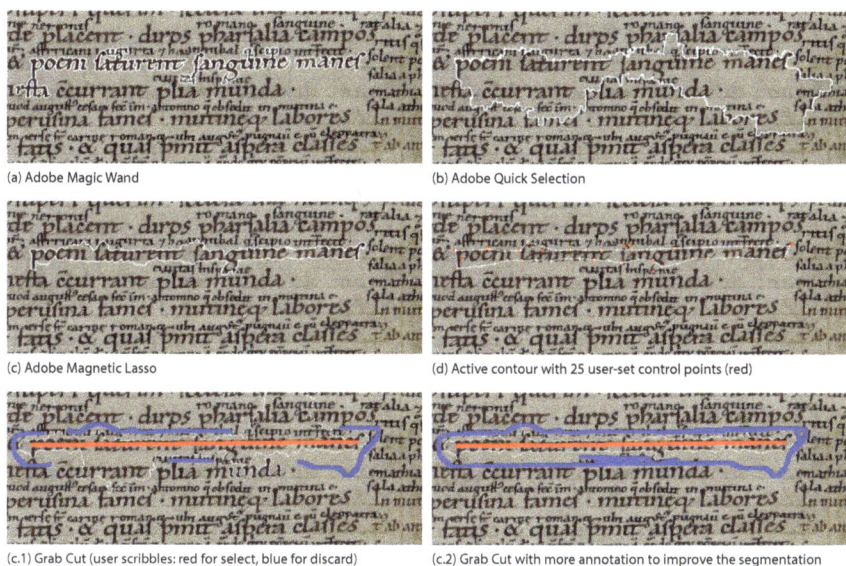

(a) Adobe Magic Wand

(b) Adobe Quick Selection

(c) Adobe Magnetic Lasso

(d) Active contour with 25 user-set control points (red)

(c.1) Grab Cut (user scribbles: red for select, blue for discard)

(c.2) Grab Cut with more annotation to improve the segmentation

Fig. 8.4: Selecting a text line with the five segmentation tools.

specific textures, such tools are either bound to be cumbersome, requiring a lot of manual corrections, or imprecise. Figure 8.4 compares the five segmentation tools for selecting a part of a text line of a historical manuscript: the *Magic Wand*, the *Quick Selection*, the *Magnetic Lasso* of Photoshop CS6, *Active Contours*, and GrabCut. Even though the *Magic Wand* tool makes a rather precise selection — aside from touching glosses — it required a lot of manual interaction (clicking on each independent component). The *Quick Selection* tool, although good for natural images, fails in presence of the special texture of such documents. The selection with the *Magnetic Lasso* is rather satisfactory; however, it required precise tracing of the characters boundaries, making it tedious when done over an extended period of time. *Active Contours* required 25 control points for the shown segmentation, and still the spline does not satisfactorily adjust to the text line. For GrabCut to work sufficiently well, a lot of scribbling is necessary; this is obviously cumbersome to do for an entire page, and even more for a full document.

In contrast to these pixel-based segmentation approaches, our proposal draws from the inherent structure of the document image represented by graphs rather than its pixel differences; thus avoiding the mentioned problems. The next section will describe in detail the graphs developed for representing document pages.

8.3   Document Graphs

For the proposed graph-based annotation system, we extract a sparse graph representation of a document's foreground starting from the image. The foreground estimation of a document image follows the assumption that strong gradient changes in the pixel data indicate its presence [Garz *et al.* (2012)], i.e., it is rich in terms of local information contents (such as significant 2D texture). We then extract points along those gradient changes as graph nodes. The graph's edges are obtained from triangulating its nodes, and finally, we employ a Minimum Spanning Tree (MST) to cluster the graph, providing a sparse structural representation of the document (c.f. Fig. 8.5 for an example). The sparse document graph is the very essence of the proposed method; subgraphs that constitute layout elements are then extracted from it in a semi-automatic fashion with a pen-based interaction. Their physical location and extent are finally described by polygons derived from the graph.

8.3.1   *Basic Definitions for Graphs*

A labeled *graph* is a 4-tuple

$$G = (V, E, \mu, \nu) \tag{8.1}$$

where V is the finite set of *nodes*, and $|V|$ is the *order* of the graph; the set $E \subseteq V \times V$ contains the graph's *edges*. This chapter considers *undirected* graphs, where each edge is an unordered pair $e = \{v, w\}$ with v and w being called the edge's *endpoints*. If $\{w, u\} \in E$, w is a neighbor of u; we call each node's set of neighbors its *neighborhood*. $\mu : V \to L_V$ is the node labeling function with the domain L_V, and $\nu : E \to L_E$ is the edge labeling function with the domain L_E. Furthermore, we constrain the graphs to *planar graphs*, that are graphs that can be drawn on a plane in $\mathbb{R}^2$ in such a way that its edges intersect only at their endpoints, i.e., edges do not cross in $\mathbb{R}^2$.

A partition of a graph's nodes V into two non-empty sets S and $T = V \setminus S$ with $S, T \in V$, $S \cup T = V$, $S \cap T = \emptyset$ we call a *cut*; with the *cut size* being the number of edges that connect nodes from either sets:

$$c(S, T) = |\{\{u, v\} \in E | u \in S, v \in T\}| \tag{8.2}$$

If there is a *path* from u to v, that is the sequence of edges that lead the way starting from node $u_0 = u$ and ending in $u_{k+1} = v$, the nodes u and v are *connected*; there might be several such paths.

$$\{u, u_1\}, \{u_1, u_2\}, \dots, \{u_{k-1}, u_k\}, \{u_k, v\} \tag{8.3}$$

Table 8.3: Method Parameters (▶ marks the preferred graph nodes). Table adapted from [Garz *et al.* (2016)].

Name	Description	Val
Binarization (Section 8.3.2)		
DoG Binarization	standard deviation	$\sigma_1 = 15.0$ px
	standard deviation	$\sigma_2 = 1.5$ px
	threshold	$T_b = 0.8$
Graph Nodes (Section 8.3.2)		
▶ Contour points	density	$d = 2.0$ px
Topological contour points	error [Douglas and Peucker (1973)]	$\epsilon = 0.5$ px
Harris-Laplace points	initial blur	$\sigma = 3.0$ px
	detection scale	$\sigma = 2\text{-}5$ px
DoG points	Gaussian standard deviation	$\sigma = 1.6$ px
	# octaves	$o = 4.0$
	# levels	$s = 2.0$
	detection threshold	$T_d = 11.0$
Edge Weights (Section 8.3.4)		
Weight matrix	(prefers horizontal edges)	$W = \left(\begin{smallmatrix} 0.5 & 0 \\ 0 & 1.5 \end{smallmatrix}\right)$
Split Layout Elements (Section 8.3.5)		
Threshold		$T = $ user def
Polygonization (Section 8.3.7)		
Polygon tightness	edge length threshold [Duckham *et al.* (2008)]	$T_a = $ user def
Topological simplification	error [Douglas and Peucker (1973)]	$\epsilon = 1.0$ px

A path's *length* is then its number of edges, and the *distance* between the nodes u and v is the length of the *shortest path* connecting them.

A subgraph $G_S = (S, E_S, \mu, \nu)$ of $G = (V, E, \mu, \nu)$ consists of a subset of graph G's nodes $S \subseteq V$, and edges $E_S \subseteq E$. A connected acyclic subgraph comprising all nodes with the minimum number of edges $(|V| - 1)$ is called a *spanning tree*. A Minimum Spanning Tree (MST) is a spanning tree with the smallest sum of edge weights.

Figure 8.5 summarizes the graph extraction process discussed below, with Table 8.3 providing a comprehensive list of the system parameters; note that of the sources for graph nodes listed, only one is chosen in practice.

8.3.2 *Graph Nodes*

Depending on the characteristics and density of graph nodes chosen, different uses of a document graph are facilitated: from high-level applications, e.g., coarse graphs of the entire page that capture the structure to derive the reading order; to fine granularity that capture the details, e.g., for character (a.1) Original image   (a.2) DoG image (contrast improved)   (a.3) Binarized image

(b) Graph Nodes V   (c) Graph G$_T$ (d) Graph G$_M$ (M$_{ST}$)

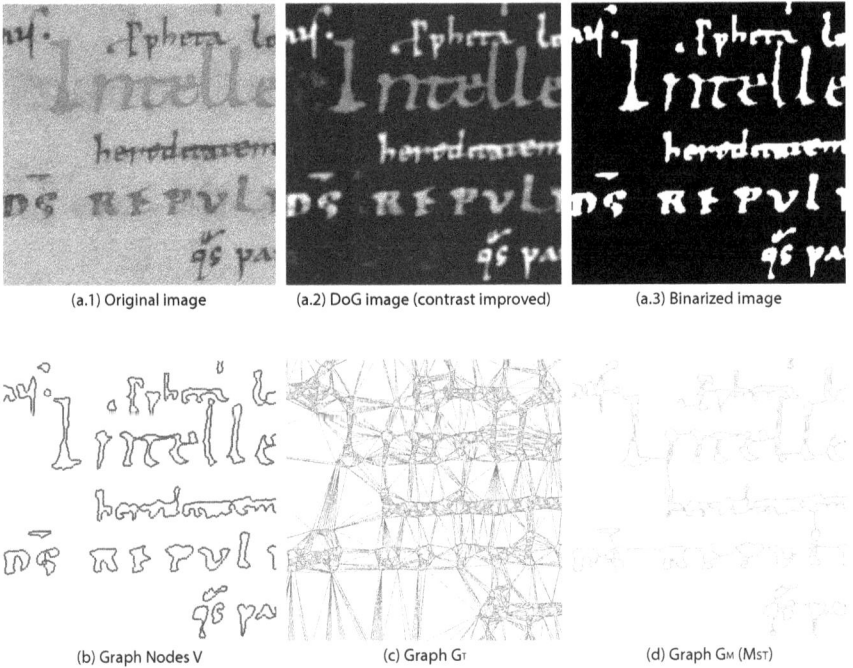

Fig. 8.5: Graph creation from the original image (a.1), with the DoG image shown in (a.2), and the binarized version in (a.3). Nodes (from contour points, c.f. Section 8.3.2) are depicted as blue disks (b), the document graph G_T in blue (c), and the MST G_M in orange (d).

recognition. For our application, a graph that represents the foreground relatively detailed is needed.

We define the nodes of the graph $v \in V$ labeled with their image coordinates:

$$\mu(v) = (x, y) \in \mathbb{R}^2 \tag{8.4}$$

We consider four sources for graph nodes, where two each originate from binarized and from gray-scale images, respectively (see Fig. 8.6). First, we describe nodes derived from binary images, followed by nodes originating from gray-scale images. We prefer nodes extracted from an image over a connected-component-based approach for two reasons: firstly, we do not need to split connected components that join adjacent lines with a heuristic, and secondly, we achieve a more dense and precise representation of the document's structure.

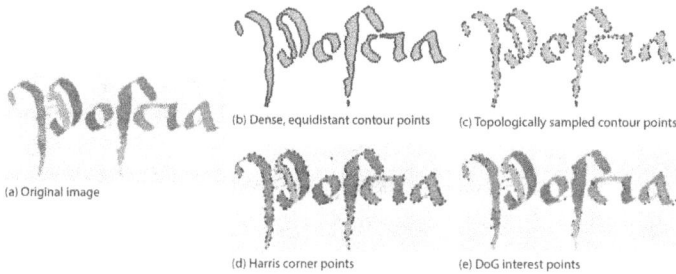

Fig. 8.6: Graph nodes from binary (b–c) and gray-scale images (d–e). Figure adapted from [Garz *et al.* (2016)].

Graph Nodes from Binary Images   We binarize a document image by applying a global threshold T_b to its gradient image $D(x, y, \sigma_1, \sigma_2)$ following the procedure proposed for creating the IAM-HistDB [Fischer *et al.* (2010)]. The gradient image is created using a Difference-of-Gaussian (DoG) approach which enhances intensity differences, thus allowing us to capture e.g., faded ink, and providing a spatial band-pass filter for noise suppression that accounts for both, big stains as well as pixel noise.

To create $D(x, y, \sigma_1, \sigma_2)$ we subtract two Gaussian-blurred versions of the original image with different amounts of blur σ:

$$D(x, y, \sigma_1, \sigma_2) = L(x, y, \sigma_1) - L(x, y, \sigma_2), \qquad (8.5)$$

where $L(x, y, \sigma)$ is the convolution of the original image $I(x, y)$ with the symmetric Gaussian kernel $G(x, y, \sigma)$ with standard deviation σ. Finally, the actual binarization is done with a global threshold T_b. We derive following graph nodes from binary images:

Dense Contour Points (CPs)
   The Suzuki contour tracing algorithm [Suzuki and Abe (1985)] identifies the contours in a binary image in a hierarchical nesting. Rather than using all contour pixels as graph nodes, we reduce their number by $10\% \pm 1.4$ in order to speed up computation with two actions: firstly, we only select every other pixel along a contour, and secondly, we discard holes and nested structures.

Topologically Sampled Contour Points (TCPs) To reduce number of CPs further while maintaining the document structure we apply the Douglas-Peucker curve simplification algorithm [Douglas and

Peucker (1973)] (see Section 8.3.7 for details) with a small error $\epsilon = 0.5$ px (average node reduction by 67 % ± 2.2).

Graph Nodes from Gray-Scale Images   For historical manuscript images that cannot be binarized satisfactorily we suggest two methods to derive nodes from gray-scale images. Naturally, other interest point detectors [Schmid *et al.* (2000); Tuytelaars and Mikolajczyk (2008)] can also be used.

Harris Laplacian corner points detected at locations of high curvature in gray-scale images, i.e., strong gradients in all directions at the pre-defined scales [Harris and Stephens (1988); Mikolajczyk and Schmid (2001)].

DoG interest points detected at blob-like structures in gray-scale images in a scale-invariant manner, which are defined as extrema in a DoG scale space [Lowe (2004)].

8.3.3   *Graph Edges*

Defining the neighborhood in the document graph, i.e., establishing the edges between the nodes, is not trivial: a grid-like approach that can successfully be applied to constraint domains such as printed business documents and Manhattan layouts, cannot appropriately model complex layouts.

Relationships in handwritten documents are not straightforward — neither global orientations (e.g., text lines are not necessarily aligned in a horizontal grid), nor spacing are guaranteed (e.g., line spacing might be larger than word spacing); and furthermore, adjacent elements might belong to different classes.

Delaunay Triangulation   Following these considerations we triangulate the nodes to form the graph's edges: Triangles are considered the most versatile way of partitioning space, and any polygonal domain can be discretized using only triangles; i.e., a set of disjoint triangles can represent — respectively approximate — arbitrary shapes [Frey (1987)]. Rado [Radó (1925)] proved that every (finite) surface can be triangulated.

The triangulation of a set $P = \{p_i : i \in \{0, ..., |V|\}\}$ of points in the plane of size $|V|$ is the partition of a plane $O \subset \mathbb{R}^2$ into a set of non-overlapping triangles. For a given set of points there exist several different solutions

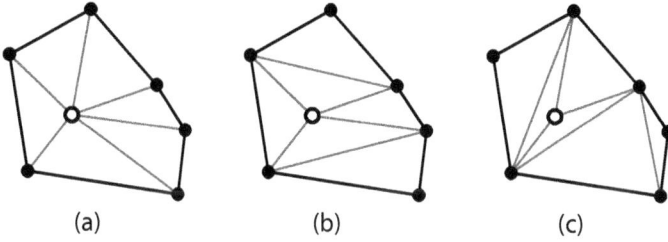

Fig. 8.7: Three possible triangulation solutions of point set P. Convex hull and exterior nodes ($|B| = 6$) are shown as black strokes and disks; interior edges and node ($|I| = 1$) as blue strokes and white disk, respectively. Each solution describes different relations between the nodes (a–c); however, given their distribution (a) appears the most natural. Figure adapted from [Garz et al. (2016)].

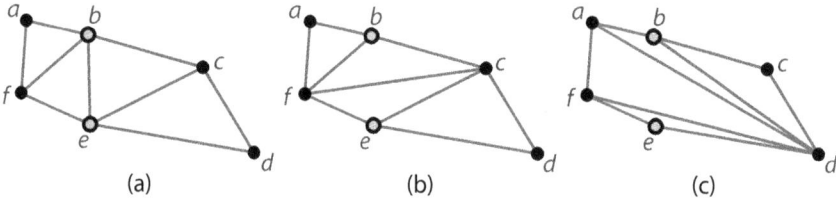

Fig. 8.8: Different neighborhood definitions of (a–c): the relation between node b and e (orange) is different in each. Given the distribution of points, (a) seems most natural.

for subdividing the space into triangles. However, not all solutions lead to an appropriate topology (c.f. Fig. 8.7(b,c)). *Delaunay Triangulation* (c.f. Fig. 8.8) achieves such a topology as it maximizes the minimum angle and enforces that no point p_i is inside the circumcircle of any triangle and thus avoids narrow triangles. Thus, we employ to generate the edges E (c.f. Fig. 8.7(a)) of the triangulated document graph G_T which models both, relations within and between layout elements (c.f. Fig. 8.5(c)).

8.3.4 Edge Weights

Having selected each node's neighbor by triangulation, we use edge weights to define each neighbor relationship: we want it to be small for pairs of nodes belonging to the same layout element, and large otherwise. An appropriate selection of edge weights will have a significant impact on the final segmentation result. The Euclidean distance is not suitable for modelling relationships in handwritten documents: it is not guaranteed that node distances within an element are smaller than between elements.

Hence, each edge $e = (u, v) \in E$ is assigned a weighted distance that takes into account to the predominant orientation of layout elements expressed as weight matrix W, i.e., favoring edges close to that orientation:

$$\nu(e) = ||(\mu(u) - \mu(v)) \times W||, \tag{8.6}$$

where $\mu(u) - \mu(v)$ is the vector difference or Euclidean distance of the node labels which is weighted with $W = \begin{pmatrix} 0.5 & 0 \\ 0 & 1.5 \end{pmatrix}$, which favors horizontal edges. Note that this is the default setting for W for a user-defined parameter of the proposed document graphs. Alternatively, the weight can be learned from the local distribution of graph nodes [Yin and Liu (2009)].

8.3.5   *Graph Clustering*

Finally, the goal is to represent each layout element as a distinct subgraph. As a first step towards this objective extract a sparse representation from the complete triangulated document graph $G_T = (V, E, \mu, \nu)$ using graph clustering; i.e., we group a graph's nodes such that they are similar with respect to a predefined property [Schaeffer (2007)]. Graph clustering which can create clusters of arbitrary shape — ideal for our purpose. We use a method inspired by human perception of 2D point sets [Zahn (1971)]: the Minimum Spanning Tree (MST)

$$G_M = (V, E_M, \mu, \nu) \tag{8.7}$$

which is an *acyclic* subgraph (no loops) of G_T, such that $E_M \subseteq E$. It connects all nodes V with exactly $|E_M| = |V| - 1$ edges, such that the sum of the edge weights is minimal.

Kruskal's algorithm [Kruskal (1956)] is a method to create an MST which treats the graph as a forest and starts with each node as an individual tree. We iteratively add edges that join trees only and only if, it has the least cost among all available options and does not violate MST properties. The cost for adding an edge is the edge weighting function ν. This clustering already reveals the main structures of a document, i.e., most edges are within-element, and some between-element (c.f. Fig. 8.5(d)). In case of large word distances and close lines, or touching ascenders and descenders, words of consecutive lines are connected.

8.3.6   Split Layout Elements

Even though the structures in the document already become apparent when clustering the triangulated graph, all subgraphs (each of which is assumed to represent a layout element) are connected in an MST. Hence, fragmented subgraphs have to be joined with additional edges to be inserted, and edges connecting different layout elements have to be deleted.

Joining two fragmented subgraphs is equivalent to joining two disjoint sets $C = A \cup B$ with an additional edge, hence $|E_C| = |E_A| + |E_B| + 1$. Deleting an edge in a MST is equivalent so splitting a graph into two disjoint subgraphs, also called a *cut*. A graph cut is partitioning its nodes V into two non-empty sets A and B such that

$$A \cup B = V,$$
$$A \cap B = \emptyset. \tag{8.8}$$

We avoid fully manual graph cuts by the user in the interactive annotation process, by partitioning the graph prior to the interactive stage. We identify edges that are very likely connecting two different layout elements by their weights and apply a global threshold T to delete those edges with a weight $\nu(e) > T$. This threshold T is a parameter that can be calibrated by the user, determined based on e.g., statistical distributions, or learned from a training sample. When using a weighted distance (c.f. Section 8.3.4), edges orthogonal to the estimated orientation of the layout elements are cut due to higher weights obtained, while within-links of the same length are preserved.

8.3.7   Polygonal Graph Representation

Rather than presenting the graph to a user, we have adopted polygons to display the segmentation results; not only are polygons more intuitively understood, they also outline the final segmentation or selection of the user. A user then manipulates the graph indirectly via the polygon interface. A polygonal description offers following benefits over e.g., pixel labeling: firstly, it facilitates encoding rich information such as the representation of relationships, hierarchies, annotations with different target domains (e.g., transliterations), and additional (semantic) data that can be linked to each element. Secondly, polygonal description is independent of the (binarized) image version used for generating the segmentation; and finally, polygons allow for overlapping regions, i.e., more than one class for a pixel. Although one could argue that a segmentation represented by polygons is coarse, evaluations are not restricted to polygon-matching (area overlap): by combining

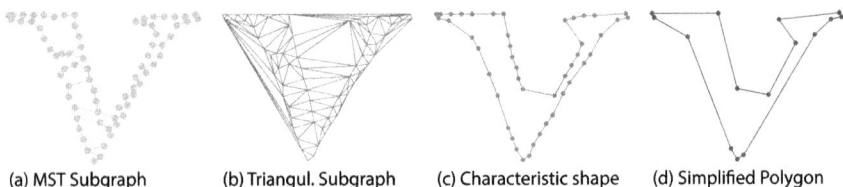

(a) MST Subgraph   (b) Triangul. Subgraph   (c) Characteristic shape   (d) Simplified Polygon

Fig. 8.9: Extracting simplified polygons of layout elements. Nodes are indicated by disks.

polygons with a high-quality binarized image, pixel-level evaluations are facilitated [Garz *et al.* (2013)].

Optimally, a layout element is described by a non-convex polygon that closely follows its contours without being too tight. Given the triangulation of each MST with its boundary being the convex hull, we can efficiently derive non-convex polygons: starting from the convex hull, we iteratively cut the longest exterior edge exceeding a threshold T_a until the desired tightness is attained provided the respective resulting polygon satisfies three constraints [Duckham *et al.* (2008)]:

    i) it contains all nodes of the subgraph and is enclosed by or equal to the convex hull,

    ii) comprises neither holes nor islands,

    iii) and each exterior node has exactly two exterior edges.

A default-value for T_a that consistently leads to an adequate acuteness for different kinds of layout element and document is hard to determine, since it is highly dependent on the actual node distribution of the respective graph and particularly user preference. [Duckham *et al.* (2008)] suggest to initialize T_a as the mean of the longest edge in the MST and the shortest edge of the triangulated graph:

$$T_a = \mathrm{mean}\left(\max_{e \in E_M} |e|, \min_{e \in E} |e| \right). \tag{8.9}$$

In our application, T_a is a user-defined parameter that can be adjusted to fine-tune the polygons to the required tightness. Figure 8.10 depicts the effect of different thresholds T_a on the appearance of a polygon.

Polygon Simplification   To efficiently represent and store the polygon representation, we want to approximate the accurate shape with the smallest possible number of vertices. We use a well-known algorithm for simplifying

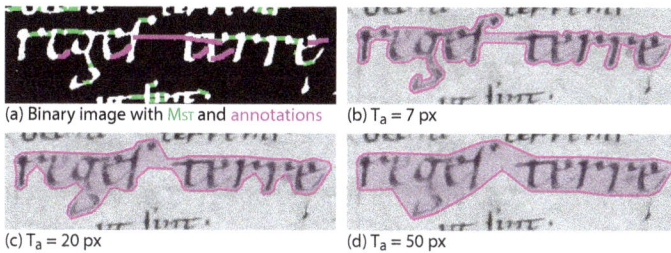

Fig. 8.10: Tightness of a polygon extracted from the given sample (a) for different thresholds T_a. Figure adapted from [Garz *et al.* (2016)].

curves [Douglas and Peucker (1973)] that, given a curve composed of line segments uses piece-wise linear interpolation with an error parameter ϵ to find a similar curve with fewer vertices. We use an adapted version with additional constraints to prevent polygons from self-intersecting, holes, or collapsing to lines [Vivid Solutions (2004)].

Given a curved line, the algorithm recursively divides it. At each step a sequence of points is approximated by a line from the first to the last point. We accept the approximation the distance of all points of the sequence is below the threshold ϵ. Otherwise the point sequence is split a the point furthest away from the line and algorithm is recursively applied to the two sub-sequences. This algorithm, though not optimal, has generally been found to produce the highest subjective- and objective-quality approximations when compared with other heuristic algorithms.

8.3.8 *Graph Evaluation*

This section evaluates the quality of document graphs with respect to the desired segmentation on the DIVA-HisDB. The quality measure also provides an estimate of the amount of manual labour we expect a user will have to do in order to make the final segmentation from the document graph.

We measure it with the Graph Edit Distance (GED) [Sanfeliu and Fu (1983)], which expresses how (dis)similar two graphs are as '*amount of distortion that is needed to transform one graph into another*' [Riesen and Bunke (2009)]. Distortions in this context are three so-called edit operations to transform it into another: substitution, deletion, and insertion operations on both, nodes and edges. For this application we only consider operations on edges, that is the number of edges that need to be inserted or deleted, respectively, in order to transform the given graph into a graph that corresponds to the desired segmentation.

We disregard node operations in order to isolate the evaluation of the graph itself from the effect of choosing different node sources. In practice, this means that the evaluation does not consider parts of the manuscript lost due to the choice of nodes, i.e., it answers the question '*What is the best graph that can be retrieved from the given nodes?*'

Hence, we define two relative measures based on the GED to measure the amount of distortion required

i) with respect to the *correct* graph edges, i.e., those that correspond to the ground truth graph; providing a global quality measure; and

ii) with respect to the number of layout elements, which gives an estimation of the user effort required to segment a single layout element.

The *insertion measure* I then assesses how fragmented the layout elements are, i.e., the amount of within-element edges that are missing and have to be inserted by the user. It is the ratio between the number of insertions and the number of correct edges in the document graph:

$$I = \frac{\#\text{insertions}}{\#\text{correct edges}} \tag{8.10}$$

The corresponding measure I_L with respect to an individual layout element then measures how many edges a user has to insert in order to complete a layout element.

The *deletion measure* evaluates the connectedness of layout elements, i.e., the how many between-element edges linking layout elements have to be deleted. Again, it is a ratio with respect to the correct edges:

$$D = \frac{\#\text{deletions}}{\#\text{correct edges}} \tag{8.11}$$

The analogous number of deletions with respect to an individual layout element is denoted D_L. Substitutions are not considered within our measure.

We selected 10 representative pages of each of the three datasets of the DIVA-HisDB for evaluation. Unless stated otherwise, measures are expressed as mean and standard deviation $(\mu \pm \sigma)$, and median $\tilde{x}$ over the pages of the evaluation dataset.

Table 8.4: **GED between the MST graphs and the best achievable graph** G_{GT} given the nodes with respect to correct edges. Unit: percentage of edges with respect to the correct edges.

	CSG 18			CSG 863			CB 55			u
	μ $\pm$ σ		$\widetilde{x}$	μ $\pm$ σ		$\widetilde{x}$	μ $\pm$ σ		$\widetilde{x}$	
Dense Contour Point (CP)										
I	0.10 $\pm$ 0.06		0.13	0.09 $\pm$ 0.08		0.08	0.11 $\pm$ 0.03		0.10	%
D	0.31 $\pm$ 0.11		0.33	0.21 $\pm$ 0.12		0.22	0.25 $\pm$ 0.04		0.24	%
Topologically Sampled Contour Point (TCP)										
I	0.16 $\pm$ 0.10		0.22	0.17 $\pm$ 0.17		0.16	0.21 $\pm$ 0.03		0.20	%
D	0.45 $\pm$ 0.16		0.48	0.38 $\pm$ 0.26		0.41	0.45 $\pm$ 0.06		0.44	%
Harris Corner Points										
I	0.46 $\pm$ 0.28		0.65	0.38 $\pm$ 0.37		0.38	0.41 $\pm$ 0.08		0.38	%
D	1.66 $\pm$ 0.63		1.89	0.98 $\pm$ 0.65		1.04	1.00 $\pm$ 0.14		0.95	%
DoG Interest Points										
I	1.70 $\pm$ 0.50		1.84	2.54 $\pm$ 0.66		2.57	1.45 $\pm$ 0.15		1.49	%
D	5.90 $\pm$ 1.90		6.54	7.20 $\pm$ 1.97		7.68	3.51 $\pm$ 0.24		3.53	%

Table 8.5: **Comparison of the original and pre-processed MST graphs** using GED between the respective graph and the best achievable graph G_{GT} given the nodes with respect to the layout elements. Unit: number of insertions and deletions required to segment a layout element.

	CSG 18			CSG 863			CB 55			u
	μ $\pm$ σ		$\widetilde{x}$	μ $\pm$ σ		$\widetilde{x}$	μ $\pm$ σ		$\widetilde{x}$	
MST (Contour Points)										
I_L	0.86 $\pm$ 0.56		0.98	1.31 $\pm$ 0.84		1.15	2.73 $\pm$ 0.72		2.71	#
D_L	3.06 $\pm$ 0.74		2.93	3.72 $\pm$ 0.93		3.97	6.54 $\pm$ 1.18		6.33	#
Seam Carving [Arvanitopoulos and Susstrunk (2014)]										
I_L	1.56 $\pm$ 0.90		1.67	5.20 $\pm$ 2.65		5.03	6.92 $\pm$ 1.54		6.55	#
D_L	2.13 $\pm$ 0.80		1.96	2.75 $\pm$ 0.97		2.77	5.08 $\pm$ 1.19		5.03	#
OCRopus page segmentation [Breuel (2008)]										
I_L	3.86 $\pm$ 1.71		4.79	5.42 $\pm$ 2.58		4.77	17.56 $\pm$ 23.20		10.76	#
D_L	2.03 $\pm$ 0.88		2.10	3.02 $\pm$ 1.03		3.00	5.69 $\pm$ 1.20		5.72	#

Table 8.4 lists the insertion I and deletion D measures for graphs with different node sources on each dataset of the DIVA-HisDB. Most notably, graphs based on CPs achieve a better GED compared to all other node sources on all datasets. Graphs based on other node sources perform particularly worse on documents with a large amount of touching components (CB 55). All following evaluations will accordingly be performed on CPs graphs.

Table 8.5 gives the insertion I_L and deletion D_L measures with respect to the layout elements, i.e., how many interactions a user has to do to segment a single layout element in a dataset. Furthermore, the table compares the proposed MST graph with graphs pre-processed by combing the obtained MST graph with the respective results of two page segmentation methods [Arvanitopoulos and Susstrunk (2014); Breuel (2008)] (provided by [Würsch *et al.* (2016)]). We removed all edges from the MST graph which intersect the boundaries of the polygons obtained from the respective segmentation methods. Note that edges which connect two fragmented subgraphs within one such polygon have not been inserted since this would require heuristic rules.

The quantitative evaluation showed that the effort of correcting the new errors introduced by pre-processing is about equivalent to correcting the original graph; i.e., different pre-processing methods merely change the nature of error, but do not reduce it.

An additional qualitative analysis showed an over-segmentation on the one hand, and layout entities that have been cut through producing errors that are hard to spot for a user, on the other. The over-segmentation might induce a '*sense of false security*' in the user since the result, when looked at globally does look quite alright, but when scrutinising the segmentation lots of errors are revealed that require precise and attentive labour — the opposite of what we try to achieve (see Fig. 8.11 and Fig. 8.12). Novel methods are needed in the future to provide better automatic suggestions for the complex manuscript layouts considered in this chapter.

8.4   Graph-User-Interaction: Scribbling

The proposed user interaction can be compared to the process of marking structures of interest using a highlighter pen which automatically propagates the highlighting throughout the structure. As stated earlier, the hypothesis of the proposed method is that graphs capture the structure of a document in a way similar to our perception; and thus, the propagation of the segmentation is not random but follows a human's expectations. This means that the graph supports our manual labour by providing hypotheses about the segmentation and saves time in the manual annotation process. Such semi-automatic suggestions are particularly important when annotating large amount of data.

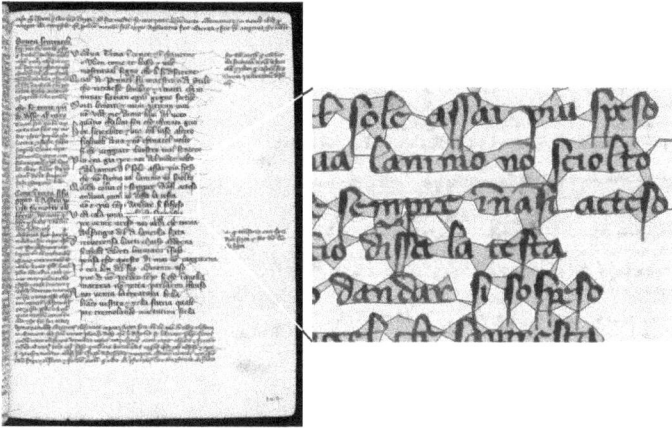

Fig. 8.11: Segmentation by OCRopus on CB 55, folio 109 recto.

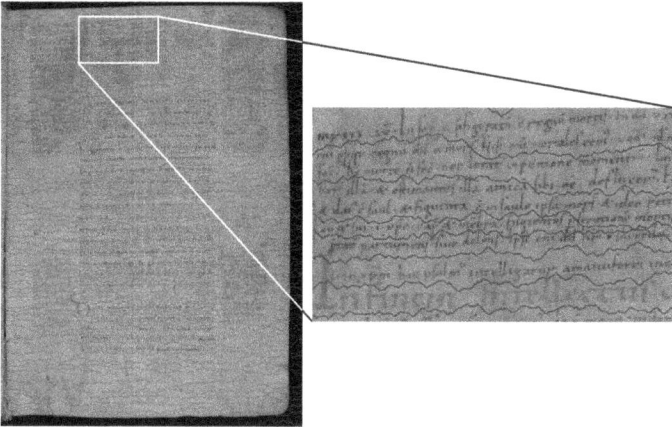

Fig. 8.12: Segmentation by Seam Carving on CSG 18, page 95.

8.4.1 *Scribbling as User Interaction Pattern*

The user can either interact directly with a visualization of the document graphs by drawing strokes that cut existing edges of the graph (deleting edges) and drawing strokes that connect fragmented subgraphs (inserting edges), or alternatively, indirectly manipulate the graph by interacting with a polygon-representation of the graph superimposed on the original document image.

The user's interactions with the proposed document graph are encoded in the graph as following operations:

i) inserting edges between fragmented components of a layout element
(within-element edges), and
ii) deleting edges that link several layout elements (between-element
edges).

Scribbling is commonly defined as '*[writing] hastily or carelessly without
regard to legibility or form*'[6] or '*to produce (marks, a drawing, etc.) or
portray [...] by rapid and irregular strokes like those of hurried writing.*'[7]
These definitions illustrate the key aspects of scribbling as swift and imprecise
interaction:

i) a user grasps the idea easily and quickly, and
ii) the interaction itself can be done with great speed.

Although a general rule is that increasing the speed of a movement reduces
its accuracy. To fix ideas, consider unlocking your door: you have to slow
down as you approach the lock to make sure the key goes in [Fairbrother
(2010)]. We can circumvent this rule using a precise graph as foundation.
Having captured the main structures of a document in a graph, the user
only needs swift and coarse interactions: they can '*hastily*' draw imprecise,
'*rapid, and irregular strokes*' over the graph '*without regard to legibility or
form,*' and still obtain a precise segmentation owing to the underlying graph.

Even though fast and approximate scribble interactions are sufficient in
most cases, scribbling also allows for precise input, necessary e.g., in regions
of touching characters. Furthermore, it allows for both, small modifications
(short strokes, clicks) as well as coarse, large-scale interactions (long strokes).
It also facilitates efficient "batch" operations, i.e., deleting or inserting
several edges with a single stroke.

When inserting missing edges within a layout element, the user is not
required to exert precision: it is enough to connect fragmented components
with a stroke that touches any part of the separate subgraphs in order to
join them. Using different "crayons" (colors) for these actions, the user can
simultaneously assign a label to each layout element. In this application,
we consider decorations, main text, and glosses as labels. Deleting edges
can be done with either scribbles as for inserting, or clicking onto individual
edges. Parts of the graph that have not been labelled are disregarded.

---

[6]http://www.merriam-webster.com/dictionary/scribble
[7]http://www.oed.com/view/Entry/173487

Foreground that is missing in the graph due to the node source chosen, can be attributed by the user in a fast and simple way by checking back with the original image and scribbling over. In particular, reconstructing characters is made simple and straightforward by consulting the original image and tracing the letter in question.

8.4.2 User Interaction Evaluation

We ran a preliminary user study in order to evaluate whether scribbling as interaction pattern was preferred over established mouse-interaction such as clicking.

This preliminary study included a single participant who was trained prior to the study. The user did not have thorough knowledge about the method but had already annotated several document pages beforehand. The three datasets of DIVA-HisDB were chosen for the study. Following the graph evaluation in Section 8.3.8, graphs based on CPs were used for the user study. The user was asked to annotate a total of 30 manuscript pages, that is 10 pages of each dataset of the DIVA-HisDB. Annotating in this context includes deleting connections between distinct layout elements, inserting edges between fragments of a layout element, labelling it with a class (text line, gloss, decoration), and adding missing content (e.g., faded ink that was lost in binarization). The user effort needed in order to create the ground truth is evaluated per layout element, e.g. per text line. It is expressed by the interaction time and the average number of insertion (which includes labeling) and deletion interactions required.

The study was carried out in our lab, where the participant had their own desk. A graphic tablet, the Wacom Intuos Tablet CTH-480/S, was used as pen input device; it was plugged into a standard notebook with an external monitor. These tablets have a battery-free pen powered by electromagnetic resonance; furthermore, finger swipes can be used, e.g., for zooming. The tablet's orientation can be switched for left- or right-handed operation. In a briefing prior to the start of the study, we explained the purpose and tasks to execute. A focus was laid on recognizing different classes of layout elements, as this is not always straightforward in a handwritten manuscript with annotations. The participant was given several days to get familiar with the setup, the *GraphManuscribble* tool, and the task; during that training time, feedback was directly incorporated into the system and the study leader was available for questions. The user study was then carried out without supervision.

First, the user visually fine-tuned a threshold on the edge length, which resulted in a personalized trade-off between expected edge insertions and deletions. After fixing this threshold, for each layout element, there were about 1.87 ± 1.22 edges missing on average that had to be inserted, and 5.17 ± 2.44 edges connecting different layout elements that had to be deleted. The high number of surplus edges can be explained by the proximity of the text lines, especially for interlinear glosses.

On average, the user spent about 14.92 ± 3.93 seconds in order to process a single layout element with an average of 5.06 ± 1.62 interactions. The ratio of insertions and deletions was approximately 2:3. Note that the number of interactions is smaller than the number of edge insertions and deletions indicated above. This is due to the fact that the user is able to connect or disconnect several layout elements with a single scribble. Finally, it is worth pointing out that the user clearly preferred the scribbling interaction (87 % of all interactions) over clicking with the mouse, although both options were available.

This initial user study has demonstrated that the sparse document graph structure is already very close to the desired ground truth annotation despite the chosen documents' complexity and only few user interactions are needed obtain the desired segmentation. This makes the proposed system an efficient tool to annotate challenging documents.

More importantly, pen-based scribbling as a user interaction has also been confirmed as swift and natural for human annotation. However, we noticed that getting used to the specific input device used required some amount of training. The graphic tablet used is an indirect input device like a mouse; an indirect input device requires the user to mentally translate the physical into the virtual movement on the screen. This translation also includes scaling, e.g., a small movement in the real world may produce a large movement on a screen; thus, it is cognitively demanding [McLaughlin *et al.* (2009)].

8.5   Conclusions and Outlook

We have shown that graphs have the capability of mimicking the human perception in the ways Gestalt psychologists have described. For the document graphs proposed for the *GraphManuscribble* tool we have been guided by the following laws of perception introduced by Gestalt psychology:

- proximity (objects that are close to one another as form a group):

defined by the neighborhood selection based on triangulation and edge weights on the graphs, and

- closure (perceive shapes or letters as being whole despite them not being complete): the document graph is capable of e.g., closing gaps, or reconstructing characters.

The remaining laws of perception may give promising directions towards future work:

- similarity (from cues such as e.g., shape, color, or shading) can be encoded by attributing graph nodes (as e.g., shape descriptors),
- "Good Gestalt": layouts usually follow some kind of regular and orderly pattern, even in complex cases, such that a global energy function over the entire page might be of use.
- familiarity: transfering labels from an annotated and segmented document graph to the graph of an unseen page.

Furthermore, when interacting with a manuscript, e.g., with the intention to extract an illumination from a document page, a user's interactions will provide a clue as to how to segment an element, i.e., how to find its boundaries. Not limited to document image analysis, such knowledge is also used in computer vision, particularly in object detection and image segmentation. Whereas methods in computer vision predominantly rely on pixel-level decision, we believe that a sparse graph representation allows for more generic learning about the abstract concept of an element's boundary. By severing or introducing graph edges and nodes, the user guides the segmentation process. A promising line of future research will be to learn from this user interaction.

References

Arvanitopoulos, N. and Susstrunk, S. (2014). Seam carving for text line extraction on color and grayscale historical manuscripts, in *ICFHR, 2014 14th International Conference on* (IEEE), pp. 726–731.

Barney Smith, E. H. (2010). An Analysis of Binarization Ground Truthing, in *International Workshop on Document Analysis Systems*, pp. 27 34.

Biller, O., Asi, A., Kedem, K., and Dinstein, I. (2013). WebGT: An Interactive Web-Based System for Historical Document Ground Truth Generation, in *International Conference on Document Analysis and Recognition*, ISBN 978-0-7695-4999-6, pp. 305–308, doi:10.1109/ICDAR.2013.68.

Bourgeois, F. L. and Emptoz, H. (2007). DEBORA: Digital AccEss to BOoks of the RenAissance, *Int. Journal on Document Analysis and Recognition* **9**, pp. 193–221.

Breidbach, O. and Jost, J. (2006). On the Gestalt Concept, *Theory in Biosciences* **125**, 1, pp. 19–36, doi:10.1016/j.thbio.2006.02.001.

Breuel, T. M. (2008). The ocropus open source ocr system, in *Electronic Imaging 2008*, pp. 68150F–68150F.

Brock, R. (2006). *Intuition and Integration: Insights from Intuitive Students*, MPhil in Educational Research, University of Cambridge.

Clausner, C., Pletschacher, S., and Antonacopoulos, A. (2011). Aletheia - An Advanced Document Layout and Text Ground-Truthing System for Production Environments, in *International Conference on Document Analysis and Recognition*, pp. 48–52.

Clavelli, A., Karatzas, D., and Lladós, J. (2010). A Framework for the Assessment of Text Extraction Algorithms on Complex Colour Images, in *IAPR International Workshop on Document Analysis Systems* (ACM), pp. 19–26.

Conte, D., Foggia, P., Sansone, C., and Vento, M. (2004). Thirty years of graph matching in pattern recognition, *Int. Journal of Pattern Recognition and Artificial Intelligence* **18**, 3, pp. 265–298.

Coüasnon, B., Camillerapp, J., and Leplumey, I. (2007). Access by content to handwritten archive documents: Generic document recognition method and platform for annotations, *Int. Journal on Document Analysis and Recognition* **9**, 2, pp. 223–242.

Doermann, D., Zotkina, E., and Li, H. (2010). GEDI - A Groundtruthing Environment for Document Images, in *International Workshop on Document Analysis Systems*, pp. 519–522.

Douglas, D. and Peucker, T. (1973). Algorithms for the Reduction of the Number of Points Required to Represent a Digitized Line or its Caricature, *Cartographica: International Journal for Geographic Information and Geovisualization* **10**, 2, pp. 112–122, doi:10.3138/FM57-6770-U75U-7727.

Duckham, M., Kulik, L., Worboys, M., and Galton, A. (2008). Efficient Generation of Simple Polygons for Characterizing the Shape of a Set of Points in the Plane, *Pattern Recognition* **41**, 10, pp. 3224–3236, doi:10.1016/j.patcog.2008.03.023.

Fairbrother, J. (2010). *Fundamentals of Motor Behavior* (Human Kinetics), ISBN 9780736077149.

Fischer, A., Baechler, M., Garz, A., Liwicki, M., and Ingold, R. (2014). A combined system for text line extraction and handwriting recognition in historical documents, in *Proc. 11th Int. Workshop on Document Analysis Systems*, pp. 71–75.

Fischer, A., Indermühle, E., Bunke, H., Viehhauser, G., and Stolz, M. (2010). Ground truth creation for handwriting recognition in historical documents, in *Proc. 9th Int. Workshop on Document Analysis Systems*, pp. 3–10.

Frey, W. (1987). Selective Refinement: A new Strategy for Automatic Node Placement in Graded Triangular Meshes, *International Journal for Numerical Methods in Engineering* **24**, 11, pp. 2183–2200, doi:10.1002/nme.1620241111.

Garz, A. (2017). *A Human-Centered Approach to Structural Image Analysis for Complex Historical Manuscripts*, Ph.D. thesis, University of Fribourg.

Garz, A., Fischer, A., Bunke, H., and Ingold, R. (2013). A Binarization-Free Clustering Approach to Segment Curved Text Lines in Historical Manuscripts, in *International Conference on Document Analysis and Recognition*, pp. 1290–1294.

Garz, A., Fischer, A., Sablatnig, R., and Bunke, H. (2012). Binarization-free Text Line Segmentation for Historical Documents Based on Interest Point Clustering, in *2012 10th IAPR International Workshop on Document Analysis Systems* (IEEE), pp. 95–99.

Garz, A., Seuret, M., Fischer, A., and Ingold, R. (2016). A user-centered segmentation method for complex historical manuscripts based on document graphs, *IEEE Trans. on Human-Machine Systems* **47**, 2, pp. 181–193.

Gordo, A., Llorens, D., Marzal, A., Prat, F., and Vilar, J. (2008). State: A multimodal assisted text-transcription system for ancient documents, in *Proc. 8th Int. Workshop on Document Analysis Systems*, pp. 135–142.

Greig, D. M., Porteous, B. T., and Seheult, A. H. (1989). Exact Maximum A Posteriori Estimation for Binary Images, *Journal of the Royal Statistical Society. Series B (Methodological)*, pp. 271–279.

Han, S., Humphreys, G., and Chen, L. (1999). Uniform Connectedness and the Classical Gestalt Principles of Grouping, *Perception & Psychophysics* **61**, 4, pp. 661–674, doi:10.3758/BF03205537.

Harris, C. and Stephens, M. (1988). A Combined Corner and Edge Detector, in *Alvey Vision Conference*, pp. 147–151.

Kandel, A., Bunke, H., and Last, M. (eds.) (2007). *Applied Graph Theory in Computer Vision and Pattern Recognition, Studies in Computational Intelligence*, Vol. 52 (Springer).

Kanungo, T., Lee, C. H., Czorapinski, J., and Bella, I. (2000). TRUEVIZ: a Groundtruth/Metadata Editing and Visualizing Toolkit for OCR, in *Photonics West 2001 – Electronic Imaging* (International Society for Optics and Photonics), pp. 1–12.

Karatzas, D., Mestre, S. R., Mas, J., Nourbakhsh, F., and Roy, P. P. (2011). ICDAR 2011 Robust Reading Competition-Challenge 1: Reading Text in Born-Digital Images (Web and Email), in *International Conference on Document Analysis and Recognition* (IEEE), pp. 1485–1490.

Karatzas, D., Robles, S., and Gomez, L. (2014). An On-line Platform for Ground Truthing and Performance Evaluation of Text Extraction Systems, in *International Workshop on Document Analysis Systems*, pp. 242–246, doi:10.1109/DAS.2014.49.

Karatzas, D., Shafait, F., Uchida, S., Iwamura, M., i Bigorda, L. G., Mestre, S. R., Mas, J., Mota, D. F., Almazan, J. A., and de las Heras, L. P. (2013). ICDAR 2013 Robust Reading Competition, in *International Conference on Document Analysis and Recognition* (IEEE), pp. 1484–1493.

Kass, M., Witkin, A., and Terzopoulos, D. (1988). Snakes: Active Contour Models, *International Journal of Computer Vision* **1**, 4, pp. 321–331.

Kassis, M. and El-Sana, J. (2016). Scribble Based Interactive Page Layout

Segmentation Using Gabor Filter, in *International Conference on Frontiers in Handwriting Recognition*, pp. 13–18.

Koffka, K. (1935). *Principles of Gestalt Psychology*, reprinted edn. (Routledge).

Kruskal, J. B. (1956). On the shortest spanning subtree of a graph and the traveling salesman problem, *Proceedings of the American Mathematical society* **7**, 1, pp. 48–50.

Lee, C. H. and Kanungo, T. (2003). The Architecture of TRUEVIZ: A groundTRUth/metadata Editing and VIsualiZing Toolkit, *Pattern Recognition* **36**, 3, pp. 811–825.

Lowe, D. G. (2004). Distinctive image features from scale-invariant keypoints, *International journal of computer vision* **60**, 2, pp. 91–110.

McLaughlin, A. C., Rogers, W. A., and Fisk, A. D. (2009). Using Direct and Indirect Input Devices: Attention Demands and Age-Related Differences, *ACM Transactions on Computer-Human Interaction (TOCHI)* **16**, 1, p. 2.

Mikolajczyk, K. and Schmid, C. (2001). Indexing Based on Scale Invariant Interest Points, in *International Conference on Computer Vision*, pp. 525–531.

Mortensen, E. N. and Barrett, W. A. (1998). Interactive Segmentation with Intelligent Scissors, *Graphical Models and Image Processing* **60**, 5, pp. 349–384, doi:http://dx.doi.org/10.1006/gmip.1998.0480.

Nafchi, H. Z., Ayatollahi, S. M., Moghaddam, R. F., and Cheriet, M. (2013). An Efficient Ground Truthing Tool for Binarization of Historical Manuscripts, in *International Conference on Document Analysis and Recognition*, pp. 807–811.

Radó, T. (1925). Über den Begriff der Riemannschen Fläche, *Acta Litt. Sci. Szeged* **2**, 101–121, p. 10.

Riesen, K. and Bunke, H. (2009). Approximate Graph Edit Distance Computation by Means of Bipartite Graph Matching, *Image and Vision Computing* **27**, 7, pp. 950–959, doi:http://dx.doi.org/10.1016/j.imavis.2008.04.004, iAPR-TC15 Workshop on Graph-based Representations (GbR 2007).

Romero, V., Toselli, A. H., Rodríguez, L., and Vidal, E. (2007). Computer assisted transcription for ancient text images, in *Proc. 4th Int. Conf. on Image Analysis and Recognition*, pp. 1182–1193.

Rother, C., Kolmogorov, V., and Blake, A. (2004). GrabCut: Interactive Foreground Extraction Using Iterated Graph Cuts, *ACM Transactions on Graphics* **23**, 3, pp. 309–314, doi:10.1145/1015706.1015720.

Russell, B. C., Torralba, A., Murphy, K. P., and Freeman, W. T. (2008). LabelMe: A Database and Web-based Tool for Image Annotation, *International Journal of Computer Vision* **77**, 1-3, pp. 157–173.

Sanfeliu, A. and Fu, K. S. (1983). A distance measure between attributed relational graphs for pattern recognition, *IEEE Trans. on Systems, Man, and Cybernetics* **13**, 3, pp. 353–363.

Saund, E., Lin, J., and Sarkar, P. (2009). PixLabeler: User Interface for Pixel-Level Labeling of Elements in Document Images, in *International Conference on Document Analysis and Recognition*, pp. 646–650, doi:10.1109/ICDAR.2009.250.

Schaeffer, S. (2007). Graph Clustering, *Computer Science Review* **1**, 1, pp. 27–64, doi:10.1016/j.cosrev.2007.05.001.

Schmid, C., Mohr, R., and Bauckhage, C. (2000). Evaluation of Interest Point Detectors, *International Journal of Computer Vision* **37**, 2, pp. 151–172, doi:10.1023/A:1008199403446.

Shahab, A., Shafait, F., and Dengel, A. (2011). ICDAR 2011 Robust Reading Competition-Challenge 2: Reading Text in Scene Images, in *International Conference on Document Analysis and Recognition* (IEEE), pp. 1491–1496.

Suzuki, S. and Abe, K. (1985). Topological Structural Analysis of Digitized Binary Image by Border Following, *Computer Vision, Graphics and Image Processing* **30**, 1, pp. 32–46.

Toselli, A. H., Romero, V., Pastor, M., and Vidal, E. (2010). Multimodal interactive transcription of text images, *Pattern Recognition* **43**, 5, pp. 1814–1825.

Tuytelaars, T. and Mikolajczyk, K. (2008). Local Invariant Feature Detectors: A Survey, *Foundation and Trends in Computer Graphics and Vision* **3**, 3, pp. 177–280, doi:10.1561/0600000017.

Vento, M. (2013). A one hour trip in the world of graphs, looking at the papers of the last ten years, in *Proc. Int. Workshop on Graph-Based Representations*, pp. 1–10.

Vivid Solutions (2004). JTS Java Topology Suite. `http://www.vividsolutions.com/jts/jtshome.htm(2004-03-11)`.

Würsch, M., Ingold, R., and Liwicki, M. (2016). SDK Reinvented: Document Image Analysis Methods as RESTful Web Services, in *International Workshop on Document Analysis Systems*, pp. 90–95.

Yanikoglu, B. A. and Vincent, L. (1998). Pink Panther: A Complete Environment for Ground-Truthing and Benchmarking Document Page Segmentation, *Pattern Recognition* **31**, 9, pp. 1191–1204.

Yin, F. and Liu, C. L. (2009). Handwritten Chinese Text Line Segmentation by Clustering with Distance Metric Learning, *Pattern Recognition* **42**, 12, pp. 3146–3157, doi:10.1016/j.patcog.2008.12.013.

Zahn, C. (1971). Graph-Theoretical Methods for Detecting and Describing Gestalt Clusters, *IEEE Transactions on Computers* **C-20**, 1, doi:10.1109/T-C.1971.223083.

PART 2
Related Research Projects

Chapter 9

OldDocPro: Old Greek Document Recognition

[1]Basilis Gatos, [1]Georgios Louloudis, [1]Nikolaos Stamatopoulos,
[1,2]George Retsinas, [1,3]Giorgos Sfikas, [3]Angelos Giotis,
[4]Foteini Simistira Liwicki, [5]Vassilis Papavassiliou and
[5]Vassilis Katsouros

[1]*Institute of Informatics and Telecommunications,*
National Center for Scientific Research "Demokritos", Greece
[2]*School of Electrical and Computer Engineering,*
National Technical University of Athens, Greece
[3]*Department of Computer Science and Engineering,*
University of Ioannina, Greece
[4]*EISLAB, Luleå University of Technology, Sweden*
[5]*Institute for Language and Speech Processing,*
Athena Research Center, Greece
bgat@iit.demokritos.gr, louloud@iit.demokritos.gr,
nstam@iit.demokritos.gr, gretsinas@central.ntua.gr,
sfikas@iit.demokritos.gr, agiotis@cs.uoi.gr, foteini.liwicki@ltu.se,
vpapa@athenarc.gr, vsk@athenarc.gr

9.1 Introduction

After many years of scholar study, old Greek machine-printed and hand-written collections continue to be an important source of novel information for scholars, concerning both the history of earlier times as well as the development of cultural documentation over the centuries. Although the accurate recognition of Latin machine-printed text is now considered largely a solved problem, recognition of scripts having a large number of character classes is still the subject of active research. Old Greek polytonic (multi accent) scripts have a large variety of diacritic marks (see Figure 9.1) and as a result a large number of character classes (more than 270). Due to that, Greek polytonic machine-printed and handwritten documents cannot be successfully processed by current OCR technologies. Some approaches that use general purpose OCR engines for the recognition of Greek polytonic documents are mainly based on intense training or post-processing without significant successful results. Taking into consideration that the Greek polytonic system was used from around 200 BC to modern times

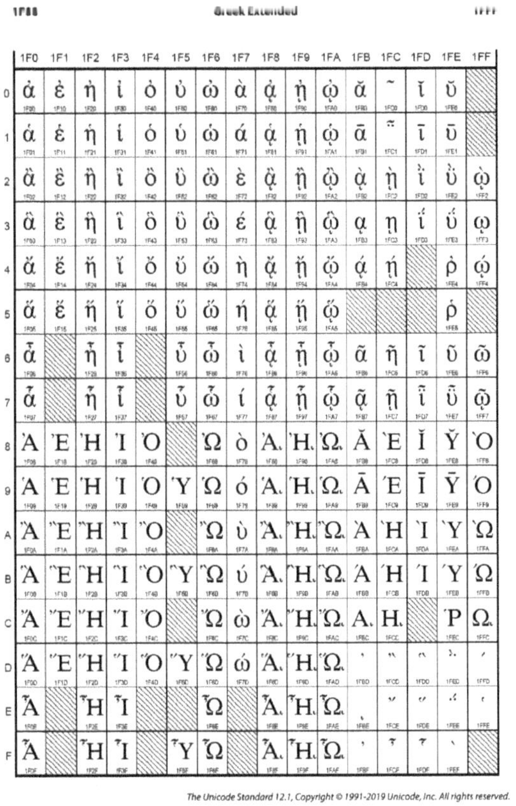

Fig. 9.1: Extended Greek characters: Diacritic marks modifying characters (from http://www.unicode.org/charts/PDF/U1F00.pdf).

until 1982, we can easily observe that a large amount of scanned Greek documents still remains without full text search capabilities. To this end, in the OldDocPro project ("novel techniques to advance the frontiers of old Greek document recognition"),[1] a group of document image processing experts worked together and focused their research efforts towards the recognition of Greek machine-printed and handwritten polytonic documents. The aim of OldDocPro was to assist the content holders in turning archives of old Greek documents into digital collections with full text access and indexing capabilities while facilitating current and future efforts in old Greek document digitization and processing. In this chapter, the main achievements of the OldDocPro project are presented focusing on the creation of the old Greek polytonic database GRPOLY-DB as well as in the development of new methods for the segmentation, recognition and keyword spotting (KWS) of old Greek documents.

9.2 The GRPOLY-DB Database

Public databases help researchers to advance the state of the art since they permit a fair and objective comparison under a common scenario (for an overview of existing databases, see (Valveny, 2014)). In the Old-DocPro project, we introduced the first publicly available old Greek polytonic database GRPOLY-DB (Gatos et al., 2015).[2] It consists of four subsets that have been semi-automatically annotated with ground-truth information at different levels using the PAGE (Page Analysis and Ground-Truth Elements) format (Pletschacher and Antonacopoulos, 2010). An overview of GRPOLY-DB subsets is presented in Table 9.1. For every segmentation level (except character level in some cases), the correspondence with the polytonic text is provided (see Figure 9.2).

For the creation of the GRPOLY-DB, we used the original images of all pages as well as the corresponding transcription. We first binarized (Gatos et al., 2006b) the original images (whenever it was necessary) and then applied sequentially the methods for layout analysis, text line and word segmentation (Gatos et al., 2014). At a next step, several users were involved in order to correct the segmentation results using the Aletheia tool (Clausner et al., 2011). An automatic transcript mapping procedure was also applied in order to assign the text information to the corresponding text line (Stamatopoulos

---

[1]http://www.iit.demokritos.gr/~bgat/OldDocPro
[2]http://www.iit.demokritos.gr/~nstam/GRPOLY-DB

Table 9.1: Overview of the GRPOLY-DB Datasets.

	Date	Pages	Number of Text Lines with GT	Number of Words with GT	Number of Characters with GT
GRPOLY-DB-Hand-written	1838-1916	46	693	4939	-
GRPOLY-DB-Machine-Printed-A	1950-1965	5	691	4998	28591
GRPOLY-DB-Machine-Printed-B (1-4)	1864	6	653	5895	30533
	1931	5	522	4473	22923
	1953	18	1673	13076	72750
	1977	4	374	3340	16714
GRPOLY-DB-Machine-Printed-C	1912	315	10478	65875	-
Total		**399**	**15084**	**102596**	**171511**

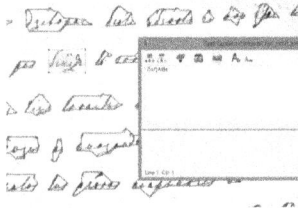

(a)

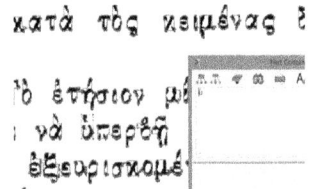

(b)

Fig. 9.2: Examples of GRPOLY-DB ground-truth regions at word (left) and character (right) level.

et al., 2010) which was again verified and corrected by a set of users. Example pages for all subsets of GRPOLY-DB can be found in Figure 9.3.

GRPOLY-DB-Handwritten contains 46 colour page images from a historical manuscript written by Sofia Trikoupi (1838–1916) (Figure 9.3(a)). The corresponding ground-truth contains segmentation at text line and word level. Concerning GRPOLY-DB-MachinePrinted-A, it consists of 5 binary page images obtained from the Hellenic National Printing House (Figure 9.3(b)). The publication year of these documents ranges between 1950 and 1965. The corresponding ground-truth contains segmentation at text line, word and character level. The GRPOLY-DB-MachinePrinted-B set consists of 33 grayscale page images from the parliament session proceedings dated from 1864 to 1977 originating from the archive of the Hellenic Parliament (Figure 9.3(c)). The corresponding ground-truth contains segmentation at

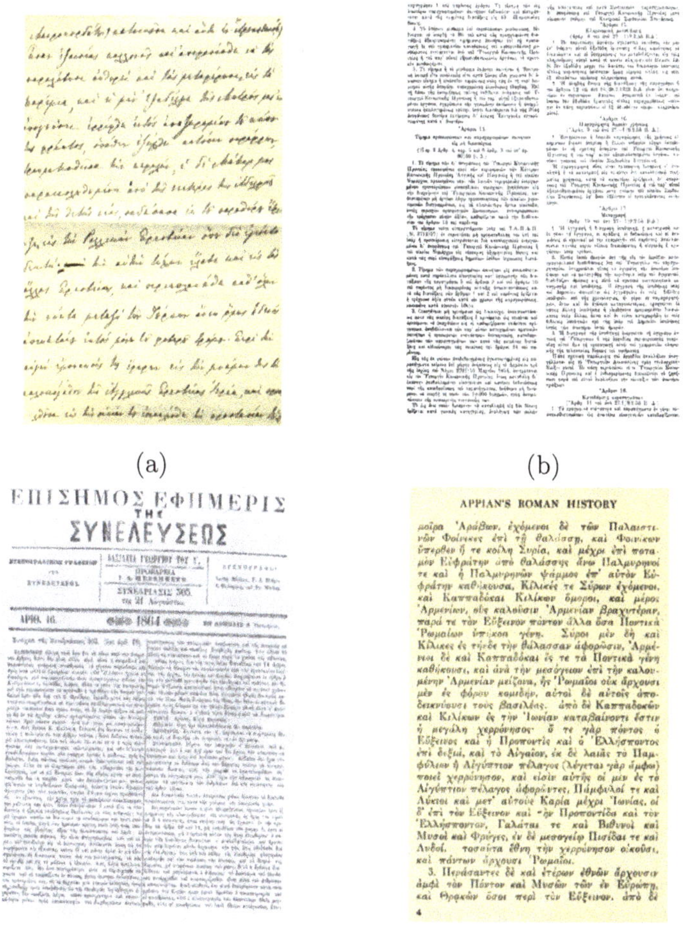

(a)   (b)

(c)   (d)

Fig. 9.3: Example pages of the GRPOLY-DB-Handwritten (a), the GRPOLY-DB-MachinePrinted-A (b), the GRPOLY-DB-MachinePrinted-B (c) and the GRPOLY-DB-MachinePrinted-C (d) datasets.

text line, word and character level. Finally, GRPOLY-DB-MachinePrinted-C contains 315 colour page images from Appian's Roman History Books I–VIII (Figure 9.3(d)) and the corresponding ground-truth segmentation at text line and word level. It is a set of better quality compared to other machine-printed GRPOLY-DB sets.

9.3   Page Segmentation

In the OldDocPro project, we used existing methods for layout analysis, text line and character segmentation (Louloudis *et al.*, 2009; Nikolaou *et al.*, 2010) while we developed a new technique for word segmentation (Louloudis *et al.*, 2016). Furthermore, we developed a new performance evaluation methodology for page segmentation techniques (Stamatopoulos *et al.*, 2015) and proposed an efficient document image segmentation representation (Retsinas *et al.*, 2016).

9.3.1   *Performance Evaluation of Page Segmentation*

The automatic evaluation of page segmentation algorithms is an important issue both for quantitative comparisons among different techniques as well as for qualitative analysis of segmentation results. In the OldDocPro project, a goal-oriented performance evaluation methodology is proposed (Stamatopoulos *et al.*, 2015) that reflects the percentage of the text information in which the subsequent processing, such as text line segmentation and recognition, can be applied successfully. It is a pixel-based approach which deals only with text regions. Moreover, the proposed evaluation technique avoids the dependence on a strictly defined ground-truth since the ground-truth for page segmentation is quite ambiguous and may differ between users (Figure 9.4).

9.3.2   *Word Segmentation*

Segmentation of a text line image into words is a challenging stage that is necessary mainly for KWS applications. Potential challenges include but are not limited to the appearance of skew and slant angle (even with different direction) in a text line image, the existence of punctuation marks that tends to reduce the distance of adjacent words and the non-uniform spacing of words. A word segmentation methodology usually comprises three stages: i) preprocessing (noise removal, skew and slant correction) ii) distance computation (selection of a distance measure in order to calculate the distance of adjacent components) and iii) gap classification (classification of the previously calculated distances as either between-word gaps or within-word gaps). In the OldDocPro project, we proposed a novel word segmentation method which uses the Student's-t distribution for the gap classification stage (Louloudis *et al.*, 2016). The main advantage of the Student's-t distribution concerns its robustness to the existence of outliers.

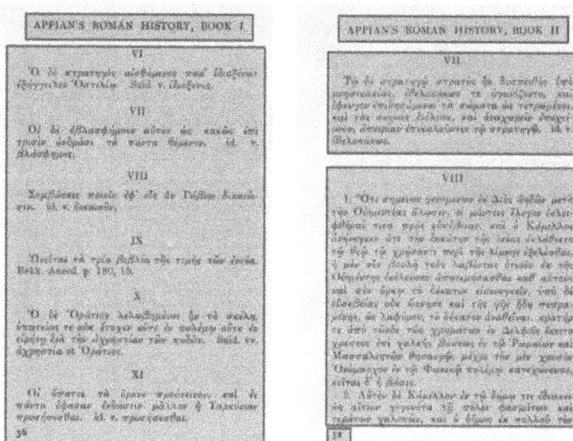

Fig. 9.4: Document Images with the corresponding acceptable ground-truth regions.

We evaluated the performance of the proposed word segmentation method against four state-of-the-art methods which follow the same protocol for the first stages of the word segmentation procedure while differentiate from the proposed method at the gap classification stage. These methods comprise: a) Gaussian mixture modeling (GMM) (Louloudis *et al.*, 2009), b) sequential clustering (Kim *et al.*, 2001), c) average linkage clustering (Kim *et al.*, 2001) and d) modified max clustering (Kim *et al.*, 2001). The evaluation method we followed is robust and well established since it corresponds to the protocol of the ICDAR 2009 Handwriting Segmentation Contest (Gatos *et al.*, 2009). The accuracy was measured in terms of Recall (R), Precision (P) and the final performance metric F-Measure (FM). The above-mentioned metrics use the number of ground truth words (N), the number of result words (M) and the number of one-to-one matches (o2o). Two different scenarios (S) were defined. According to the first scenario (S1), all the distances appearing in the document image were used for the gap classification stage. For the second scenario (S2), the largest distances appearing in each document image which correspond to the 2% of the total number of distances, were excluded from the classification. The idea for the definition of two scenarios was to check the effectiveness of methods into a scenario were outliers are defined using an empirical criterion and are 'manually' discarded. We assume that 2% of the distances correspond to outliers. Table 9.2 presents comparative experimental results for the GRPOLY-DB-MachinePrinted-C dataset and for

Table 9.2: Word Segmentation Comparative Results for the GRPOLY-DB-MachinePrinted-C dataset.

Word Segmentation method	S	M	o2o	R(%)	P(%)	FM(%)
GMM	S1	68101	64795	98.36	95.15	96.73
(Louloudis *et al.*, 2009)	S2	67581	65153	98.9	96.41	97.64
Sequential Clustering	S1	64052	62079	94.24	96.92	95.56
(Kim *et al.*, 2001)	S2	65390	63812	96.87	97.59	97.23
Average Linkage	S1	32060	24930	37.84	77.76	50.91
(Kim *et al.*, 2001)	S2	64712	62781	95.3	97.02	96.15
Modified Max	S1	18131	9383	14.24	51.75	22.34
(Kim *et al.*, 2001)	S2	56653	53419	81.09	94.29	87.19
Student's-t	S1	66795	65375	99.24	97.87	98.55
(Louloudis *et al.*, 2016)	S2	66688	65342	99.19	97.98	98.58

the two previously described scenarios (S1 and S2). The Student's-t always outperforms all other methods for all evaluation metrics (o2o, R, P and FM). When pruning extreme value inputs (S2), the Student's-t result remain largely the same, with only a very slight difference upwards or downwards. On the other hand, all other methods show improved results for scenario S2 compared to S1. This means that pruning values using a manually chosen threshold is required for them to obtain optimal performance, unlike the Student's-t which in a sense has a built-in mechanism of dealing with extreme values/outliers.

9.3.3 *Document Image Segmentation Representation*

The result of a document image segmentation task, e.g. text line or word segmentation, is usually a labeled image with each label corresponding to a different segmented region. For many applications, the segmented regions need to be stored and represented in an efficient way, using simple geometric shapes. A challenging task is to restrict all pixels corresponding to a specific label inside a polygon with a minimum number of vertices. Such a polygon promotes the description simplicity and the storage efficiency, while providing a much more user friendly representation that can be edited easily. In the OldDocPro project, we proposed a cost-effective approximation of the minimum-edges polygon problem, computing a contour enclosing only pixels of a certain label and using a greedy algorithm in order to reduce the contour into a minimum-link polygon that retains the separability property between the labeled set of pixels (Retsinas *et al.*, 2016) (Figure 9.5).

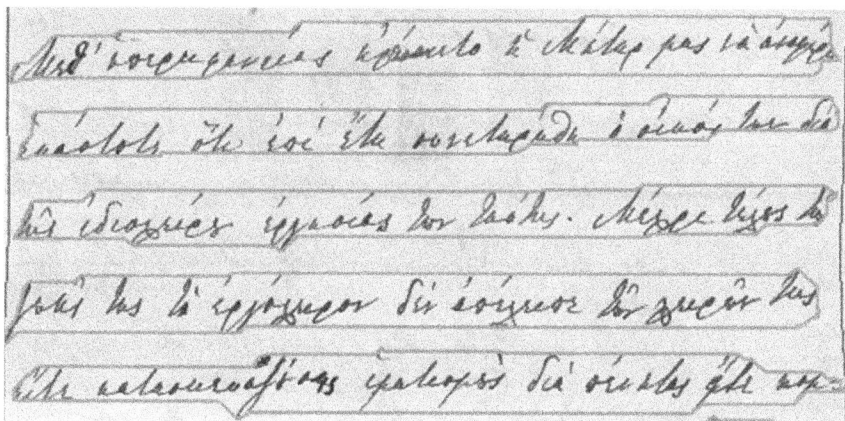

Fig. 9.5: Example of the proposed polygon representation of the segmentation result.

9.4 Text Recognition

In OldDocPro, we worked on text recognition of old Greek documents assuming as input the isolated characters (Retsinas *et al.*, 2015) as well each text line (Katsouros *et al.*, 2016; Simistira *et al.*, 2015).

9.4.1 *Isolated Character Recognition*

The proposed method for isolated character recognition (Retsinas *et al.*, 2015) relies upon the application of a projection-based feature extraction stage, which resembles the Radon transform, on both the original image and a set of generated images corresponding to different gradient orientations of the original image. It incorporates popular ideas from state-of-the-art feature extraction methods, such as Histogram of Oriented Gradients (HoG) (Dalal and Triggs, 2005), based on the fact that the gradient information has proven very useful for a variety of object recognition problems. After computing the Discrete Fourier Transform coefficients of the projection vector, only the first $n_c + 1$ are used to form the projection-based descriptor. The final feature vector is the concatenation of the projection-based descriptor applied in the initial binary image as well as in each of the four gradient orientation images, as it is depicted in Figure 9.6. For the classification stage, Support Vectors Machines (SVM) are used.

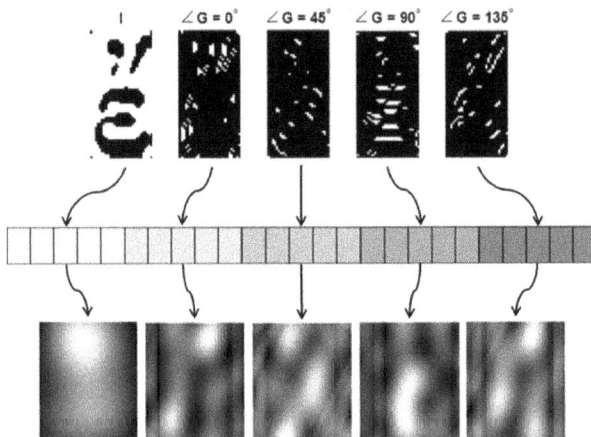

Fig. 9.6: Final descriptor as the concatenation of features of the initial image and its oriented gradients and their corresponding visualizations.

A 5-fold cross-validation was applied in order to evaluate the recognition of isolated characters of subsets GRPOLY-DB-MachinePrinted-A and GRPOLY-DB-MachinePrinted-B. We first selected all characters belonging to classes with at least 30 instances (125 classes). Two different scenarios were defined. According to the first scenario (SC-1), all instances were used (143051 instances) while at the second scenario (SC-2), only 30 randomly selected instances per class were used (3750 instances). We compared the proposed technique with two state-of-the-art character recognition techniques based on HoG features (Dalal and Triggs, 2005) combined with an SVM classifier and adaptive windows features (Gatos *et al.*, 2011) combined with a KNN classifier. The recognition results for the two scenarios of the GRPOLY-DB database are shown in Table 9.3. Specifically, we evaluated both the cases for $n_c = 3$ (POG3), which was the optimal for the other databases and the resulting descriptor is fairly small (180 features), and for $n_c = 6$ (POG6), which was chosen as the optimal for this database, even though it is a four times larger descriptor. The proposed technique exhibits superior performance, while the POG6 descriptor shows better performance compared to POG3 (especially in SC-2, which is a more qualitative scenario) at the cost of the length of the feature vector.

Table 9.3: Character recognition results for the GRPOLY-DB-MachinePrinted-B dataset and the two scenarios SC-1 and SC-2 for HoG (Dalal and Triggs, 2005), AdWin (Gatos *et al.*, 2011), POG3 (Retsinas *et al.*, 2015) and POG6 (Retsinas *et al.*, 2015).

	HoG	AdWin	POG3	POG6
SC-1	98.37%	97.71%	98.49%	**98.60%**
SC-2	92.00%	88.69%	93.67%	**94.35%**

9.4.2 *Text Line Recognition*

For text line recognition, in OldDocPro we developed two systems. The first was based on Hidden Markov Models (HMM) (Katsouros *et al.*, 2016) and the other on Long Short Term Memory (LSTM) Networks (Simistira *et al.*, 2015). In the HMM-based approach (Katsouros *et al.*, 2016), we modeled each character with a multistate, left-to-right HMM, with Gaussian Mixture Models (GMMs) as emission probability density function over the feature space. A text line is modeled by concatenating the models for each character in the text line. Note that space is also modeled as a separate character. GMMs are parameterized by the weights, the means and the variances for each Gaussian mixture. The number of mixtures for the GMMs, number of states of the HMMs and the transitions allowed among the states are also parameters of the model. The 1D-LSTM-based recognizer (Simistira *et al.*, 2015) used the OCRopus framework. The input text line image is scanned by a fixed-height window of 1-pixel width to convert the 2D-image into a one dimensional sequence (Figure 9.7).

We compared the text line recognition performance of the two proposed systems at character and word levels using (a) the open source OCR engine of Tesseract[3] and (b) the commercial OCR FineReader Engine v.ll[4] on the dataset GRPOLY-DB MachinePrinted-B. For Tesseract no training was necessary, as we used the model for Greek polytonic which was created by Nick White (White, 2012). For the ABBYY FineReader Engine we used 367 text lines of GRPOLY-DBMachinePrinted-B that do not belong to the test set in a way so that each target character class appears at least 5 times. The corresponding character error rates (CER) and word error rates (WER) are presented in Table 9.4. It can be observed that a) the HMM-based

---

[3] https://code.google.com/p/tesseract-ocr/
[4] https://www.abbyy.com/en-ca/ocr-sdk/

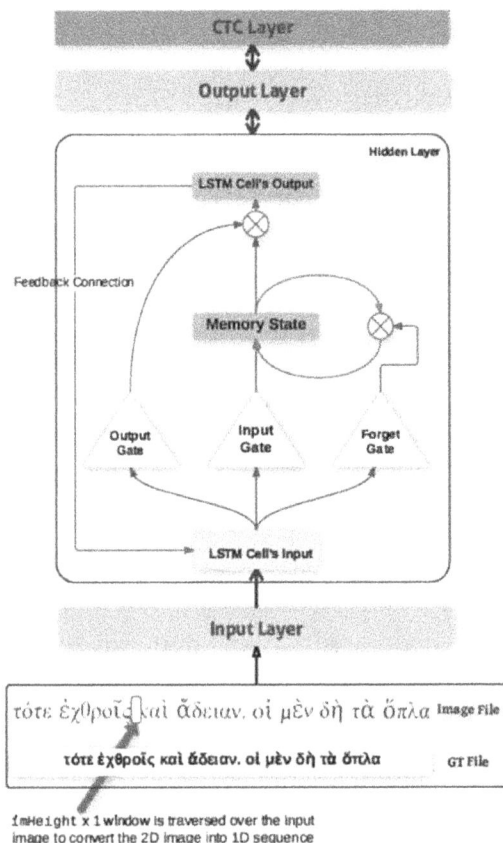

Fig. 9.7:   The 1D-LSTM architecture.

recognition system overcomes the problem of character segmentation and clearly outperforms the open source and commercial engines of Tesseract and ABBYY FineReader, respectively, for both accuracy measures (i.e. CER and WER) and b) The LSTM-based recognizer is the most promising achieving the best results for both measures and a remarkable low character error rate of 5.51%.

9.5   Keyword Spotting

In OldDocPro, we prepared a survey of keyword word spotting techniques (Giotis *et al.*, 2017) which attempts to fill the gaps in recent advances of

Table 9.4: Text line recognition comparative results for the GRPOLY-DB-MachinePrinted-B dataset.

OCR Engine	CER (%)	WER (%)
Tesseract[3]	30.37	71.43
ABBYY FineReader[4]	19.2	48.6
HMM-based (Katsouros et al., 2016)	8.61	25.3
LSTM-based (Simistira et al., 2015)	**5.51**	**24.13**

keyword spotting methods and emphasize on several topics not discussed by previous related studies. Additionally, we introduced two new keyword spotting systems. The first system supports a shape-based matching between handwritten words represented by local contour features (Giotis et al., 2015). The query image is first aligned with the test image according to a similarity measure using the corresponding feature descriptors and then the aligned images are matched with the use of a deformable non-rigid point matching algorithm. Each word image is first skeletonized and then represented by the pairs of adjacent segments (PAS) (Figure 9.8). The proposed PAS-based approach was evaluated against: a) hybrid feature extraction (zones and projections) combined with appropriate normalization (skew, slant, position, stroke thickness) (Gatos et al., 2006a), b) adaptive zoning features that are extracted after adjusting the position of every zone based on local pattern information (Gatos et al., 2011) and c) dynamic time warping (DTW) using word profiles (Rath and Manmatha, 2003). Comparative results that are presented in Table 9.5 using the Mean Average Precision (MAP) show that the proposed PAS-based approach achieves the best results.

Fig. 9.8: The extracted PAS features from the word image skeleton.

The second system (Sfikas et al., 2015) is an extension of the attribute-based model for word spotting and recognition recently presented in (Almazán

Table 9.5: Keyword spotting comparative results for the GRPOLY-DB-Handwritten dataset.

Keyword Spotting Method	Mean Average Precision (%)
Hybrid features (Gatos *et al.*, 2006a)	39.4
Adaptive Zoning (Gatos *et al.*, 2011)	40.4
DTW (Rath and Manmatha, 2003)	56.2
PAS-based (Giotis *et al.*, 2015)	**60.0**

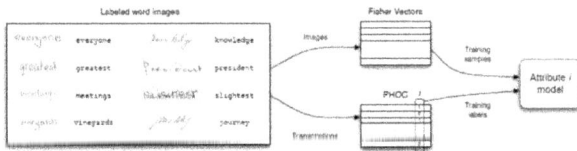

Fig. 9.9: The attribute-based model. The two descriptors (FV and PHOC) are used together to learn a projection to a new space.

Table 9.6: Keyword spotting comparative results for the GRPOLY-DB-MachinePrinted-B dataset.

Keyword Spotting Method	Mean Average Precision (%)
Adaptive Zoning (Gatos *et al.*, 2011)	57.8
DTW (Rath and Manmatha, 2003)	62
A-PHOC (Sfikas *et al.*, 2015)	52.5
PH-PHOC (Sfikas *et al.*, 2015)	56.6
MB-PHOC (Sfikas *et al.*, 2015)	**74.4**

et al., 2014) for use with polytonic old greek documents. The word image data is used to create a Fisher Vector (FV) descriptor, while the transcription is used to create a histogram-based descriptor named Pyramidal Histogram of Characters (PHOC). The two descriptor sets are used together to learn a projection to a new space and create a new descriptor (Figure 9.9). In the proposed work (Sfikas *et al.*, 2015), three different ways to extend PHOC to polytonic greek are proposed based on the number and meaning of the bins used for PHOC (A-PHOC, PH-PHOC and MB-PHOC). Comparative results that are presented in Table 9.6 show that the MB-PHOC descriptors significantly outperform other methods based on adaptive zones (Gatos *et al.*, 2011) and DTW (Rath and Manmatha, 2003) in terms of mean average precision for the GRPOLY-DB-MachinePrinted-B dataset.

The attribute-base model for Greek polytonic characters (Sfikas *et al.*, 2015) can be also used for the task of handwritten word recognition. To perform recognition, we use a lexicon that is made up of the transcriptions appearing in the full dataset. Each PHOC descriptor of the lexicon words is compared to each of the words of the test set. This corresponds to a lexicon size of 2141 unique words. The representation of the lexicon word that gives the smallest Euclidean distance is selected as the recognized transcription. We used the same training/test set settings for the trials performed for word spotting, and the MB-PHOC model. Recognition accuracy is evaluated over the GRPOLY-DB-Handwritten set and measured as the percentage of correctly recognized words. In the GRPOLY-DB-Handwritten set, this amounts to 2000 total words in the test set, out of which 1518 have been correctly recognized and 482 missed, for a correct word ratio of 75.9%. Note that we count as a miss the difference of one or more letters or diacritics between the recognized word and the ground truth. An example of recognition result can be seen in Figure 9.10.

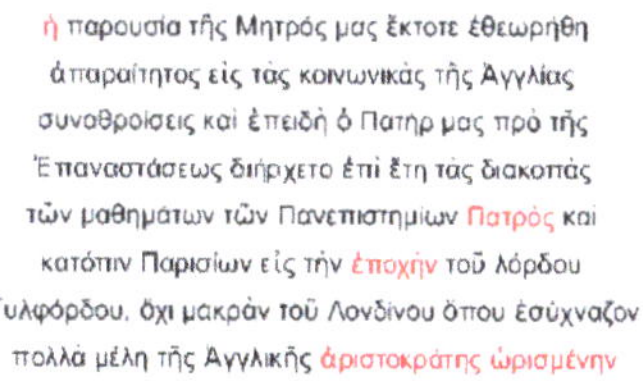

ἡ παρουσία τῆς Μητρός μας ἔκτοτε ἐθεωρήθη
ἀπαραίτητος εἰς τάς κοινωνικάς τῆς Ἀγγλίας
συναθροίσεις καί ἐπειδή ὁ Πατήρ μας πρό τῆς
Ἐπαναστάσεως διήρχετο ἐπί ἔτη τάς διακοπάς
τῶν μαθημάτων τῶν Πανεπιστημίων Πατρός καί
κατόπιν Παρισίων εἰς τήν ἐποχήν τοῦ λόρδου
Γυλφόρδου, ὄχι μακράν τοῦ Λονδίνου ὅπου ἐσύχναζον
πολλά μέλη τῆς Ἀγγλικῆς ἀριστοκράτης ὡρισμένην

(a) 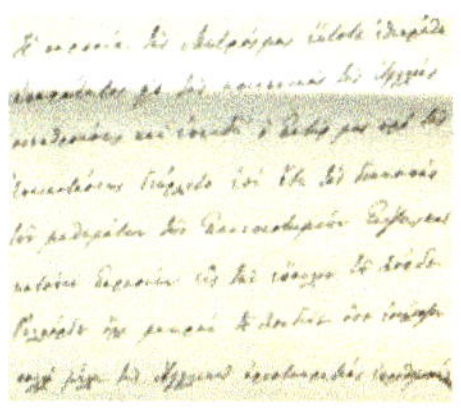   (b)

Fig. 9.10: Word recognition result (a) of image (b) from the GRPOLY-DB-Handwritten set. All words are recognized correctly except for the words coloured red.

9.6   Conclusions

The main achievements of the OldDocPro project are presented focusing in the creation of the old Greek polytonic database GRPOLY-DB as well as in the development of new methods for the segmentation, recognition and KWS of old Greek documents. GRPOLY-DB (Gatos *et al.*, 2015) is the first publicly available old Greek polytonic database and consists of four subsets that have been semi-automatically annotated with ground-truth information at different levels using the PAGE format. This dataset was used to test and compare with existing techniques the new methods which were developed during the OldDocPro project and are the following: a) A novel word segmentation method which uses the Student's-t distribution for the gap classification stage (Louloudis *et al.*, 2016). The main advantage of the Student's-t distribution concerns its robustness to the existence of outliers. b) A method for isolated character recognition that relies upon the application of a projection-based feature extraction stage, which resembles the Radon transform, on both the original image and a set of generated images corresponding to different gradient orientations of the original image (Retsinas *et al.*, 2015). c) Two methods for text line recognition. The first was based on HMM (Katsouros *et al.*, 2016) and the other on LSTM Networks (Simistira *et al.*, 2015). d) Two new keyword spotting systems. The first system supports a shape-based matching between handwritten words represented by local contour features (Giotis *et al.*, 2015). The second system is an extension of the attribute-based model for use with polytonic old Greek documents (Sfikas *et al.*, 2015). This system can be also used for the task of handwritten word recognition.

References

Almazán, J., Gordo, A., Fornés, A., and Valveny, E. (2014). Word spotting and recognition with embedded attributes, *IEEE transactions on pattern analysis and machine intelligence* **36**, 12, pp. 2552–2566.

Clausner, C., Pletschacher, S., and Antonacopoulos, A. (2011). Aletheia - An Advanced Document Layout and Text Ground-Truthing System for Production Environments, in *International Conference on Document Analysis and Recognition*, pp. 48–52.

Dalal, N. and Triggs, B. (2005). Histograms of oriented gradients for human detection, in *2005 IEEE computer society conference on computer vision and pattern recognition (CVPR'05)*, Vol. 1 (IEEE), pp. 886–893.

Gatos, B., Kesidis, A. L., and Papandreou, A. (2011). Adaptive zoning features for character and word recognition, in *2011 International Conference on Document Analysis and Recognition* (IEEE), pp. 1160–1164.

Gatos, B., Louloudis, G., and Stamatopoulos, N. (2014). Segmentation of historical handwritten documents into text zones and text lines, in *2014 14th International Conference on Frontiers in Handwriting Recognition* (IEEE), pp. 464–469.

Gatos, B., Pratikakis, I., Kesidis, A., and Perantonis, S. (2006a). Efficient off-line cursive handwriting word recognition, in *10th International Workshop on Frontiers in Handwriting Recognition, IWFHR*.

Gatos, B., Pratikakis, I., and Perantonis, S. J. (2006b). Adaptive degraded document image binarization, *Pattern Recognition* **39**, 3, pp. 317–327.

Gatos, B., Stamatopoulos, N., and Louloudis, G. (2009). Icdar2009 handwriting segmentation contest, in *Proceedings of 10th International Conference on Document Analysis and Recognition*, 10, pp. 1393–1397.

Gatos, B., Stamatopoulos, N., Louloudis, G., Sfikas, G., Retsi nas, G., Papavassiliou, V., Simistira, F., and Katsouros, V. (2015). GRPOLY-DB: An old Greek Polytonic document image database, in *ICDAR, 2015 13th International Conference on*, pp. 646–650.

Giotis, A. P., Sfikas, G., Gatos, B., and Nikou, C. (2017). A survey of document image word spotting techniques, *Pattern Recognition* **68**, pp. 310–332.

Giotis, A. P., Sfikas, G., Nikou, C., and Gatos, B. (2015). Shape-based word spotting in handwritten document images, in *2015 13th International Conference on Document Analysis and Recognition (ICDAR)* (IEEE), pp. 561–565.

Katsouros, V., Papavassiliou, V., Simistira, F., and Gatos, B. (2016). Recognition of greek polytonic on historical degraded texts using hmms, in *2016 12th IAPR Workshop on Document Analysis Systems (DAS)* (IEEE), pp. 346–351.

Kim, S.-H., Jeong, S., Lee, G.-S., and Suen, C. Y. (2001). Word segmentation in handwritten korean text lines based on gap clustering techniques, in *Proceedings of Sixth International Conference on Document Analysis and Recognition* (IEEE), pp. 189–193.

Louloudis, G., Gatos, B., Pratikakis, I., and Halatsis, C. (2009). Text line and word segmentation of handwritten documents, *Pattern recognition* **42**, 12, pp. 3169–3183.

Louloudis, G., Sfikas, G., Stamatopoulos, N., and Gatos, B. (2016). Word segmentation using the student's-t distribution, in *2016 12th IAPR Workshop on Document Analysis Systems (DAS)* (IEEE), pp. 78–83.

Nikolaou, N., Makridis, M., Gatos, B., Stamatopoulos, N., and Papamarkos, N. (2010). Segmentation of historical machine-printed documents using adaptive run length smoothing and skeleton segmentation paths, *Image and Vision Computing* **28**, 4, pp. 590–604.

Pletschacher, S. and Antonacopoulos, A. (2010). The page (page analysis and ground-truth elements) format framework, in *Pattern Recognition (ICPR), 2010 20th International Conference on* (IEEE), pp. 257–260.

Rath, T. M. and Manmatha, R. (2003). Word image matching using dynamic time warping, in *IEEE Conference on Computer Vision and Pattern Recognition, Proceedings*, Vol. 2 (IEEE).

Retsinas, G., Gatos, B., Stamatopoulos, N., and Louloudis, G. (2015). Isolated character recognition using projections of oriented gradients, in *2015 13th International Conference on Document Analysis and Recognition (ICDAR)* (IEEE), pp. 336–340.

Retsinas, G., Louloudis, G., Stamatopoulos, N., and Gatos, B. (2016). Efficient document image segmentation representation by approximating minimum-link polygons, in *2016 12th IAPR Workshop on Document Analysis Systems (DAS)* (IEEE), pp. 293–298.

Sfikas, G., Giotis, A. P., Louloudis, G., and Gatos, B. (2015). Using attributes for word spotting and recognition in polytonic greek documents, in *2015 13th International Conference on Document Analysis and Recognition (ICDAR)* (IEEE), pp. 686–690.

Simistira, F., Ul-Hassan, A., Papavassiliou, V., Gatos, B., Katsouros, V., and Liwicki, M. (2015). Recognition of historical greek polytonic scripts using lstm networks, in *2015 13th International Conference on Document Analysis and Recognition (ICDAR)* (IEEE), pp. 766–770.

Stamatopoulos, N., Louloudis, G., and Gatos, B. (2010). Efficient transcript mapping to ease the creation of document image segmentation ground truth with text-image alignment, in *2010 12th International Conference on Frontiers in Handwriting Recognition* (IEEE), pp. 226–231.

Stamatopoulos, N., Louloudis, G., and Gatos, B. (2015). Goal-oriented performance evaluation methodology for page segmentation techniques, in *2015 13th International Conference on Document Analysis and Recognition (ICDAR)* (IEEE), pp. 281–285.

Valveny, E. (2014). Datasets and annotations for document analysis and recognition, in *Handbook of Document Image Processing and Recognition* (Springer), pp. 983–1009.

White, N. (2012). Training tesseract for ancient greek ocr, *Eutypon*, pp. 1–11.

Chapter 10

Advances in Handwritten Keyword Indexing and Search Technologies

Joan Puigcerver, Alejandro H. Toselli and Enrique Vidal

Pattern Recognition and Human Language Technology Research Center,
Universitat Politècnica de València, Spain
joapuipe@prhlt.upv.es, ahector@prhlt.upv.es, evidal@prhlt.upv.es

Nowadays there is a great need for accessing the textual content of many vast digitized handwritten collections held by digital libraries, archives, cultural institutions, etc. The manual transcription of such huge material would be overly expensive and unaffordable in a reasonable time. On the other hand, fully automatic, or assisted handwritten text recognition technologies, respectively, still can not face this challenge with acceptable recognition accuracy or fairish processing time. The solution proposed here focuses on probabilistic indexing and search techniques under the precision-recall tradeoff paradigm. Query-by-string, word-segmentation-free, line-level keyword spotting techniques are employed to obtain the word relevance probabilities required for probabilistic indexing. Empirical results on several historical image datasets, entailing different complexity levels, confirm the viability and adequateness of the proposed indexing and search approach.

10.1 Introduction

In last few decades, large collections of historical handwritten documents have been scanned and converted into digital images, both to ensure preservation and to make them available through web sites of libraries and archives all over the world. Archives, in particular, hold billions of documents containing very important data about the evolution of daily human activities over the centuries. However, the wealth of information conveyed by the text captured in these images remains largely inaccessible, hidden behind thousands of terabytes of digital image data. To exploit and make profit of such mass-digitization efforts, affordable information retrieval methods are required which allow the users to accurately and efficiently search for textual contents in large collections of handwritten text images.

Of course, a first idea to provide the required access to textual information is to transcribe the text images. This is very appealing since it would be useful not only for information retrieval, but also for many other tasks such as producing scholarly digital (critical) editions. However, *manually* transcribing such historical documents, typically by paleography experts, is generally overly expensive and plainly unaffordable for the vast amounts of images constituting most archive collections of interest.

Another obvious idea is to rely on *automatic* transcription based on Handwritten Text Recognition (HTR). This technology has been experiencing great advances in the last few years, after the introduction of Convolutional and Recurrent Neural Networks for optical modeling. Nevertheless, while academic publications and results of public competitions might suggest that almost perfect transcription is close to be achieved, practical end-to-end results on historical archive handwritten images generally fall short from the expectations. Failures come from many causes; an important one is related with automatic layout analysis and/or line detection problems, which often prevent establishing a correct reading order and severely hinder the final quality of the transcripts.

An alternative to fully automatic processing is to rely on *computer-assisted* transcription. This was successfully explored empirically in [Toselli *et al.* (2010); Romero *et al.* (2012); Alabau *et al.* (2014)], following new, powerful concepts of pattern recognition-based human-machine interaction introduced in [Vidal *et al.* (2007)] and [Toselli *et al.* (2011)]. Following the good results of these laboratory studies, preliminary evaluation by real users was carried out in [Toselli *et al.* (2017)].

In the last few years, the TRANSCRIPTORIUM and the READ projects[1] have further explored the practical capabilities of these automatic and assisted, interactive HTR (IHTR) technologies to speed-up the conversion of raw text images into electronic text. Despite great advances achieved

---

[1]http://transcriptorium.eu, https://read.transkribus.eu

in these developments, current conclusions are not very optimistic about the potential effectiveness of either HTR or IHTR to process *very large* manuscript collections. Some nuances of this claim are analyzed hereafter:

In some cases, fully automatic transcripts of text images can be useful for plaintext indexing and search purposes. However, in many historical text image collections of interest, the typical level of transcription accuracy achieved severely hinders the search *recall*; i.e., the system ability to ensure that all or most of the images containing a given query text can actually be retrieved.

Similarly, fully automatic transcription of most historical text images do not reach either the level of accuracy needed for typical scholarly editions of the corresponding image collections.

In both cases, the required level of accuracy can obviously be obtained by means of additional user effort. To this end, rather than just letting the users edit the noisy automatic transcripts, IHTR can be used to achieve the desired transcription accuracy in a cost-effective way. This can lead to significant effort reductions with respect to just manually editing the automatic transcripts. But the overall human effort demanded by IHTR is still substantial. Therefore, while IHTR is proving useful to produce scholarly editions of moderately sized historical collections, the required effort to deal with the kind of massive image collections, which are the typical target of indexing and search, is by all means entirely prohibitive.

According to this analysis, textual information searching approaches, specifically designed for large text image collections, are needed. In these approaches, indexing and search must be implemented on the images themselves, without resorting to previously obtained image transcripts. On the other hand, rather than "exact" searching (as in plaintext), search has to be performed with a *relevance threshold*, somehow specified by the user as part of the query in order to meet the *precision-recall trade-off* which is considered most adequate in each query.

Keyword spotting (KWS) is a traditional way to address search problems within this framework [Manmatha *et al.* (1996); Rath and Manmatha (2007); Cao *et al.* (2009); Rodriguez and Perronnin (2009); Kamel (2010); Fischer *et al.* (2012); Frinken *et al.* (2012); Wshah *et al.* (2012); Toselli and Vidal (2013); Toselli *et al.* (2016); Puigcerver *et al.* (2016)]. More precisely, KWS aims at determining locations on a text image or image collection which likely contain instances of a query word, without explicitly transcribing the image(s).

In the traditional literature, two different KWS paradigms are assumed: Query-by-Example (QbE) and Query-by-String (QbS). In QbE the query word is specified by means of a cropped example-image of the query word, while just a textual character string is needed in QbS. While the QbE scenario can be useful in some applications, it is clearly not adequate in our large-scale indexing and search scenario and only QbS is considered here.[2] Similarly, traditional "word segmentation-based" KWS is obviously inadequate either for the kind of image collections considered. Instead, in the experiments presented in this work, we assume the (word-unsegmented) *line image* as the smallest search target, as in [Terasawa and Tanaka (2009), Kolcz *et al.* (2000); Fischer *et al.* (2012); Frinken *et al.* (2012); Wshah *et al.* (2012); Toselli and Vidal (2013); Toselli *et al.* (2016)], among others.

On the other hand, KWS techniques can be considered to belong to one of these two broad classes: *training-based* and *training-free*. Training-based KWS methods are generally based on statistical optical (and language) models and typically adopt the QbS paradigm, while most training-free techniques are based on direct (image) template matching and assume the QbE framework. The approaches proposed here are training-based and therefore need some amount (tens to hundreds) of manually transcribed images to train the required optical and language models. Clearly, in large handwritten collections, the effort or cost to produce training data is more than rewarded by the benefits of accurately making the textual contents of these collections available for exploration and retrieval.

10.2   Proposed Indexing and Search Technology

The indexing and search technology we are developing assumes the so called *precision-recall trade-off search model* which requires to compute *word relevance probabilities* for adequate regions of the text images of interest. Here we outline how to appropriately choose adequate indexing regions and how to compute the required probabilities.

---

[2]Note, however, that highly accurate QbE performance can be easily achieved by using just QbS technology [Vidal *et al.* (2015)].

10.2.1   *Pixel-Level Word Relevance Probabilities: the "Posteriorgram"*

A basic concept on which the proposed approach relies is the so called *pixel-level "posteriorgram"*. Basically, it is a posterior probability map computed for a given image $\mathcal{X}$ and a possible query word v. At each location (i, j) of $\mathcal{X}$, the posteriorgram provides the posterior probability that the word v is written in some subimage of X which includes the pixel (i, j). Formally:

$$P(Q = v \mid X = \mathcal{X}, L = (i, j)) \;\;\equiv\;\; P(v \mid \mathcal{X}, i, j) \qquad (10.1)$$

Fig. 10.1 illustrates this concept.

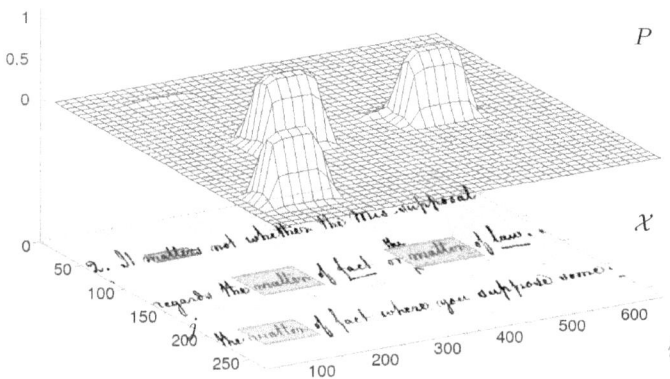

Fig. 10.1: Pixel-level posteriorgram, P, for a text image X and word $v =$ "matter". To compute P an accurate, contextual (n-gram based) *word classifier* was used. This helped to achieve very low posteriors in a region of X around $(i = 130, j = 70)$, where a very similar (but *different*) word, "matters", is written.

The value of P at each image location (i, j) can be easily obtained by statistical *marginalization*: consider that v may have been written in any possible bounding box of the image $\mathcal{X}$ which includes the pixel (i, j). The marginalization process simply adds the word recognition probabilities for all these bounding boxes. Therefore a posteriorgram can be simply obtained by repeated application of any word classification system capable of recognizing isolated (pre-segmented) words. Obviously, the better the classifier, the better the corresponding posteriorgram estimates. As illustrated in Fig. 10.1, using a context-aware word classifier provides very accurate pixel-level word posteriors.

Directly obtaining a full pixel-level posteriorgram in this way entails a formidable amount of computation. However, as it will be discussed later, it can be very efficiently computed by clever combinations of subsampling of the image positions (i, j) and adequate choices of the marginalization bounding boxes.

10.2.2   *Image Region Word Relevance Probabilities*

Posteriorgrams could be directly used for KWS: Given a relevance threshold τ, a word v is just spotted in all image positions (i, j) where P is greater than τ. Varying the threshold, adequate *precision–recall* tradeoff can be achieved. However, for large image collections, indexing word relevances for every pixel of every images in the collection is obviously unfeasible. For indexing purposes, what we really need is the probability that a word v is written within a (pre-specified) image region, such as a line, a column, or a full page, without explicitly taking into account exactly where the word is written within the region or how many instances of the word may appear in this region. In the field of Information Retrieval, this is called the *"relevance probability"* of the image region. For a probabilistic formulation, three random variables are used: *Relevance* is modeled by a binary variable R, image regions or "zones" are modeled by Z and "query" words by Q. Then, the probability that a region $Z = z$ is relevant for a query word $Q = v$ is expressed as:

$$P(R = 1 \mid Z = z, Q = v) \;\equiv\; P(R \mid z, v) \tag{10.2}$$

Therefore indexing an image collection requires computing $P(R \mid z, v)$ for each region z and word v to be indexed.

Exactly computing these relevance probabilities can become complex. Nevertheless, as discussed in [Toselli *et al.* (2016)], a very simple and intuitively appealing approach is to obtain the region relevance probability for a word v just as the maximum pixel-level probability for v over all the pixels of the region. Formally:

$$P(R \mid z, v) \;\approx\; \max_{i,j} P(v \mid z, i, j) \tag{10.3}$$

where i, j range over all the pixel locations of z. For instance, if $\mathcal{X}$ in Fig. 10.1 is considered the region z to be indexed, the probability that $\mathcal{X}$ is relevant for the query "matter" is adequately approximated just the maximum of the four picks of the posteriorgram shown in this figure.

10.2.3 *Minimal Searchable Image Regions: Line-Level KWS*

In our work so far, line-shaped regions have been adopted as the smallest image region to be indexed. From the user point of view, lines are are sufficiently precise target image positions for most practical document image search and retrieval applications. On the other hand, line-shaped image regions allow for efficient computation of posteriorgrams by adequately choosing the bounding boxes needed for the underlying marginalization process and by clever vertical subsampling of image positions.

First, *marginalization bounding boxes* for a line-shaped image region can be simply defined just by horizontal segmentation. On the other hand, with line-shaped image regions, *vertical subsampling* may simply be done by running, with some overlap, a vertical-sliding window of the expected height of the text in the image. Moreover, in many cases of interest, text lines are fairly regular and recently developed line detection techniques yield results which are sufficiently accurate to be used as an advantageous proxy for the required vertical subsampling. This allows to save computation costs and tends to increase indexing accuracy. Finally, and most importantly, line-shaped text image regions typically contain most of the relevant linguistic context needed for precise computation of word classification probabilities using a language-model based recognizer, as discussed above.

10.2.4 *Efficient Computation of Posteriorgrams and Relevance Probabilities*

In our approaches, line-level posteriorgrams are very efficiently computed using *Word Graphs*, obtained as a byproduct of recognizing full line-region images with a holistic HTR system based on *optical character models* and (N-gram) *Language Models* [Toselli *et al.* (2016)]. When applied to a line-shaped image region, these systems can take advantage of most of the linguistic context which is present in the image to provide very accurate word classification probabilities. On the other hand, a WG obtained in this way provides lots of alternative horizontal word-level segmentations. These segments directly define very adequate sets of bounding boxes, exactly as required by the marginalization process used to compute the posteriorgrams.

10.3   Datasets

Many historical collections of handwritten text images have been considered for testing the proposed indexing and search technologies. Most of this work was carried out within the TRANSCRIPTORIUM project mentioned in Section 10.1. General information and specific features of the datasets used in this work are presented below.

The first two datasets (BENTHAM and AUSTEN) correspond to collections which are rather modern (18–19th century), entailing similar, relatively mild challenges in terms of writing style, homogeneity and language usage. The last three datasets (PLANTAS, ALCARAZ and WIENSTULRICH) belong to more challenging, earlier handwritten collections (16–17th centuries), which exhibit many of the difficulties entailed by early modern and medieval manuscripts.

Bentham Dataset   This dataset composed of 433 page images is part of the Bentham collection containing more than 80 000 images of manuscripts written by the renowned English philosopher and reformer Jeremy Bentham (1748–1832) and his secretarial staff [Causer and Wallace (2012)]. It includes texts about legal reform, punishment, the constitution, religion, and his famous *"panopticon"* prison paradigm. The dataset used here is exactly the same adopted for the ICFHR-2014 HTRtS competition[3] of handwritten text recognition [Sánchez *et al.* (2014)]. The 433 pages of this dataset were written by many hands, resulting in a large writing style variability, thereby requiring many training samples to adequately train multi-writer optical character models. Page examples of this dataset are shown in Fig. 10.2 and basic statistics in Table 10.1. Additional details can be found in [Sánchez *et al.* (2014)].

Austen Dataset   The AUSTEN dataset is an autograph from a single notebook containing early works by Jane Austen (1775–1817), the famous romantic fiction English novelist. The notebook is known as "Juvenilia - Volume the Third" and includes two novels *Evelyn* and *Catharine, or the Bower* that were written between the years 1787 and 1793.[4] Most of this manuscript was written by Jane Austen's hand (almost 90% of the lines), although there are a few pages written by her nephew, James Edward

---

[3]www.transcriptorium.eu/~htrcontest/contestICFHR2014/public_html/HTRtS2014

[4]http://www.janeausten.ac.uk/manuscripts/blvolthird/1.html

Austen (11 pages, 185 lines), and her niece, Jane Anna Elizabeth Lefroy (5 pages, 99 lines).

Page examples of this 128 pages dataset are shown in Fig. 10.2 and basic statistics in Table 10.1. Additional details can be found in [Villegas *et al.* (2015)]. Lines are curved and compressed, see Figure 2(d).

Plantas Dataset   This dataset of 1 035 pages and around 20 000 handwritten text lines is one of the seven volumes of the book "Historia de las plantas", written using a quill-pen by the botanist Bernardo de Cienfuegos in the early 17th century. The book was writing mainly in Spanish, with a significant number of words and full sentences in Latin and other languages. It includes 49 pages at the beginning comprising indices, reference tables, a multilingual botanical glossary, and a 36-page preface. This is followed by 887 numbered pages that contain 152 chapters about cereals and related plants, including 126 botanical illustrations [Toselli *et al.* (2017)].

Alcaraz Dataset   The ALCARAZ dataset belongs to the written records from the Inquisition process (1534–1539) against Pedro Ruiz de Alcaraz, a member of the 16th century Spanish *alumbrados* religious movement. The full manuscript is composed of 953 page images written, probably by several hands, using mainly two types of early modern Spanish calligraphies, known as *Cortesana* and *Procesal encadenada*. Many of the records were written quickly, without consistent blank spaces between and within words, and with plenty of (rather inconsistent, often improvised) abbreviations. The main language is Spanish, with many words, abbreviations and full passages in Latin. From the complete dataset, ground truth transcripts were produced for a subset of 44 pages, using modernized transcripts available from [Kinder (1966–1997)]. These pages correspond to some of the declarations made by Pedro Ruiz de Alcaraz and are mainly written in *Cortesana* calligraphy. See Fig. 10.2 for sample pages and Table 10.1 for basic statistics. More details can be found in [Villegas *et al.* (2015)].

WienStUlrich Dataset   This dataset is a 52 pages subset of a Wiensanktulrich birth register book, written by a single writer in the 16th century.

It was endowed with two types of ground truth annotations. First, a layout analysis of each page was manually done to indicate columns, records and lines, resulting in a dataset of 3 618 lines grouped in 494 birth records.

Second, the dataset was diplomatically transcribed line by line by expert paleographers. Words of both Germanic and Latin origin appear in the records. Latin words are generally written in *italic* (cursive) style, while *fraktur* style is used for most German words. Figure 10.2 and Table 10.1 show sample pages and basic statistics for this dataset. See [Romero *et al.* (2016)] for additional details.

BENTHAM   AUSTEN

PLANTAS   ALCARAZ   WIENSTULRICH

Fig. 10.2: Page images examples of all the datasets used in this work.

Table 10.1: Basic statistics of all the datasets used in this work.

Number of:	BENTHAM	AUSTEN	PLANTAS	ALCARAZ	WIENSTULRICH
Pages	433	128	871	44	52
Lines	11 473	2 693	19 544	1 728	3 618
Running words	106 905	25 291	197 617	23 481	15 693
Different words	9 716	3 567	21 148	3 405	2 303
Query words	6 962	2 281	9 945	2 669	2 256
Different characters	86	81	77	31	74
Training / Test pages	400 / 33	50 / 78	224 / 647	10-fold CV	5-fold CV

10.4   Experimental Framework

System setup details, dataset usage, criteria for selecting the query sets and assessment measures adopted are presented in this section.

10.4.1   *System Setup*

Probabilistic indices for each dataset were built as explained in Sec. 10.2. The optical and language models needed to compute the posteriorgrams and the line-level word relevance probabilities were trained from transcribed line images of the corresponding datasets.

Optical modelling was based on left-to-right character hidden Markov models (HMMs), trained from transcribed line images. HMM training was carried out with the Embedded Baum–Welch algorithm [Jelinek (1998); Young *et al.* (1997)]. On the other hand, image transcripts were used to train a 2-gram word language model, back-off smoothed with the Kneser–Ney technique [Kneser and Ney (1995)]. Line images were represented as 24-dimensional feature vector sequences computed as in [Kozielski *et al.* (2012)].

Meta-parameters associated with 2-gram and HMM training (grammar scale factor, word insertion penalty, number of states per HMM and number of gaussians per state) were tuned using validation subsets of the training sets. See [Toselli *et al.* (2017); Sánchez *et al.* (2014); Villegas *et al.* (2015); Romero *et al.* (2016)] for more details about these settings for each dataset. Finally, using the previously trained models, line-level word relevance probabilities, $P(R \mid x, v)$, were obtained as in Eq. (10.3), computed as outlined in Sec. 10.2.4.

10.4.2   *Dataset Usage Details and Query Set Selection*

Experimental results for the BENTHAM, AUSTEN and PLANTAS datasets were obtained using the corresponding train/test partitions outlined in Table 10.1. Around 10% of the training data of each dataset were used for validation. For the AUSTEN-B experiment (see Fig. 10.3), no training data was used. Instead, we used optical and language models previously trained for the experiment with the BENTHAM dataset, as explained in Sec. 10.5. Finally, for the smaller datasets ALCARAZ and WIENSTULRICH, rather than fixed training/test partitions, N-fold cross validation was adopted for evaluation, with the values of N reported in Table 10.1.

Regarding the selection of query words, several keywords selecting criteria have been used in previous works for KWS assessment. Clearly, any given KWS system may perform better or worse depending on the specific keywords used for evaluation and how they are distributed in the test set. Since our approach is aimed at indexing applications, testing with a large set of keywords is mandatory.

Taking into account these observations, the main keyword selection criterion adopted in this work is to use all the words that appear in the training sets of each dataset. This is exactly true for BENTHAM, AUSTEN and PLANTAS, whose respective query set sizes (after removing/normalizing text diacritics) were 6 962, 2 281 and 9 945, as reported in Table 10.1. On the other hand, as previously commented, N-fold cross-validation was used for experiments with the small-sized ALCARAZ and WIENSTULRICH datasets. Therefore, to simplify the experimentation, in these cases all the different words of each dataset were considered query word (after text normalizing and removing diacritics). The resulting query set sizes, also reported in Table 10.1, were 2 669 for ALCARAZ and 2 256 for WIENSTULRICH.

10.4.3   *Evaluation Measures*

The standard *recall* and *interpolated precision* measures [Manning *et al.* (2008)] are used to assess the retrieval effectiveness in all the search experiments.

For a given query and relevance threshold, *recall* is the ratio of relevant image regions (lines) correctly retrieved by the system (often called "hits"), with respect to the total number of relevant regions existing in the image test set. *Precision*, on the other hand, is the ratio of hits with respect to the total number of (correctly or incorrectly) retrieved regions.

By varying the relevance threshold, different related values of recall and precision can be obtained. These values can be plotted into the so-called *Recall-Precision* curve. Clearly, for a perfect system this curve would go straight from the point $(1, 0)$ vertically up to $(1, 1)$ and then horizontally left to $(0, 1)$. That is, such a system should exhibit a full precision (1) independently of the relevance threshold. This would in fact be the behaviour of a conventional plaintext retrieval system tested on a the perfect transcripts of the test set images. A reasonable KWS system should provide curves above the diagonal of the graph, the closer to the upper right corner (point $(1, 1)$), the better.

Results are also reported in terms of overall *average precision* (AP), which is obtained by computing the area under Recall-Precision curves. AP is a popular scalar assessment measure for KWS. Please refer to [Toselli *et al.* (2016)] for details on this assessment measure.

10.5   Laboratory Results

Indexing and search results for the datasets described in Sec. 10.3 are presented in Figs. 10.3 and 10.4.

Results of Fig. 10.3 correspond to the relatively modern (and easier) collections BENTHAM and AUSTEN. In the case of AUSTEN, two experiments were carried out. In the first one (labelled "AUSTEN") a conventional training-testing setting was adopted; i.e., optical and language models were trained with the AUSTEN training set and performance was measured on the independent test set of the same collection. In the second experiment (labelled "AUSTEN-B"), the models trained with the BENTHAM training set (and used to obtain the BENTHAM results of Fig. 10.3) were used to index the test set images of the AUSTEN collection. This experiment was aimed to explore whether a handwritten image collection can be fully automatically indexed without previous training an that collection, by using optical and language models previously trained with images of text of the same language and similar historic period and handwriting style.[5]

Good results are achieved for all the datasets. As expected, the results are somewhat inferior for the more difficult early modern datasets. But even at this level of performance, a system can be used in practice to reliably find relevant information. The results for AUSTEN without training (i.e., using models trained for other not too different collections) are also somewhat inferior, but still sufficiently good to grant a successful use in practice.

Overall these results are actually very competitive as compared with results reported in the literature for classical KWS systems [Rath and Manmatha (2007); Rodriguez and Perronnin (2009); Wshah *et al.* (2012); Fischer *et al.* (2012); Frinken *et al.* (2012); Toselli and Vidal (2013); Toselli *et al.* (2016)]. However, one may argue whether these great laboratory results actually translate into a similarly good practical search experience. To help the reader's intuition in this respect, the demonstration systems described in

---

[5]The writing style of AUSTEN is similar to the style of some of the writers of the BENTHAM collection.

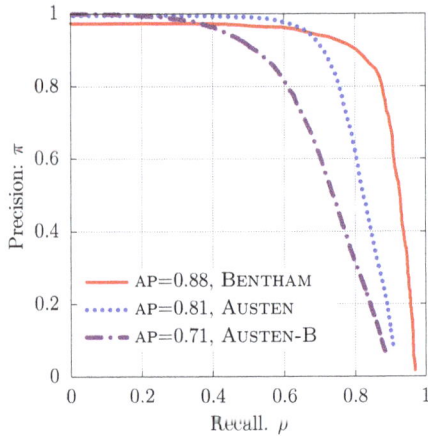

Fig. 10.3: Results on 18–19th century handwritten text image collections.

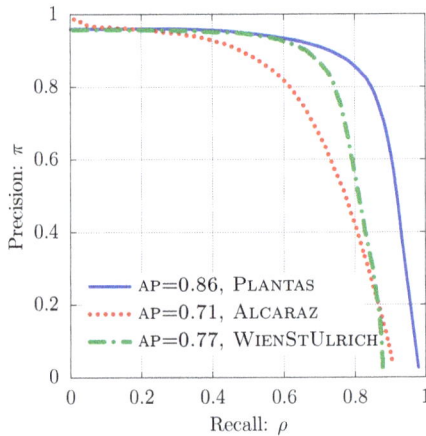

Fig. 10.4: Results on early modern (16th c.) handwritten text image collections.

the next section can provide first-hand experience about the capabilities of these systems and the significance of the results presented in this section.

10.6   Demonstration Systems

The indexing and search engines used to obtain the results presented in Sec. 10.5, are also used to support demonstration systems which are publicly available through Internet. Most of these demonstrators are hosted in the Demonstrations section of the TRANSCRIPTORIUM web site. A list of all demonstrators available is in this link:

http://transcriptorium.eu/demots/KWSdemos

It should be pointed out, however, that for the PLANTAS collection, the demonstration is *not* on the Vol. I of the collection, used in the laboratory experiments presented in the previous section.[6] In this case, the demonstrator is actually a real working system, useful to find information in the 739 pages of the *untranscribed* Vol. VII of the same PLANTAS collection. The same optical and language models trained with pages of Vol. I and used to obtain the results of Fig. 10.4, were used to fully index the new, untranscribed Vol. VII in a totally automatic way. So this demonstrator can be seen as a typical and real example of the interesting possibilities of the technology presented in this paper.

10.7 Conclusion and Outlook

A formal probabilistic framework has been adopted for indexing and searching large collections of handwritten documents. Empirical results with a variety of historic collections exhibiting different challenges and levels of complexity assess the usefulness of these methods. Models trained for a given collection can provide quite useful indexing and search performance on images of similar collections, without need of any (re-)training. Several demonstrators have been implemented and made publicly available through the Internet for first-hand experience of real use in practice.

All the techniques and experiments described in this paper assume that a user query is just a single word. However, techniques are also being developed for combined, multiple word queries. In particular, Boolean and word sequence combinations are already supported in the demonstrators outlined in Sec. 10.6 and preliminary formal evaluation results are reported in [Toselli *et al.* (2018)].

The techniques presented here require a predefined, possibly very large list of words to be indexed. To overcome this limitation, two simple approaches were developed and tested in [Puigcerver *et al.* (2016)]. The first one amounts

---

[6]An older demonstrator for the used dataset for the Vol. I of PLANTAS is available at http://cat.prhlt.upv.es/kws-demos.

to relevance probability *smoothing*, based on edit-distance word similarities derived from character confusion probabilities. The second was a *back-off* approach where only the queries involving non-indexed words were handled using much more computationally expensive character-level lexicon-free search based on the so-called "filler model" [Fischer *et al.* (2012); Frinken *et al.* (2012); Toselli and Vidal (2013)]. The first of these approaches is implemented in most of the demonstrators outlined in Sec. 10.6.

These techniques do prove adequate as a means to extend the capabilities of lexicon-based indexing approaches beyond the restriction of allowing only queries for predefined words. However, as the manuscript collections considered become truly large (hundreds or millions of images), even the very concept of "word" often proves elusive. This happens because of inconsistent word usage over the time-span of the collection and/or because of the casual mix of several languages in the same manuscripts. In these cases, native lexicon-free approaches are needed, which moreover should lend themselves to efficient probabilistic indexing and fast query search and retrieval.

In our recent work, the concept of "word" is relaxed to the so called "pseudo-word". Pseudo-words are character sequences which have high probability of being words actually written in images. In order to probabilistic index pseudo-words, character-based (rather than lexicon-based) optical and language models are needed. In this framework, we develop methods to determine when a sequence of characters qualify for a to-be-indexed pseudo-word and then index pseudo-words more or less as explained in this paper for real words. First ideas towards these new, fully lexicon-free probabilistic indexing and search technologies have been developed in [Puigcerver (2018)] and successfully tested and used in [Lang *et al.* (2018)] and in [Bluche *et al.* (2017)] for real large-scale indexing.

In the coming future, work is also planed to address the issue of which type of image region is most suitable for indexing. So far line-regions are considered the most elementary regions to index. This entails a requirement for automatic line detection and extraction. While fairly accurate automatic text line detection techniques are already available nowadays, results often lack robustness; that is, these techniques can not consistently and reliably deal with the large variability of image quality and layout usually exhibited by really large manuscript collections. So, from time to time, a batch of page images appears where line detection fails dramatically and, as a result, these pages become badly indexed. In an attempt to completely circumvent this line detection bottleneck, our current work aims at considering full page images as the smallest indexing regions. Yet, these page-level probabilistic indexing methods should still be able to provide, as a byproduct, the location (bounding box) of each spotted word within the corresponding page image.

Acknowledgments

The author's work was partially supported by the Generalitat Valenciana under the Prometeo/2009/014 project grant ALMAMATER, and through the EU projects: HOME (JPICH programme, Spanish grant Ref. PCI2018-093122).

References

Alabau, V., Martinez-Hinarejos, C., Romero, V., and Lagarda, A. (2014). An iterative multimodal framework for the transcription of handwritten historical documents, *Pattern Recognition Letters* **35**, pp. 195–203, frontiers in Handwriting Processing.

Bluche, T., Hamel, S., Kermorvant, C., Puigcerver, J., Stutzmann, D., Toselli, A. H., and Vidal, E. (2017). Preparatory KWS Experiments for Large-Scale Indexing of a Vast Medieval Manuscript Collection in the HIMANIS Project, in *2017 14th IAPR Int. Conf. on Document Analysis and Recognition (ICDAR)*, Vol. 01, pp. 311–316.

Cao, H., Bhardwaj, A., and Govindaraju, V. (2009). A probabilistic method for keyword retrieval in handwritten document images, *Pattern Recognition* **42**, 12, pp. 3374–3382, doi:10.1016/j.patcog.2009.02.003.

Causer, T. and Wallace, V. (2012). Building a volunteer community: results and findings from Transcribe Bentham, *Digital Humanities Quarterly* **6**, 2.

Fischer, A., Keller, A., Frinken, V., and Bunke, H. (2012). Lexicon-free handwritten word spotting using character HMMs, *Pattern Recognition Letters* **33**, 7, pp. 934–942.

Frinken, V., Fischer, A., Manmatha, R., and Bunke, H. (2012). A novel word spotting method based on recurrent neural networks, *IEEE Trans. on Pattern Analysis and Machine Intelligence* **34**, 2, pp. 211–224.

Jelinek, F. (1998). *Statistical Methods for Speech Recognition* (MIT Press).

Kamel, I. (2010). On indexing handwritten text, *Int. Journal of Multimedia and Ubiquitous Engineering* **5**, 2.

Kinder, A. G. (1966–1997). Inquisition documents concerning Pedro Ruiz de Alcaraz, in *The Kinder Collection in the John Rylands University Library* (The University of Manchester Library).

Kneser, R. and Ney, H. (1995). Improved backing-off for m-gram language modeling, in *Proc. Int. Conf. on Acoustics, Speech, and Signal Processing*, pp. 181–184.

Kolcz, A., Alspector, J., Augusteijn, M., Carlson, R., and Viorel Popescu, G. (2000). A Line-Oriented Approach to Word Spotting in Handwritten Documents, *Pattern Analysis & Applications* **3**, pp. 153–168, 10.1007/s100440070020.

Kozielski, M., Forster, J., and Ney, H. (2012). Moment-based image normalization for handwritten text recognition, in *Proceedings of the 2012 International Conference on Frontiers in Handwriting Recognition*, ICFHR '12 (IEEE Computer Society, Washington, DC, USA), ISBN 978-0-7695-4774-9, pp. 256–261, doi:10.1109/ICFHR.2012.236, http://dx.doi.org/10.1109/ICFHR.2012.236.

Lang, E., Puigcerver, J., Toselli, A. H., and Vidal, E. (2018). Probabilistic Indexing and Search for Information Extraction on Handwritten German Parish Records, in *Frontiers in Handwriting Recognition (ICFHR), 2018 16th International Conference on*, pp. 44–49.

Manmatha, R., Han, C., and Riseman, E. (1996). Word spotting: A new approach to indexing handwriting, in *Proc. Int. Conf. on Computer Vision and Pattern Recognition*, pp. 631—637.

Manning, C. D., Raghavan, P., and Schtze, H. (2008). *Introduction to Information Retrieval* (Cambridge University Press, New York, NY, USA), ISBN 0521865719, 9780521865715.

Puigcerver, J. (2018). *A Probabilistic Formulation of Keyword Spotting*, Ph.D. thesis, Universitat Politècnica de València.

Puigcerver, J., Toselli, A. H., and Vidal, E. (2016). Querying out-of-vocabulary words in lexicon-based keyword spotting, *Neural Computing and Applications*, pp. 1–10 doi:10.1007/s00521-016-2197-8.

Rath, T. M. and Manmatha, R. (2007). Word spotting for historical documents, *IJDAR* **9**, 2–4, pp. 139–152.

Rodriguez, J. and Perronnin, F. (2009). Handwritten word-spotting using hidden Markov models and universal vocabularies, *Pattern Recognition* **42**, 9, pp. 2106–2116.

Romero, V., Toselli, A., and Vidal, E. (2012). *Multimodal Interactive Handwritten Text Recognition*, Machine Perception and Artificial Intelligence, Vol. 80 (World Scientific).

Romero, V., Toselli, A. H., Sánchez, J. A., and Vidal, E. (2016). Handwriting transcription and keyword spotting in historical daily records documents, in *Document Analysis Systems (DAS), 2016 12th IAPR Workshop on* (IEEE), pp. 275–280.

Sánchez, A., Joan, Romero, Verónica, Toselli, A. H., and Vidal, E. (2014). ICFHR2014 Competition on Handwritten Text Recognition on Transcriptorium Datasets (HTRtS), in *Frontiers in Handwriting Recognition (ICFHR), 2014 14th International Conference on*, pp. 785–790.

Terasawa, K. and Tanaka, Y. (2009). Slit style hog feature for document image word spotting, in *ICDAR'09*, pp. 116–120.

Toselli, A., Vidal, E., and Casacuberta, F. (2011). *Multimodal Interactive Pattern Recognition and Applications*, 1st edn. (Springer).

Toselli, A. H., Leiva, L. A., Bordes-Cabrera, I., Hernández-Tornero, C., Vicent, B., and Vidal, E. (2017). Transcribing a 17th century botanical manuscript: Longitudinal interactive transcription evaluation and ground truth production, *Digital scholarship in the humanities* doi:https://doi.org/10.1093/llc/fqw064.

Toselli, A. H., Romero, V., Pastor, M., and Vidal, E. (2010). Multimodal interactive transcription of text images, *Pattern Recognition* **43**, 5, pp. 1814–1825.

Toselli, A. H. and Vidal, E. (2013). Fast HMM-Filler approach for Key Word Spotting in Handwritten Documents, in *Proc. of the 12th International Conference on Document Analysis and Recognition (ICDAR '13)* (IEEE Computer Society, Washington, DC, USA), pp. 501–505.

Toselli, A. H., Vidal, E., Puigcerver, J., and Noya-García, E. (2018). Probabilistic multi-word spotting in handwritten text images, *Pattern Analysis and Applications*, pp. 1–10.

Toselli, A. H., Vidal, E., Romero, V., and Frinken, V. (2016). HMM word graph based keyword spotting in handwritten document images, *Information Sciences* **370–371**, pp. 497–518.

Vidal, E., Rodríguez, L., Casacuberta, F., and García-Varea, I. (2007). Interactive pattern recognition, in *International Workshop on Machine Learning for Multimodal Interaction* (Springer), pp. 60–71.

Vidal, E., Toselli, A. H., and Puigcerver, J. (2015). High performance query-by-example keyword spotting using query-by-string techniques, in *Document Analysis and Recognition (ICDAR), 2015 13th International Conference on* (IEEE), pp. 741–745.

Villegas, M., Sanchez, J. A., and Vidal, E. (2015). Optical modelling and language modelling trade-off for handwritten text recognition, in *Document Analysis and Recognition (ICDAR), 2015 13th International Conference on* (IEEE), pp. 831–835.

Wshah, S., Kumar, G., and Govindaraju, V. (2012). Script independent word spotting in offline handwritten documents based on hidden markov models, in *Frontiers in Handwriting Recognition (ICFHR), 2012 International Conference on*, pp. 14–19.

Young, S., Odell, J., Ollason, D., Valtchev, V., and Woodland, P. (1997). *The HTK Book: Hidden Markov Models Toolkit V2.1*, Cambridge Research Laboratory Ltd.

Chapter 11

Browsing of the Social Network of the Past: Information Extraction from Population Manuscript Images

[1]Alicia Fornés, [1]Josep Lladós and [2]Joana Maria Pujadas-Mora

[1]*Computer Vision Center, Computer Science Department,*
Universitat Autonoma de Barcelona, Spain
[2]*Open University of Catalonia and Center for Demographic Studies,*
Universitat Autonoma de Barcelona, Spain
afornes@cvc.uab.es, josep@cvc.uab.cat, jpujadasmo@uoc.edu

This chapter describes a complete system for the extraction of information of historical population documents. This system has been constructed as a result of several multidisciplinary projects bringing together researchers in computer vision, pattern recognition and historical demography. The chapter describes different contributions ranging from low level processing for document image enhancement, to the semantic recognition of named entities and their linkage. The proposed system gives a key role to the user, in the transcription and validation processes. User engagement experiences of crowdsourcing and gamesourcing are described. The resulting knowledge base is organized in a social network model, so the browsing of the data can be provided accordingly.

11.1 Introduction

For centuries, historical documents (mostly handwritten) were the main repository of knowledge shared among people. Preserved through ages in archives and libraries, documents have been incrementally gathering the history of societies. These institutions have invested a lot of resources in the last decade in digitizing large collections of historical documents not only for preserving them in a digital format, but also to give access to scholars and citizens at large through web-based digital repositories. Web-based consultation tools developed so far allow a limited access, consisting in browsing through images, or querying based on metadata. The most advanced ones consist of transcribed documents and hence allow to retrieve information based on the document contents. However, most of the existing digital libraries and archives with transcribed contents have been produced by manual human labour, which is a tedious and time consuming task.

Population records stored in public, ecclesiastical or private archives and libraries are a special case of historical documents. These sources range from censuses, birth, marriage or death registers (through Parish books and civil Registers), to dynamically updated population registers, among others. They are usually handwritten, and have value not only by themselves, but by their contents. In this way, historical population documents constitute a backbone of the history of societies. Since every person has been registered at some time, these documents can be considered the "democratization" of the history. Whether because of their continuity along time and/or their widespread use by societies of the past, they constitute a key part of the rich documentary heritage of church and public administration and help shaping collective identities. Mostly modern censuses cover individually every inhabitant, irrespective of age, sex or social status for the 19th and 20th centuries, even existing previously. Demographic events are still recorded nowadays around the world, being common, objective and trustworthy. These citizen-centered documents contain a complete, factual and reliable memory of the communities of our ancestors.

There has been an important progress in document image analysis and recognition techniques, in particular with the successful adoption of deep learning to handwritten text recognition (HTR) and key word spotting (KWS). It has boosted the introduction of (semi)automatic transcription in the construction of digital libraries and archives. Nowadays, the historical document collections that are digitized are often indexed. However, narrowing the semantic gap regarding the interpretation of the contents is still a challenge. To really extract semantic knowledge from historical documents, it is necessary not only to transcribe them, but also to associate the transcribed words to the corresponding semantic class. Population documents are a good example: a transcribed census record is not useful unless the relevant words are classified as family names, cities, occupations, etc. Although the progress of intelligent reading techniques, a completely automatic process is still a challenge. Historical documents convey several difficulties: physical degradation, obsolete languages, multi-writer styles, lack of dictionaries and grammatical normalization, etc. that prevents fully automatic systems to be efficient. The inclusion of the human in the loop has been a successful strategy to compensate it. Thus, crowdsourcing and gamesourcing experiences are implemented as entry tools for document transcription, data annotation and validation.

In this chapter we describe some recent results of projects in the context of information extraction from demographic historical documents. In particular, we describe the progress of the projects *5CofM: Five Centuries of Marriages;*[1] *Tools: Tools and Procedures for Massive Computerization of Historical Population Sources*; and *Networks: Citizen technology and innovation in the construction of historical social networks for the understanding of the demographic legacy.*[2] These projects have been implemented in a cross-disciplinary framework, bringing together scientists from computer vision and pattern recognition, and historical demography [Pujadas-Mora *et al.* (2016)].

Our vision is inspired by the revolution of lifelogging and social networks to create browsing experiences of the big data from the population of the past. The hypothesis underlying this vision is that historical population data can be articulated into a searchable social network representational model. Thus, we have developed information extraction methods for images of population documents (in particular marriage and census records). Named entities have been recognized in handwritten document images and record linkage techniques have been afterwards applied. As stated above, due to the difficulties of fully automatic processes, we have designed crowdsourcing and gamesourcing methods to both efficiently transcribe the documents, and validate the automatic tools.

The use of a social network paradigm to browse the past through people, their relations and their events requires the definition of equivalences between the demographic variables and the social media terms. For example, social profiling, defined as the process of constructing a signature based on the user's social data (attributes, shared media, relations), can be mapped into the digital heritage space of population data and extract the historical profiles of people and communities (co-residence patterns, family or

---

[1]Five Centuries of Marriages project: http://dag.cvc.uab.es/infoesposalles/
[2]Networks project: http://dag.cvc.uab.es/xarxes/

neighborhood structures, etc.). Life caching, i.e. storing and sharing one's life events, corresponds to the demographic concept of life courses of people and communities registered in longitudinal population data. Path finding in a social network allows to reconstruct genealogies.

The chapter is organized as follows. In Section 11.2 we describe the importance of historical population documents in the recovery of the memory of past generations. We also detail the typologies of documents, and the databases that have been constructed in our work. Section 11.3 outlines the architecture of our system to extract information from historical population documents. In Section 11.4 we describe the low level approaches for image enhancement. Section 11.5 describes the different document image analysis and recognition techniques integrated into the system, addressed to the extraction of information. Section 11.6 is devoted to describe the algorithms for semantic recognition of named entities, context-aware transcription and record linkage. In Section 11.7 we describe the crowdsourcing and game-sourcing applications for assisted transcription and validation, as well as the browsing interface to search through the document contents. Finally, Section 11.8 draws the conclusions and future perspectives.

11.2   Population Records and Datasets

Promoted by ecclesiastical official instances and public administrations, the recording of vital events of birth, marriage and death of individuals, and counting the population in censuses, has been a uniform practice over centuries. It makes these sources common, objective and trustworthy. These documents are records of individuals' events and relations in their lifetime. By tracking events (birth, marriage, death) and relations (genealogical, spatio-temporal), together with the individual observations of inhabitants based on their names (gender), surnames, ages, birth-date and birthplace and relationship with the head of the household in censuses, a huge social network of the past can be constructed, as well as the life logs of individuals.

Population records contain complete and factual data of societies that allow interpreting the history. Scholars from different areas take advantage of this information in their research: historians, anthropologists, medical doctors, biologists, etc. The analysis of individual demographic outcomes and the evaluation of their socio-demographic variables show the interplay between a micro and a macro context as a consequence of cultural, social, economic and political events. The work presented in this chapter has been based on

(a)   (b)

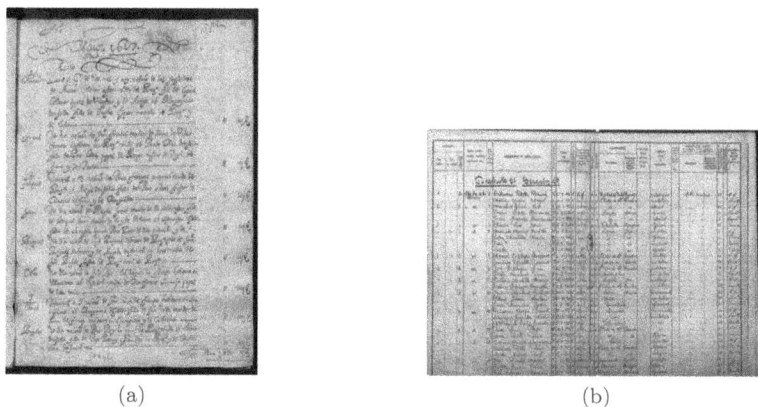

Fig. 11.1: Examples of population documents. (a) Marriage record. (b) Census record.

two types of population records: census and marriage records (see examples in Figure 11.1).

Local censuses started to be regularly taken in the nineteenth century for the purpose of rationalizing the state's population and wealth. Census records have a tabular structure collecting information of individuals in each household at a certain point in time such as names and surnames of family members, ages, place of birth, family/labour relationship with the head of the household, occupation, individual wealth (wages/assets) such as the value of their home and belongings, etc. The information is ordered by street address. Censuses are recorded in cities and villages at regular points in time. This structure and procedure is quite common world-wide. The database used in this work was constructed in the project *NETWORKS: 'Tools and procedures for the large scale digitization of historical sources of population'*. This ongoing database, up to September 2020, gathers censuses from thirteen municipalities of the county of Baix Llobregat, in Catalonia. It contains a total of 183 local censuses comprising a period between 1828 and 1965.

The *Barcelona Historical Marriage Database*, was an outcome of ERC Advanced Grand Project *5CofM: 'Five Centuries of Marriages '*. Between 1451 and 1905, a centralized fiscal register, called *Llibres d'Esposalles* (Marriage License Books) recorded all the marriages of the Barcelona Diocese and the fees charged according to the social status of the spouses (it was a tax register on marriage licenses). These books are conserved at the Barcelona Cathedral archive. It comprises 291 books with information on approximately 610,000 marriages celebrated in 250 parishes, ranging from the most urban core of the city to the most rural villages in the periphery of the Diocese. This dataset was fully digitized, transcribed using crowdsourcing tools (see Section 11.7) and studied from the historical and demographic point of view [Brea-Martínez and Pujadas-Mora (2019); Pujadas-Mora *et al.* (2018)]. In addition, part of this database has been additionally annotated with the corresponding ground truth for evaluating document image analysis and recognition algorithms. Concretely, it is composed of one volume (single writer) of the original source, with a total of 174 pages, 1,740 registers, 5,498 lines. The *Esposalles* dataset [Romero *et al.* (2013)] has been created for handwritten text recognition. The *BH2M: the Barcelona Historical Handwritten Marriages database* has been created for layout analysis, word spotting and semantic recognition. The BH2M database consists of annotated images in an XML hierarchical structure (from individual words to blocks of text). The minimum unit of information is a bounding box of an individual word, with its transcription. Additional attributes like line or register number, or category, are associated to words. This representation allows to easily retrieve a GT from the meta-data adapted to the tasks being tested (segmentation, word spotting, handwriting recognition, etc.). Three levels in the XML meta-data associated to images can be identified. The first one is designed to evaluate tasks for layout analysis, the second one for text transcription, and the third one for context dependent interpretation.

11.3   System Architecture

In this section we outline the main components of the system, shown in Figure 11.2. It consists of four main packages, referred as "spaces", namely image space, annotation space, semantic space and users space.

The image space contains the main image processing and analysis tasks addressed to the enhancement of the input image and the segmentation of the layout.

The annotation space contains the tasks for transcribing and indexing the document images in terms of their contents. This space consists of the technologies for handwritten text transcription (HTR), key word spotting (HTR) for document retrieval (in query-by-string and query-by-example scenarios).

The semantic space contains the tasks addressed to extract semantic meaning from the document terms, i.e. it is addressed to reduce the semantic gap allowing the interpretation of documents. In the particular context of historical population documents the tasks of the semantic space organize the data in a social network (graph-based) representation. Graph-based analytics are hence used to extract meaning from this conceptual model. The tasks that are included in this space are: context-aware word spotting (recognition of words based on the intrinsic context of images); named entity recognition (association of word transcriptions to semantic categories); and record linkage (construction of the network relations between image terms).

Finally, the user plays an important role in the information extraction process. The users view consists of the tasks that integrate the users feedback in the process, either for the transcription or the navigation through the knowledge network. The design of the system in terms of the social network of the past gives to the document interpretation process a dual user-centric basis. Thus, the data representation (network) is structured around the citizens of the past, and the citizens of the present have an active role in the construction of the network and the exploitation of the data.

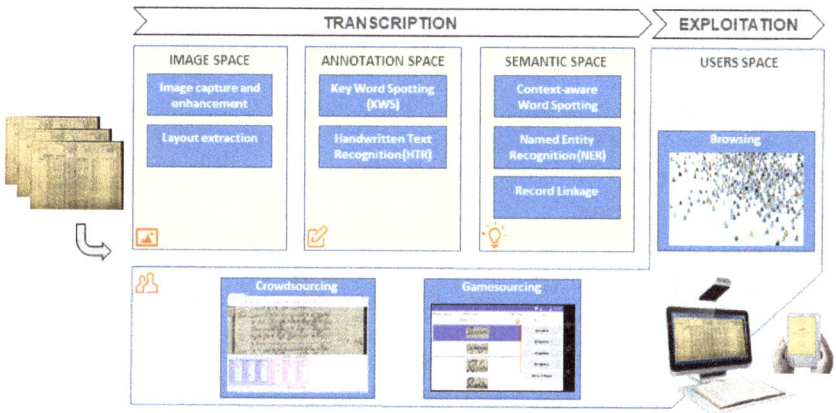

Fig. 11.2: System architecture.

In the following sections the main tasks of the architecture are further described.

11.4   Image Capture and Document Enhancement

In many cases, historical manuscripts are degraded due to paper aging and must be enhanced before their recognition. Typical degradations are background variation, illumination changes or dark spots. In addition, and in case of double-sided documents, the back side of the document may also interfere with the front side due to the paper transparency or ink bleeding, causing the undesired show-through effect.

One possibility is to match both sides of the document in order to detect the show-through components. However, this matching is not always accurate due to different skews, resolution or warping effects, and consequently, the performance decreases. For this reason, we propose to remove the show-through components using only one side of the scanned document. Our method [Fornés *et al.* (2013)] is based on a Multiresolution Contrast (MC) decomposition to estimate the contrast of features at different spatial scales. The method relies in the fact that show-through are usually low contrast components, while foreground components are high contrast ones. In addition, background variations tend to be spatially wide components, hence they can be considered low spatial frequency features.

The method first decomposes the image into a Multiresolution Contrast representation in order to obtain the contrast of components at different spatial scales, and therefore, it does not depend on the size and resolution of the image. Another positive aspect is that the contrast between pixels is invariant to global illumination changes (e.g. neighbour pixels on a shadowed area, intensity of the scanned page, etc). This decomposition is also able to remove shadowed areas by weighting spatial scales. Concretely, the image is enhanced by reducing the contrast of low spatial frequency components. Finally, the show-through phenomenon is minimized by thresholding the low contrast components. As a result, the legibility of the documents is improved, as shown in Figure 11.3.

11.4.1   *Layout Analysis and Text Line Extraction*

Once the image has been enhanced, the layout of the document is analyzed to detect and segment the different regions. In the case of tabular documents, projection profiles can be used to detect rows and columns in the document. In the case of the marriage register books of the Barcelona Cathedral, records are written in paragraphs, and more sophisticated methods are

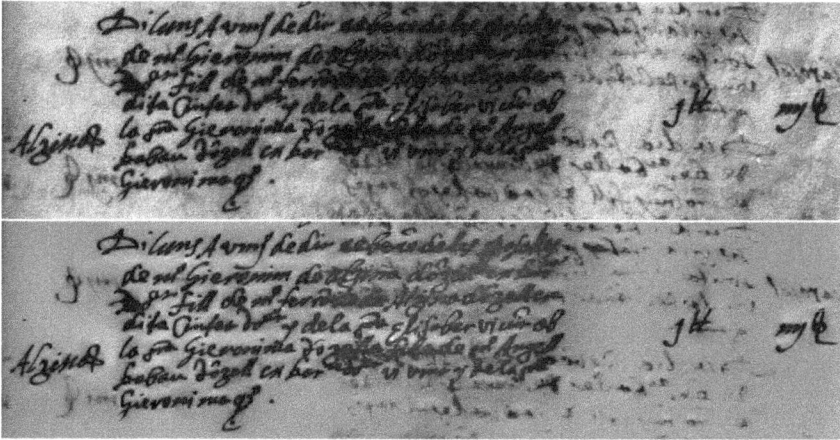

Fig. 11.3: Show-through removal. Top: original image; Bottom: enhanced image.

needed. Stochastic Context-Free Grammars (SCFG) are used to model the structure of the document [Álvaro *et al.* (2015)]. A parsing process is therefore used to address both the detection of textual zones and the analysis of structural relationships among these zones. Bidimensional SCFG (2D-SCFG) is a well known formalism that has been applied for bidimensional parsing. This type of grammars can represent contextual bidimensional relations that are relevant for document layout segmentation. Concretely, 2D-SCFG are used to compute the most likely structure and segmentation of a document. First, two sets of text classification features (Gabor and Relative Location Features) are used for an initial classification of each zone. Then, the segmentation is obtained as the most likely hypothesis according to the stochastic grammar.

After the segmentation of regions, text lines must be segmented before starting the text recognition stage. Given that many handwritten text lines are touching or overlapping ones to the others, an analysis based on projection profiles is not accurate enough. For dealing with these difficulties, we formulate line segmentation as seam carving problem solved as an optimal graph traversal. Given a graph representing the skeleton of the background, the goal is to find the central path in the area between to consecutive text lines. Concretely, our algorithm [Fernández-Mota *et al.* (2014)] creates a graph using the skeleton of the background of the image. The vertices of the graph are characteristic points in the skeleton (end or intersection points), and the edges correspond to the skeleton paths. Since touching text lines create a discontinuity in the path, we add virtual edges between ending nodes that are close. Then, the path-finding algorithm searches for the optimum path between text lines, that corresponds to the minimum cost graph traversal from the left to the right. To model the cost function that guides the minimization process, the algorithm uses the trend of the path, computed by a linear regression. That means that given an intermediate graph node of the graph, the next node of the path is chosen as the one among the neighbouring such that represents the smoothest trend. Thanks to the incorporation of the virtual edges, the algorithm is able to reconstruct the broken path, which correspond to touching lines. An example is shown in Figure 11.4.

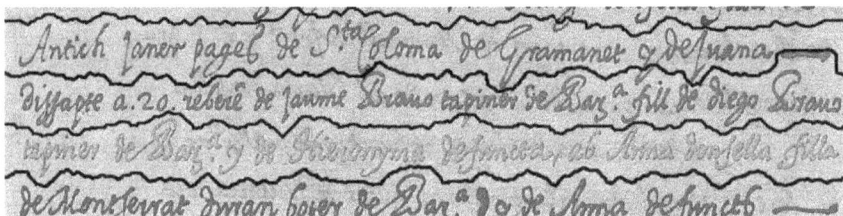

Fig. 11.4: Line segmentation.

Finally, in case some detection and recognition algorithms require already segmented words, we combine the above mentioned line segmentation with a word segmentation algorithm based on the anisotropic gaussian filter [Manmatha and Rothfeder (2005)] in order to improve the word segmentation accuracy [Fernández *et al.* (2012)].

11.5   Annotation Space

In this section we describe the main document image analysis techniques that have been developed for extracting the information from handwritten documents.

11.5.1   *Key Word Spotting*

In cases where the transcription of handwritten documents is difficult, word spotting can be used to search and index the contents. In this work we have explored several approaches for keyword spotting, including both statistical and structural representations [Lladós *et al.* (2012)]. In this section, we have selected two representatives. The first approach is a structural and learning-free method, suitable for searching information in collections where there is no training data at all. In this case, the query is a word image (namely query-by-example word spotting), so the system retrieves those documents containing word images with a similar shape appearance. The second approach corresponds to a statistical and learning-based method, appropriate for searching words in documents where training data is available. In this second case, the system can search a query word image, and also a textual query (namely query-by-string word spotting). Next, we describe these techniques in more detail.

11.5.1.1   *Word Spotting Based on Graphs*

The first approach consists in a query-by-example word spotting method based on a graph representation. Graph-based models are common in visual recognition and retrieval due to their representational power. For example, graphs are robust representations able to describe shapes in terms of the relationships between constituent parts or primitives. In the case of handwritten documents, it has been demonstrated that graphs can also effectively represent the inherent deformations of handwriting [Riba *et al.* (2015)]. In the case of handwritten documents, we construct an attributed graph from the word images as follows. First, graphemes are extracted from the shape convexities in the handwritten strokes. Those convexities are used as stable units of handwriting, and are associated to graph nodes. Then, spatial relations between them determine graph edges, which create the graph that represents each word image. Once all the graphs are constructed, word spotting is defined in terms of an error-tolerant graph matching using the bipartite-graph matching algorithm.

Nevertheless, the retrieval of query graphs from large document collections implies a high computational complexity. Therefore, we propose a graph indexation formalism [Riba *et al.* (2017)] based on binary embeddings, which are defined as hashing keys for graph nodes. The procedure is as follows. First, given a database of labeled graphs, graph nodes are complemented with vectors of attributes representing their local context. Then, a binary-valued hash function is applied to each attribute vector to convert it to a binary code. As a result, word spotting can be formulated in terms of finding target graphs in the database whose nodes have a small Hamming distance from the query nodes, which can be easily computed with bitwise logical operators. As a result, this fast indexation can significantly speed-up the inexact subgraph matching process, offering a feasible solution for large scale word spotting. Moreover, the method does not need any labelled data to train the system, and consequently, it can be applied to any kind of document collection (different languages, scripts, etc.) without restrictions.

11.5.1.2 *Word Spotting Based on PHOC Attribute Embeddings*

A statistical word spotting method was proposed in [Almazán *et al.* (2014)], based on attribute representation. It is a learning-based method that proposes a joint representation of word images and their transcriptions. First, the Pyramidal Histogram of Characters (PHOC) embeds the textual word into an attribute space. In this space, words and word images are characterized by a set of attributes. The textual transcription of the word is codified using the PHOC attributes, where each attribute represents the presence of a character in a certain part of the word. In order to take into account the position of the characters in the word, the PHOC descriptor is created using a pyramidal structure. In the first level, the left part of the vector encodes the presence of each character in the first part of the word. Similarly, the right part of the vector encodes the presence of each character in the second part of the word. The next level of the pyramid divides the word in three parts, and the attribute vector at that level will encode which character is present at each part. The next levels will divide the word into 4 and 5 parts. The final level contains the most common bigrams in the language.

The word images are encoded by extracting SIFT features and performing a clustering based on Fischer vector. Then, an individual Support Vector Machine (SVM) is trained for each attribute. Finally, Canonical Correlation Analysis (CCA) is used to put the images and the text strings in a common subspace. Thanks to this common space, not only word spotting but also word recognition become a nearest neighbor search in a very low dimensional space.

Compared to the graph-based word spotting approach, this method has two main advantages. First, since it is a learning-based method, the overall results are better because the system can learn the appearance of the text (i.e. the handwriting style). Secondly, it can either perform searches given both word images and textual queries (i.e. query-by-example and query-by-string). The main drawback is that labelled data is necessary to train the system.

11.5.2   *Handwritten Text Recognition*

Handwritten Text Recognition is the task of processing the input text image to obtain its textual transcription. Given the high variability in the handwriting style, it is necessary to learn the correspondence between the pixels in the image (i.e. shape of strokes) and the corresponding transcription. The most typical techniques are based on deep neural networks, such as recurrent neural networks.

Since word spotting based on PHOC attribute embeddings has shown its ability to recognize isolated words with good performance, in this work we have extended it to handwritten text recognition (i.e. sequence learning) towards a lexicon free approach. Our approach [Toledo *et al.* (2017)] uses the convolutional neural network, called the PHOCNet [Sudholt and Fink (2016)], to extract the attribute embedding of small pieces of text (patches of text images using a sliding window approach). Contrary to the SVMs used for word spotting, here the PHOCNet is directly trained to output the PHOC representation of a given word image. Indeed, the PHOCNet could be seen as a feature extractor.

Once the sequence of embeddings is obtained, we use Long Short-Term Memory Recurrent Neural Networks (LSTM) to obtain the transcription. Concretely, we use bi-directional LSTMs to cope with the vanishing gradient problem and improve the context by processing the sequence forwards and backwards. Finally, we use the Connectionist Temporal Classification (CTC) to obtain the transcription. Contrary to the word spotting and recognition methodology based on PHOC, this approach is able to recognize out of vocabulary (OOV) words, which are quite usual in population documents where there are migration movements. An example is shown in Figure 11.5.

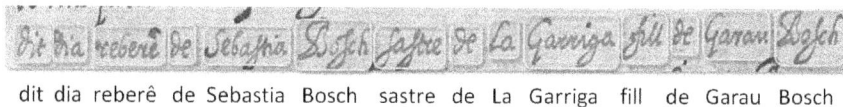

dit dia reberê de Sebastia Bosch   sastre de La Garriga   fill   de Garau Bosch

Fig. 11.5: Handwritten text recognition example. Input image and textual output.

11.6   Semantic Space

This section is devoted to describe the algorithms for semantic recognition, context-aware transcription and record linkage.

11.6.1   *Named Entity Recognition*

In addition to handwritten text recognition, it is also necessary to obtain the semantic categories (e.g. names, places, occupations) of the relevant words, namely Named Entity Recognition (NER). This is the first step to interpret the contents and store the information in semantically accessible knowledge databases.

Traditionally, named entity recognition has been applied to the results of handwriting recognition. However, given the difficulties in processing historical handwritten documents (e.g. paper degradation, different handwriting styles, etc.), errors in the transcription affect the performance of the NER. For this reason, instead of subsequent tasks, we propose to recognize the named entities directly over the word image. In our first attempt, [Toledo *et al.* (2016)], we proposed a semantic categorization method based on Convolutional Neural Networks to categorize isolated word images, without transcription, and without any use of context information.

However, in the specific case of population documents, we must take into account that, instead of tabular documents, some records are represented in the form of paragraphs. In such cases (e.g. the marriage records), the structure of the record tends to follow a regular expression (although some variations may appear). For this reason, we have improved our initial semantic categorization based on CNNs with the incorporation of context information. For this purpose, we have modelled the semantic language model of the paragraphs using a Bidirectional Long Short-Term Memory Recurrent Neural network. In this way, this approach [Toledo *et al.* (2019)] is able to model the relation among the words, taking into account the preceding words. The output of the network is the semantic category of each word, but seen in a sequence of words. Moreover, this approach can extract more information than just the semantic category, for example, to associate a semantic category to a specific person in a record (e.g. husband's surname, father's occupation). For this purpose, the output of our neural network has two outputs: the category and the person it relates to (see Figure 11.6).

Fig. 11.6: Named Entity Recognition (top) and Person Recognition (bottom).

Once the semantic categories have been established, the transcription is performed. In this case, the recognizer could even be constrained to the word categories. For example, when transcribing a word whose semantic category is a surname, the recognizer could only provide transcriptions of words that are existing in a given dictionary of surnames.

11.6.2 *Context-Aware Transcription*

The interpretation of document contents do not only rely on the image features but also on the context defined in terms of the relations among the objects. Couasnon et al. [Coüasnon (2006)] define two types of contextual knowledge, namely from inside or outside the document page. Inside (intrinsic) context refers to the presence of some terms depending on the geometric relations to other terms. In handwriting recognition it can be seen as the language model underlying a word decoder that transcribes a word image using the memory of its predecessors. The external (extrinsic) context is the correlation and cross-linkage between data of different pages, or collections. In our scenario, the recognition of some family names in a census record, can guide the search of the same words in other census images if they correspond to the same household record.

In this section we focus on the intrinsic context. In [Fernández et al. (2013)] we proposed a word spotting method that models the internal context in terms of Markov Logic Networks (MLN). The key observation is that in population documents some words have high probability of co-occurrence. There is an implicit syntax in the structure of the records. For example, in marriage records, the presence of some words like "married to", or "with" reinforces the category of the previous and subsequent words; some family names have high probabilities to be linked to city names; and many other combinations that can be learned. The use of dictionaries is a common approach to model this context. However, they are generally corpus-specific, and in historical documents, strongly depend on time period and geographic areas, especially for named entities. We therefore focus on the syntactical structure of the text lines. The main idea of our contextual word spotting approach is that given a query word image and its semantic category (e.g. family name, city name, date, etc.), the detection can be reinforced by the likelihood of this category to appear within a context, according to syntactic rules. These syntactic rules are learned and modeled using a MLN. The use of MLN to model a grammatical structure offers more flexibility in the definition of the rules, incremental and simple learning, with respect to traditional language models used in handwriting recognition.

Marriage records have a regular structure that can be modeled with a probabilistic Context Free Grammar (CFG). Figure 11.7 illustrates the structure of a marriage record. There are some keywords, terminal alphabet of the grammar, that separate the different parts of the record, namely date, husband and wife components. The husband and wife components usually contain the name, the town, the occupation and the corresponding parents' names. A MLN is a probabilistic logic which applies the ideas of a Markov network to the first-order logic, enabling uncertain inference. The MLN can be considered as a collection of first-order logic rules, where

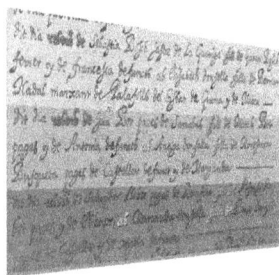

99.9	R -> D P H [HF] W [WF]
89.3	D -> name name [name]
75.3	P -> rebere de
81.0	H -> names
45.8	HF -> fill de names
88.7	W -> names
71.9	WF -> filla de names
56.4	names -> name [name] [name] [name]

Fig. 11.7: Regular structure of a marriage record, modeled with a MLN rules.

each rule has an associated weight that indicates the strength of the rule. We have represented the above structure of the records with a weighted Context-Free grammar (CFG) in Chomsky normal form. It has been mapped to a MLN framework and statistical parsing techniques are used for the recognition. The weights of the rules are learned from examples, modeling the co-occurrence probabilities of the components. The reader is referred to [Fernández *et al.* (2013)] for further details.

11.6.3 *Record Linkage*

In the previous section we have defined the extrinsic context as the relation of the image entities with other ones in external collections or images. This relation, which is usually established in terms of semantic correlations, can boost the extraction of information. Record linkage can be defined as finding instances in a data set that refer to the same entity across different data sources. In the scenario of population documents, record linkage finds relations between people in records, once individual named entities have been recognized, so it allows to generate genealogies, or to establish individual and family lifespans.

Census records have a tabular structure collecting information of individuals in each household at a certain point in time such as names of family members, ages, place of birth, family relationship, occupation, value of their home and belongings, etc. The information is ordered by street address. Census are recorded in cities at regular points in time. Therefore, there is a redundancy from one observation to the next one. Thus, we take advantage of the knowledge that an individual (or a family), may be registered at the same household in two consecutive censuses. Given an already transcribed census record at time t, a query-by-string word spotting is used to search the same entity in the census at time $t + 1$ [Mas *et al.* (2016)]. This not only is used and external context that guides the recognition, but also allows to construct links between two instances of the same person. From a demographic point of view, the constructed links define the *life course* of a person.

11.7 User Space

This section is devoted to describe the crowdsourcing and gamesourcing applications as well as the browsers.

11.7.1 *Crowdsourcing Applications*

In spite of the above mentioned approaches, the performance of document image analysis and recognition techniques is not perfect, and it must be semi-supervised or validated by human beings. Since the population documents in this work cover several centuries, they are written by many different writers. In addition, the typologies also differ, since the structure of a marriage record is different from the census records. For this reason, labelled data is necessary to train the different algorithms. We have developed several crowdsourcing applications. Crowdsourcing is a well-known paradigm that consists in splitting the work in many micro-tasks to be distributed among many users. In this way, the work can be significantly sped-up.

Next, we will describe our web-based data entry tool as well as several computer-games that have been developed for validation.

11.7.1.1 *Crowdsourcing Platform for Data Entry*

Concerning crowdsourcing platforms for transcription, there exist generic platforms such as Transkribus,[3] and also some specific for demographic documents, such as the World Archives Project tool of *Ancestry.com*.[4] However, our developed application integrates the two points of view: the contents view, and the labelling view.

The contents view is used as the data entry tool. Here, the module is used for recording the contents of the records, according to the semantic categories. The screen is divided in two regions: the upper part shows the document image, and the bottom part shows the different form fields, which have to be filled by the user. The resulting database is used for demographic research.

The labelling view corresponds to the annotation over the image. This module is used for providing a literal transcription, annotating where each text line and words are located in the document image. In addition, if the user has already filled the form corresponding to that record, the system automatically assigns the semantic categories (name, surname, occupation) to the words. In this way, our integrated platform puts into correspondence the contextual information (contents view) with the words transcription (labeling view). As a result, we can obtain ground-truth at image level for training the algorithms, as shown in Figure 11.8

---

[3] Transkribus: https://transkribus.eu/Transkribus/
[4] World Archives Project: https://www.familytreemaker.com/AWAP/

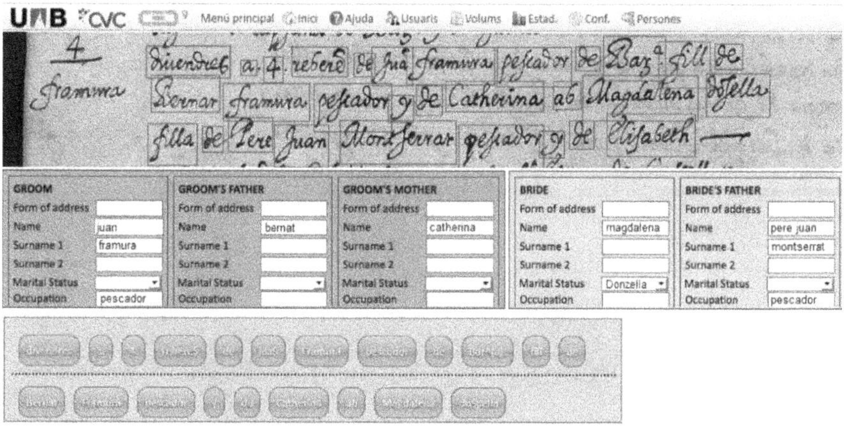

Fig. 11.8: Bi-modal crowdsourcing platform.

11.7.1.2 *Gamesourcing Strategies for Validation*

In crowdsourcing, the contribution of users tends to be voluntary, and their reward uses to be their satisfaction of collaborating in making the document contents publicly available. However, the annotation is tedious, and some users loose interest after some time. Gamification, defined as the application of game-design elements and principles in non-game contexts, has demonstrated to engage and keep the interest of users. For this reason, we have also explored how to engage users in the annotation process. With this aim, we have developed several gamesourcing (i.e. crowdsourcing via gamification) applications for mobile devices [Chen *et al.* (2018)] in order to validate the automatic transcription.

The first game is used to validate the output of the transcription algorithm. When the player selects a word in the touch-screen of the mobile, the system shows the most probable transcriptions according to the HTR.

The second game is used to validate that several word images are the same. The idea behind is that a user can visually check that many word images look the same (or not) in a very fast way. So, if several words look the same, then we can assume that they all have the same transcription, and save time. Consequently, not all words in a document collection must be validated using the first and slower game, because it is enough to validate a small percentage of these groups of similar words. An image of the two games is shown in Figure 11.9.

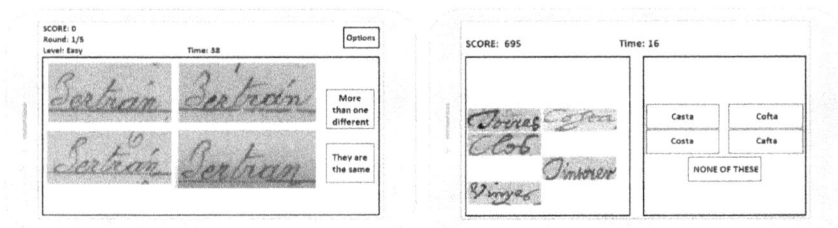

Fig. 11.9: Gamesourcing apps. Left: clusters game; Right: transcription game.

11.7.2 *The Browsers*

Finally, we show two browser prototypes. The first one can be used for browsing and searching in historical documents that have not been transcribed. The second prototype is used for browsing the historical social network. Both of them are described next.

11.7.2.1 *Browsing and Searching in Historical Documents Using a Mobile Device*

The first prototype, called *e-crowds* [Riba *et al.* (2014)], is envisioned for electronic readers, such as ebooks, tablets, or smartphones. Lately, the reading behaviour is moving from a static to a dynamic mode, in which users can jump between information via hyper-links. Thus, our prototype is designed to allow users to browse and search words within the documents, following the idea of the *active reading* paradigm. In this scenario, we suppose that documents have not been transcribed, so the search is performed using the word spotting technique described in [Almazán *et al.* (2014)].

First, the system allows users to browse the document collection using typical gestures used in mobile devices: the previous or next page is shown by left or right swiping movements, and zooming in/out is done through 2-finger pinch. The search functionality allows searching words by either touching a word in the manuscript (query-by-example) or by providing a textual query (query-by-string). Once the query word has been introduced, the system shows, in the right side panel, the list of retrieved words in the document collection. When the user touches a word in the list, the system shows, in the main panel, the page that contains that word. If there are several instances of that word in the page, they are all displayed in red bounding boxes (see Figure 11.10). In addition, the user can perform

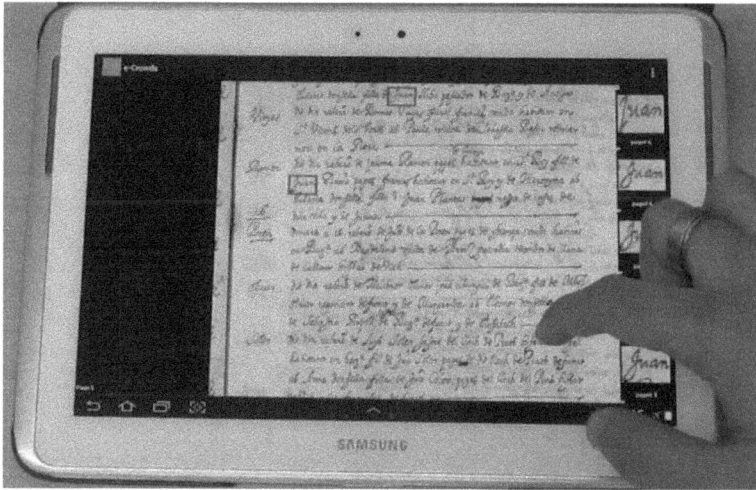

Fig. 11.10: Word Spotting application in tablet devices.

combined searches, which means that users can refine a search by adding more words to the search.

11.7.2.2 *Browsing the Social Network with a Web-Based Platform*

The web-based browser, shown in Figure 11.11, aims to facilitate the consumption and dissemination of the historical social network in an illustrative and pedagogic way. The browser allows to navigate through the social network with an interface similar to *Facebook*. Users can also use the search engine to find individuals. For each individual, the platform shows the personal data, including the location where that person lived, and, in case it is available, a photograph. The system also shows the relatives and a genealogical tree. By clicking on a relative, the user jumps to the personal website of that relative.

For each town or village, the system also shows demographic data such as the population pyramid, the most frequent names, surnames or occupations for a certain time period, as well as migration movements.

11.8 Conclusions

In this chapter we have presented a system for the extraction of information from historical population documents (marriage and census records) and

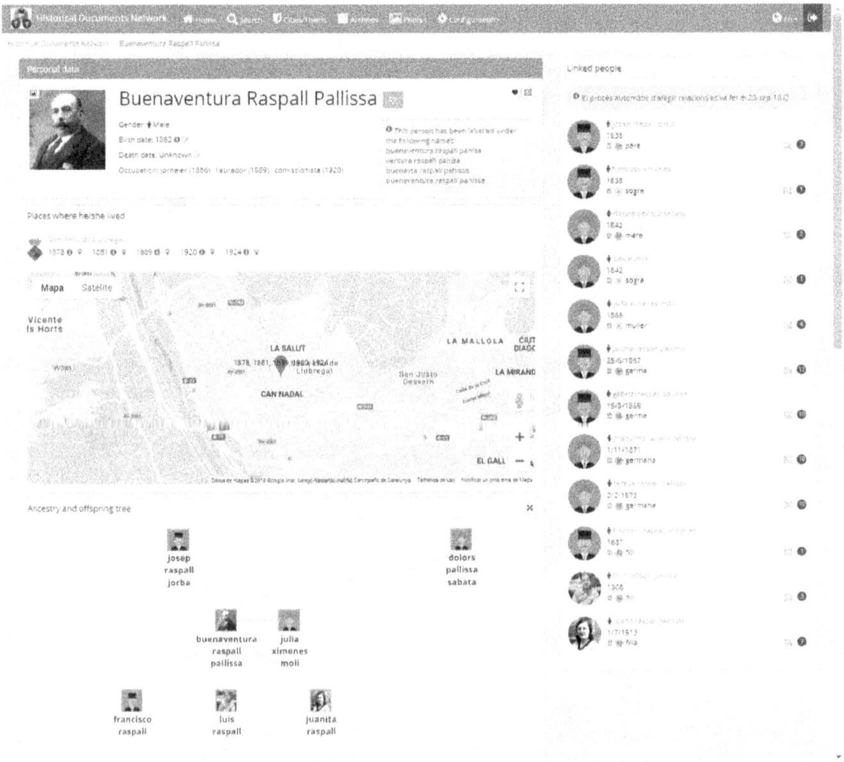

Fig. 11.11: Browser. The information of a person is shown together with their relatives.

the subsequent linkage of information. We have presented a formalism of social network as the conceptual model to represent and present the information. Technically, the presented system has been split in four components, namely the low level image processing and enhancement view, the content recognition view, the semantic space for the interpretation of named entities and the relations between data terms, and finally the users space. The last component, the user in the loop, is addressed to combine a manual entry and validation to complement the automatic algorithms.

The main conclusions that we can draw from the proposed work are summarized as follows. First, population records play a key role in the interpretation of the history. If we assume that each individual has been registered at some point in a census, birth, marriage or death record, these documents allow to construct a complete and reliable narrative of the past. From the life course of individuals, the aggregated and inter-linked describes the aggregated knowledge of the evolution of the communities of the past. Second, the automatic reading of historical manuscripts has progressed a lot in the last decade. On the one hand, the incorporation of deep neural networks in handwriting recognition has allowed to cope with complex document images; and on the other hand, several keyword spotting techniques have been proposed in the literature that are able to extract and index relevant words in holistic way even though images are in bad conditions. However, due to the heterogeneity of historical manuscripts in terms of structure, language, writing style, etc. a fully automatic recognition can not be achieved without modeling the semantic knowledge that gives context to the contents and reduces the semantic gap. This is especially noticeable in the extraction of named entities, which require the knowledge of concepts in the historical context, and the syntactic structure of the documents. A third important conclusion is the need of the inclusion of the user in the process. Contrarily to what could be expected, although the automation of document recognition progresses, the need of including the user will increase and hence more complex systems will be possible. We should probably move from the "user in the loop" concept to the "algorithm in the loop". This means that the future of universal access to historical archives will be based in user-centered systems, that will be complemented with automatic components that will be launched depending on the user intentions.

As continuation of the system proposed in this work, and based on the metaphor of a social network as a way to construct narratives of the past, we will evolve towards a more complete platform, adding information from other census, birth, marriage, death records, but also connecting the users of the past to the users of the present. Thus, users will be able to provide and link the information extracted from historical manuscripts to data in other modalities (e.g. recordings, photographs, oral history, etc.)

11.9 Acknowledgements

This research has been partially supported by the ERC Advanced Grand Project "Five Centuries of Marriages" (2011–2016) funded by the European Research Council (ERC 2010-AdG-20100407), and whose principal investigator is Professor Anna Cabré; the projects funded by Recercaixa "TOOLS: Tools and procedures for the large scale digitization of historical sources of population" (2015–2017) and "NETWORKS: Technology and citizen innovation for building historical social networks to understand the demographic past" (2017–2019), both funded by Obra Social "La Caixa" with the collaboration of the ACUP; the Spanish projects RTI2018-095645-B-C21 and RTI2018-095533-B-I00, the Ramon y Cajal Fellowship RYC-2014-16831, and the CERCA Programme/Generalitat de Catalunya.

References

Almazán, J., Gordo, A., Fornés, A., and Valveny, E. (2014). Word spotting and recognition with embedded attributes, *IEEE transactions on pattern analysis and machine intelligence* **30**, 12, pp. 2552 2566.

Álvaro, F., Cruz, F., Sánchez, J.-A., Terrades, O. R., and Benedí, J.-M. (2015). Structure detection and segmentation of documents using 2d stochastic context-free grammars, *Neurocomputing* **150**, pp. 147–154.

Brea-Martínez, G. and Pujadas-Mora, J.-M. (2019). Estimating long-term socioeconomic inequality in southern Europe: The Barcelona area, 1481–1880, *European Review of Economic History* **23**(4), 397–420.

Chen, J., Riba, P., Fornés, A., Mas, J., Lladós, J., and Pujadas-Mora, J. M. (2018). Word-hunter: A gamesourcing experience to validate the transcription of historical manuscripts, in *Frontiers in Handwriting Recognition (ICFHR), 16th International Conference on*, pp. 528–533.

Coüasnon, B. (2006). Dmos, a generic document recognition method: application to table structure analysis in a general and in a specific way, *International Journal of Document Analysis and Recognition (IJDAR)* **8**, 2, pp. 111–122, doi:10.1007/s10032-005-0148-5.

Fernández, D., Lladós, J., Fornés, A., and Manmatha, R. (2012). On influence of line segmentation in efficient word segmentation in old manuscripts, in *Frontiers in Handwriting Recognition (ICFHR), 2012 International Conference on* (IEEE), pp. 763–768.

Fernández, D., Marinai, S., Lladós, J., and Fornés, A. (2013). Contextual word spotting in historical manuscripts using markov logic networks, in *Proceedings of the 2nd International Workshop on Historical Document Imaging and Processing* (ACM), pp. 36–43.

Fernández-Mota, D., Lladós, J., and Fornés, A. (2014). A Graph-Based Approach for Segmenting Touching Lines in Historical Handwritten Documents, *International Journal on Document Analysis and Recognition* **17**, 3, pp. 293–312.

Fornés, A., Otazu, X., and Lladós, J. (2013). Show-through cancellation and image enhancement by multiresolution contrast processing, in *Document Analysis and Recognition (ICDAR), 2013 12th International Conference on* (IEEE), pp. 200–204.

Lladós, J., Rusinol, M., Fornés, A., Fernández, D., and Dutta, A. (2012). On the influence of word representations for handwritten word spotting in historical documents, *International journal of pattern recognition and artificial intelligence* **26**, 05, p. 1263002.

Manmatha, R. and Rothfeder, J. L. (2005). A scale space approach for automatically segmenting words from historical handwritten documents, *IEEE Transactions on Pattern Analysis and Machine Intelligence* **27**, 8, pp. 1212–1225.

Mas, J., Fornés, A., and Lladós, J. (2016). An interactive transcription system of census records using word-spotting based information transfer, in *2016 12th IAPR Workshop on Document Analysis Systems (DAS)* (IEEE), pp. 54–59.

Pujadas-Mora, J.-M., Brea-Martínez, G., Jordà Sánchez, J.-P., and Cabré, A. (2018). The apple never falls far from the tree: siblings and intergenerational transmission among farmers and artisans in the barcelona area in the sixteenth and seventeenth centuries, *The History of the Family*, pp. 1–35.

Pujadas-Mora, J. M., Fornés Bisquerra, A., Lladós, J., and Cabré, A. (2016). Bridging the gap between historical demography and computing: tools for computer-assisted transcription and analysis of demographic sources, *Future of historical demography: upside down and inside out*, pp. 127–131.

Riba, P., Almazán, J., Fornés, A., Fernández-Mota, D., Valveny, E., and Lladós, J. (2014). E-Crowds: A Mobile Platform for Browsing and Searching in Historical Demography-Related Manuscripts, in *International Conference on Frontiers in Handwriting Recognition* (IEEE), pp. 228–233.

Riba, P., Lladós, J., and Fornés, A. (2015). Handwritten word spotting by inexact matching of grapheme graphs, in *Document Analysis and Recognition (ICDAR), 2015 13th International Conference on* (IEEE), pp. 781–785.

Riba, P., Lladós, J., Fornés, A., and Dutta, A. (2017). Large-scale graph indexing using binary embeddings of node contexts for information spotting in document image databases, *Pattern Recognition Letters* **87**, pp. 203–211, doi:https://doi.org/10.1016/j.patrec.2016.06.015, advances in Graph-based Pattern Recognition.

Romero, V., FornéS, A., Serrano, N., SáNchez, J. A., Toselli, A. H., Frinken, V., Vidal, E., and LladóS, J. (2013). The esposalles database: An ancient marriage license corpus for off-line handwriting recognition, *Pattern Recognition* **46**, 6, pp. 1658–1669.

Sudholt, S. and Fink, G. A. (2016). Phocnet: A deep convolutional neural network for word spotting in handwritten documents, in *Frontiers in Handwriting Recognition (ICFHR), 2016 15th International Conference on* (IEEE), pp. 277–282.

Toledo, J. I., Carbonell, M., Fornés, A., and Lladós, J. (2019). Information extraction from historical handwritten document images with a context-aware neural model, *Pattern Recognition* **86**, pp. 27–36, doi:https://doi.org/10.1016/j.patcog.2018.08.020.

Toledo, J. I., Dey, S., Fornés, A., and Lladós, J. (2017). Handwriting recognition by attribute embedding and recurrent neural networks, in *Document Analysis and Recognition (ICDAR), 2017 14th IAPR International Conference on*, Vol. 1 (IEEE), pp. 1038–1043.

Toledo, J. I., Sudholt, S., Fornés, A., Cucurull, J., Fink, G. A., and Lladós, J. (2016). Handwritten word image categorization with convolutional neural networks and spatial pyramid pooling, in *Joint IAPR International Workshops on Statistical Techniques in Pattern Recognition (SPR) and Structural and Syntactic Pattern Recognition (SSPR)* (Springer), pp. 543–552.

Chapter 12

Lifelong Learning for Text Retrieval and Recognition in Historical Handwritten Document Collections

Lambert Schomaker

Bernoulli Institute, University of Groningen, Netherlands
l.r.b.schomaker@rug.nl

12.1 Introduction

Current developments in deep learning neural networks show remarkable progress, also in document-analysis systems for historical manuscript collections (Sudholt and Fink, 2018; Gurjar *et al.*, 2018; Sudholt and Fink, 2016; Bluche, 2016). However, there are still many stumbling blocks and recognition performances are still not at a level which matches the expectations in user communities. For scholars in the humanities, these expectations are indeed high, as evidenced from the criticism that large-scale digitization endeavors such as the Google Books project[1] drew (Chalmers and Edwards, 2017).[2] This state of affairs is noteworthy, because optical character recognition of machine-printed text — as opposed to handwritten manuscripts — yields performances that are already incredibly high from the point of view of current handwriting-recognition research. Practical tests reveal character recognition rates from 68% on early 20th century printed newspapers to 99.8% on modern material (Klijn, 2008). Lower rates from 71% to 98% character recognition are mentioned for newspapers from the

---

[1] https://en.wikipedia.org/wiki/Google_Books
[2] Such opinions were raised quite vocally, e.g., during plenary discussions at the Annual Seminar of the Consortium of European Research Libraries (CERL), Oslo, Norway, October 28th, 2014.

period 1803–1954 (Holley, 2009) who also reports that any performance below 90% recognition accuracy would be considered 'poor'.

If complaints on the accuracy of recognized text and its OCR-based metadata are already so strong in the recognition of machine-printed text, what can we expect from the user's reactions on current handwriting recognition algorithms? It is clear that some reflection is necessary in order to promote computer-based reading systems for opening access to historical collections. In this chapter a number of considerations and experiences will be presented concerning the development of the Monk [van der Zant *et al.* (2008, 2009); van Oosten and Schomaker (2014); Schomaker (2016)] e-Science service for historical documents at the University of Groningen in the period 2008–2019. This system aims at supporting researchers in machine learning and scholars in the humanities in doing research concerning the What, When & Who questions:

- 'What has been written?' (text recognition);
- 'When was it written?' (style-based dating of manuscripts); and
- 'Who wrote the document?' (writer identification).

By adding labels at the page-description level, adding line transcriptions at the level of line-strip images and adding zone labels for words and characters, the scholars create a growing index to documents. At the same time, machine-learning researchers can use the harvested $\{image, label\}$ tuples for training their methods. Table 12.1 gives an overview of a number of relevant statistics.

Table 12.1: Key statistics representing the data present within the Monk system (July 2018).

Number of:	(qty.)
Institutions	30
Books, multi-page documents	567
Page scans	152k
Line strips	273k
Zone (ROI) candidate images	700M
Lexical and shape classes	147k
Disk storage	120 TB
Files	1.3×10^9
Human-labeled zones words, characters, visual elements	900k

In the context of the Monk system *Human labeled* means: 'an image zone, manually labeled as an original individual text item, possibly new to the system', or, alternatively, it may imply: 'recognizer-based labels that are confirmed by a human user on the basis of a ranked hit list provided by the system'. Figure 12.1 gives an overview of the document styles, scripts, and image quality varieties in the current collection on Monk.

Fig. 12.1: Random samples from the collections currently on the Monk system. Apart from handwritten manuscripts also some machine printed material is on the system. In the philosophy of big-data methods, the classification algorithms should not be trained or designed specifically for a particular style. While this is possible to a large extent, the wide range of image quality and layout particularities remains challenging.

During the development of this system, the following issues were encountered, concerning the questions of the users and concerning the machine-learning approach to choose:

- Expectation management - How is a reading system positioned as a technological tool in terms of the promised functionality and the benefits to be expected for users, i.e., librarians, archivists and end users?

- Usage scenarios - Does the institution basically desire an e-Book reader with a key-word search enhancement, is the goal to support users in creating edited digital books from handwritten manuscripts or is the goal to just convert images of paper documents to encoded text for further processing?

- Technical realization - Is the reading system offered as a stand-alone computer tool, running on the the PC of the end user, or running on the infrastructure of a library institution under local supervision, or is it constructed as a 'cloud'-based service, somewhere on Internet, with support from remote, possibly anonymous but expert-level staff?

- Work-flow concept - Does the archive intend to perform a single-shot conversion of a given collection (from pixels to encoded text) or do the users realize that continuous efforts in quality control will be required, including labeling by experts or volunteers over a prolonged period of time?

- Quality and quantity of the material - Will there be a preselection of materials and what are the criteria? What types of material are present: books, diaries/journals, shoe boxes with letters in their original envelope, written by diverse writers?

- Industrialization and scalability - Who is responsible for image pre-processing and layout analysis? A folder with 2000 scanned raw unlabeled images of papyrus texts is not well comparable to an academic benchmark test for machine learning that is preprocessed, packaged, labeled and prepared for k-fold evaluation experiments (LeCun *et al.*, 1998; Marti and Bunke, 2002; Fischer *et al.*, 2012). In real-world applications, collections have a wide variety of document and layout formats. How to handle the consequences of success: "If it works, can we process several hundreds of such collections within a year?"

- Human effort - Who will be responsible for quality control of the meta-data input, and the linguistic quality of the labeling process?

If users perform an inconsistent labeling, they may blame the system if recognition performances are lower than expected.

- Algorithms - Finally, after having listened to signals from user communities, there is the last consideration, which mostly is the starting point for many in our research domain: The selection of the machine-learning methodology used. How to choose between word-spotting (Rath and Manmatha, 2007), word-based recognition (van der Zant *et al.*, 2008) and character-stream based handwritten-text recognition (HTR) (Sánchez *et al.*, 2013)? Even here, realistic and pragmatic considerations need to be taken into account, that are insufficiently addressed by designers of machine-learning methods. Will it be possible to enjoy improvements in algorithms, over time? How to select such methods? Are current methods in deep learning usable in practical application settings?

The answer to such questions is not easy. When maintaining a large-scale e-Science repository of handwritten document collections, it quickly becomes apparent that at least 'four Vs of Big Data' play a role here: **Volume**, **Velocity**, **Variety** and **Veracity**. The **volume** is indeed large and may be in the hundreds of thousands of page scans. This has consequences for storage but also for computation: (re)training efforts will pose a significant load on the infrastructure. Data sets can be much too large to fit in memory, especially considering the fact that training processes for multiple collections will run in parallel. **Velocity** pertains to the rate at which new scanned pages are entering the system as well as the rate at which labels are being produced by the users. New labeling may refute existing labeling. Since neural networks cannot unlearn individual input/output pairs, new insights or corrections by users usually necessitates a new training from start. **Variety** plays a role in image-quality preprocessing. Although an 'end-to-end' training is advocated these days, the generalization from, e.g., a parchment training set to a papyrus-based test set will be highly limited. A proper preprocessing increases the reusability of samples that are homogenized in their visual appearance over multiple diverse training contexts. Variety also plays a dominant role at a level where current deep learning does not provide solutions as yet: Layout structure diversity. Curvilinear line shapes, tabular text objects and marginal notes often require collection-specific layout analysis. Finally, writing style variety and linguistic variations need to be handled. As regards **Veracity**, it should be noted that the machine-learning assumption that 'ground truth is a rock solid factum' cannot be held in a live system. In many cases, a coherent labeling systematics needs to be invented by humanities researchers, on the spot: This goal may have been the whole purpose of the digitization effort for the manuscript, in the first place.

In this chapter, the evolution of the trainable search engine for handwritten historical collection, Monk will be used to illustrate the manner in which these considerations were addressed. In this process, a number of phenomena in machine learning were encountered that are hitherto not handled in great detail in the common benchmark-oriented literature but which will become apparent under large-scale, open domain conditions.

12.2   Expectation Management

Both in the Google Books[3] project and in projects aimed at digitizing vast amounts of handwritten material from a wide range of international scripts and historical periods, it is essential to create realistic expectations in end users. The end users can be archivists and librarians, for whom correctness of metadata and core text data is very important. End users have their own expectations, which are concentrated in the areas of legibility and the reading experience, i.e., usability aspects, as well as accuracy of text recognition (van der Zant *et al.*, 2009). Increasingly, there are expectations as regards multimodality, the recognition of the pictorial information next to the handwriting, and the possibility of (semi-automatic) creation of hyperlinks to semantic databases (Weber *et al.*, 2018).

Inspection of the handwriting-recognition literature will lead to unrealistic expectations. From a fundamental-science perspective, standard benchmark tests are clearly necessary. However, they also introduce a bias as well as a reduction in the diversity of data that are handled in literature, in comparison to real-world applications. The standard data sets, especially MNIST (LeCun *et al.*, 1998), but also the George Washington (GW) data set (Fischer *et al.*, 2012) have been introduced quite a number of years ago, with generations of PhD students trying to improve the recognition rate of the previous cohort, which is possible due to the vast accumulation of knowledge and skills concerning precisely these data sets (but not other unseen data sets). Even the IAM data set (Marti and Bunke, 2002), which

---

[3]https://en.wikipedia.org/wiki/Google_Books

is very realistic and challenging due to the presence of multiple writers, is of limited use as a predictor for the performance of an algorithm on historical material. The handwriting style and image quality concerns contemporary mixed-cursive and cursive handwriting. Recognition results obtained for such data sets are meaningless for an archivist with a medieval collection, a collection hieratic script on papyrus (Figure 12.2), or a collection of Russian 17th century pamphlets in an exuberant cursive style with large ascenders and descenders (Figure 12.3).

Fig. 12.2: An example of hieratic script with papyrus in two types of aging within the same text column and weak contrast differences between ink trace and papyrus fibers.

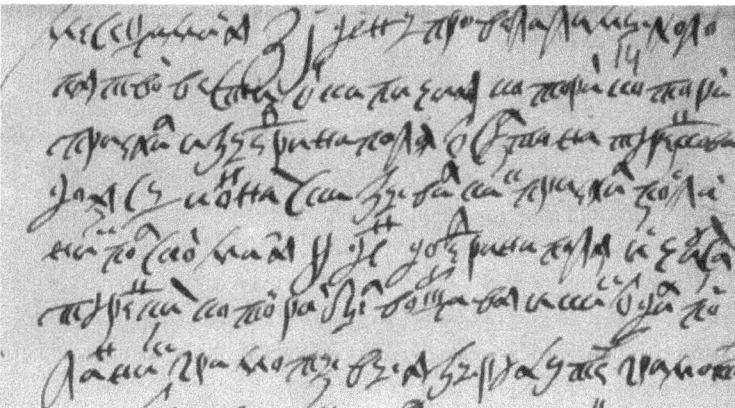

Fig. 12.3: A 17th century Russian example of an exuberant style with isolated and connected-cursive elements as well as overlap of ascenders and descenders between successive lines.

The goal of performing tests under acceptable theoretic conditions of independently sampled and identically distributed statistical properties is laudable and necessary, but it is not enough. Real collections violate both the conditions of stationarity and ergodicity which are needed for successful machine learning. A writer of a journal (diary) will usually start out with high ambitions and a clean style, in eloquent full sentences. However, as time progresses, this may evolve into sloppily produced entries containing more and more abbreviations, marginal notes in all orientations, and other idiosyncrasies (doodles) that were not present in the first pages. Both at the level of shape and at the level of language, the source processes are not stationary. Ergodicity, the requirement for a stochastic process that its statistical distribution can be estimated (read: because there is a single, underlying signal source) is also often questionable. A single document may be produced by multiple scribes (read: different writing-style signal sources) and the linguistic content may vary from chapter to chapter to such a degree that one cannot consider the overall process ergodic: it is based on a diverse set of stochastic language generators. Such considerations seem to point to the use of machine-learning models that are trained and applied, *conditional* to a known aspect of the signal source, e.g., "we are in a Chinese section of the series of page scans", which indicates that a deep-learning model trained on Chinese characters may be considered as more appropriate than other style models. More formally, if $p(x|M1, S1) > p(x|M2, S2)$, then $p(C|x, M1) > p(C|x, M2)$, for samples x, a sample class C, two styles S_i and corresponding trained models $M_i, i = 1, 2$. In words, if the data are likely to be generated by model M1 if the source is in style S1, the probability is higher that a correct class label C is computed by model M1 rather than by model M2. An alternative approach would, e.g., require the assumption that there is enough training data for all possible scripts and classes such that a true 'omniscript' neural network can be trained. In this second, ambitious approach it is assumed, unrealistically, that a) enough data are present to bypass the problems of non-stationarity and non-ergodicity and that b) the resulting model would not suffer from the competition between all the classes, i.e., the complete set of international scripts. Please note that the Chinese language alone has a dictionary set (Ytizi Zydian) of 106.203 character shapes. Although other languages have smaller character sets, the mutual competition is bound to create risks. If whole-word classification is performed, the number of classes will be equal to the sum of the word lexicon sizes of all involved styles. For the case of Chinese alone, a convolutional neural network with a 'normal' dimensionality of a thousand units in pre-final layer N-1 and 100k output units in 'one-hot' configuration would require a fully connected layer with more than 100 million weights (Figure 12.4). At this number of coefficients it is unlikely that the 'dropout trick' (Hinton *et al.*, 2012) will alleviate this situation.

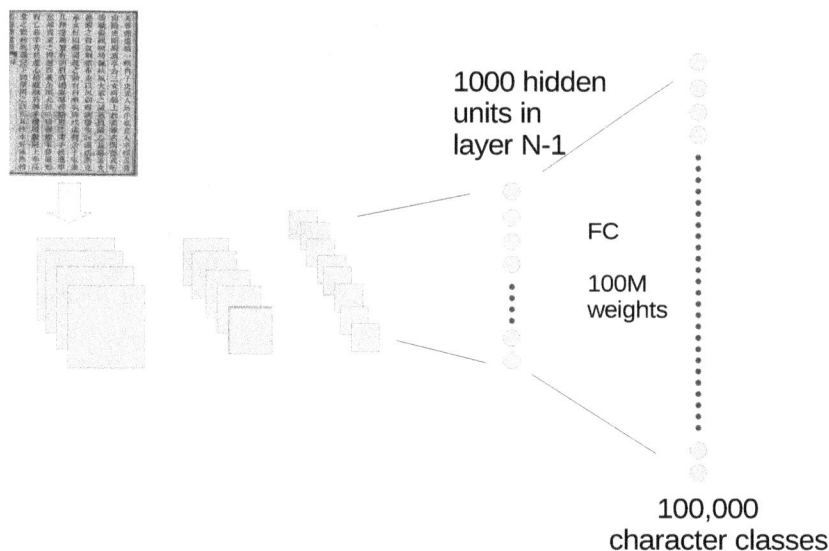

1000 hidden units in layer N-1

FC

100M weights

100,000 character classes

Fig. 12.4: In case of a very large number of output classes, the notion of a one-hot target output vector representing the classes becomes untenable. Handcrafted attribute representations need to be designed for the final layer, reducing its dimensionality (He and Schomaker, 2018).

With such a large number of incoming weights to a neuron, the collinearity problem entails that there are too many equipotential solutions for realizing a target (output) activation value, turning training into an ill-posed problem, i.e., a problem for which not one or, alternatively many solutions exist. In this example, the estimation problem is so massive that it can be argued that even in the absence of a collinearity problem, the underlying densities (the shapes of the underlying manifolds) need to be covered in sufficient detail by giving the neural network a sufficient number of training examples. Considering a lenient rule-of-thumb to have 5 samples (I/O pairs) per coefficient this would require half a billion training samples, disregarding the number of weights in the earlier layers in that network. If one would argue, that with a dropout probability of, say 0.8, the net number of coefficients is

20 million weights, this still implies that 100 million labeled samples would be needed according to the rule-of-thumb, a quantity that few research groups have at their disposal. With some additional (human) thinking, other representations than 100k-dimensional one-hot vectors can be used to solve the large set classification problem. We have proposed a solution based on attribute learning for the case of very large character sets (He and Schomaker, 2018). Within the Chinese character set, convenient attribute representations concerning the presence of radicals but also the order of strokes (e.g., the Wubi Xing method[4]). Similarly, for Western texts, an attribute method was introduced, PHOCNet (Sudholt and Fink, 2016). While very useful, such useful methods are highly script and/or language specific, thereby blocking the ambition of an 'omniscript' approach. If it is necessary to improve the recognition rates by using linguistic statistics, this introduces yet another condition that needs to be determined for processing a given image region. An e-Science service for handwriting recognition will need to be able to handle a wide variety of scripts and languages. Sometimes, it will not even be possible to flag individual pages with a code for script style and language condition. The 17th century Cuper-Braun[5] collection in Monk, concerns a series of European scholarly letters by different writers. They write in a multitude of languages, switching from Latin to French, interjecting the text with phrases in Greek and Hebrew (Figure 12.5).

Therefore, in any case, some form of modular classification approach appears to be more practical when it comes to historical manuscripts. As a consequence, dedicated training will be necessary on most of the ingested digital documents. In some cases, it will even mean that separate models are necessary for papyrus-based and for parchment-based documents of a particular writing style, due to the clear differences in the ink deposition and absorption process for the two materials. See Figure 12.2 for an example of problematic pre-processing requirements for hieratic script on papyrus.

In light of the problems lined out thus far, it may be clear that the concept of an *AI black box* that will produce a perfect Microsoft Word text file when given a scanned image of historical text is utterly unrealistic. Consequently, the conclusion was to inform potential Monk system users according to the following notes:

- Don't promise perfection

---

[4]https://en.wikipedia.org/wiki/Wubi_method
[5]The Cuper-Braun collection was kindly provided by Dr. J. Touber.

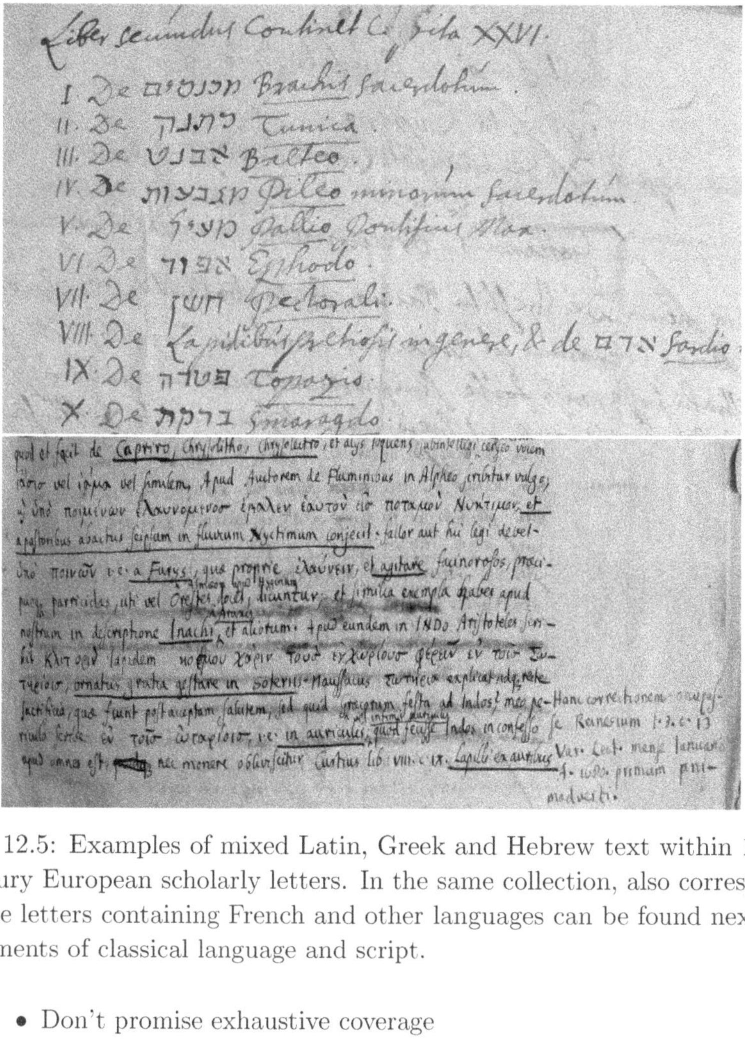

Fig. 12.5: Examples of mixed Latin, Greek and Hebrew text within 17th century European scholarly letters. In the same collection, also correspondence letters containing French and other languages can be found next to fragments of classical language and script.

- Don't promise exhaustive coverage
- Don't promise that it is a single conversion step
- Make clear that labeling will be necessary along the digital life cycle of the collection

12.3 Deep Learning

The successes of deep learning are based on a number of favorable conditions that are lacking in the context of historical document analysis. The problem of the archivist consists of a pile of scanned images, with an image quality that is not guaranteed to be amenable to optical character recognition or handwritten text recognition beforehand. The language may be known, but that does not mean that an appropriate lexicon exists. The same holds for other linguistic resources. The character shapes, i.e., allographs, are usually unknown, or constitute a variant of a known style and no labeled data for machine learning is present. In fact, the whole purpose of the digitization is to get at encoded text, given the pixels in the image. What can be done to enjoy the benefits of current machine-learning technology? One possible approach is proposed with the Transkribus (Kahle *et al.*, 2017) platform within the READ project. Scholars are required to label a sufficient amount of pages, by transcribing them at the line level. Typically 70 to 100 transcribed pages are considered to be necessary. This approach has limitations. For instance, what is the optimal set of pages to be used as the training set for a larger collection? Will it concern a single run of human transcription activity? As discussed above, starting with the first pages of a handwritten document is risky due to the intrinsic non stationarity. Secondly, the benefits of the labeling will only become apparent after the investment of human labeling has been done. In the design of the Monk system, an alternative approach is proposed, where pattern recognition starts upon the input of the first word label. From an over-segmented data set, hit lists are generated of 'mined' word zones and presented to the user, for confirmation. The user may choose to label words on the basis of a given line of text, thereby enlarging the covered lexicon. This type of process was dubbed *'widening'*. Alternatively, the user may choose to confirm labels in the hit list for a pattern, thereby improving the training set for that particular class: *'deepening'*. In labeling the hit lists, also additional catches of well-segmented words can be labeled, adding to the lexicon of known patterns. In this framework, useful computations are applied at the earliest moment in time. However, not all machine-learning methods are suitable in such an approach, as will be detailed in the next section.

12.4   The Ball-Park Principle

In fact, while a label-agglomeration process is evolving over time, the system passes different ball parks, each with its own most suitable machine-learning approaches.

No labels (zero labels). - In case no labels are available, it may be possible to rely on a pre-trained recognizer from the nearest handwriting style and a comparable lexicon. Additional training can then be applied for transfer learning. A particularly interesting solution is provided by machine-learning approaches based on attributes. Attributes are symbolic tokens that can be used to provide a text hypothesis in what basically constitutes are rule-based computation (Sudholt and Fink, 2016; He and Schomaker, 2018) known as zero-shot learning (Larochelle *et al.*, 2008). Please note that in a system such as Monk, which immediately exploits the arrival of new labels, the underlying class of patterns can directly be trained. In this manner, a secondary classification method, B, is kickstarted by the earlier applied primary method, A, which may be not optimal but still able to handle the zero-labels condition.

One label. - In case a single label is present, we enter the ball park of nearest-neighbor (1NN) classification. The labeled instance can be used for a data mining process, as in word spotting. Some appropriate distance measure is needed for comparing feature vectors. Such feature vectors can be dedicated (designed) or be trained, as is the case for embedded features tapped from some layer in an existing pre-trained neural network (Chanda *et al.*, 2018a). The resulting hit list can be presented to human users for confirmation. Upon entering a few labels, the system enters the next ball park.

One to five labels. - With a few labels, some methods are able to produce rudimentary models. It becomes possible to compute standard deviations of features, enabling the use of Bayesian modeling. Instead of 1NN, kNN can be applied but it is much more attractive to use nearest-mean (nearest centroid) classification, because this reduces the computation load. After all, in a data mining context, if the reference set is large and the pool of patterns to be mined is huge, computational costs are too high. Taking, again, the extremal example of the Chinese dictionary set of 106k characters, the presence of 5 examples per class would require 530k times N comparisons, N being the huge number of candidate patterns in the data-mining pool.

Twenty to hundred labels. - As the number of labeled instances increases, more powerful classification methods can be used. For instance, with 50 positive examples of a class and an appropriate number of counter examples, support-vector machines (SVMs) can be trained for a more advanced form of targeted (specialized) pattern mining in the pool of unknown objects.

More than one hundred labels. - Here, finally, a level of coverage is obtained which allows training of contemporary deep-learning methods. However, this is only sensible if there are enough classes, such that the total number of patterns is in balance with the number of weights (model coefficients) in the classifier. This amount of labeling is just a starting point. As is long known in professional OCR classifiers for machine print, each class requires thousands of examples. Similarly, for handwritten digits large data sets are currently being collected with 830k samples (Uchida *et al.*, 2016).

As Figure 12.6 shows (upper left), the word (or pattern) accuracy performance of single classes may approach 100% recognition with thousands of examples, but not in all classes. Such scatter plots provide a deeper insight in where the friction towards a higher performance resides. Consider,

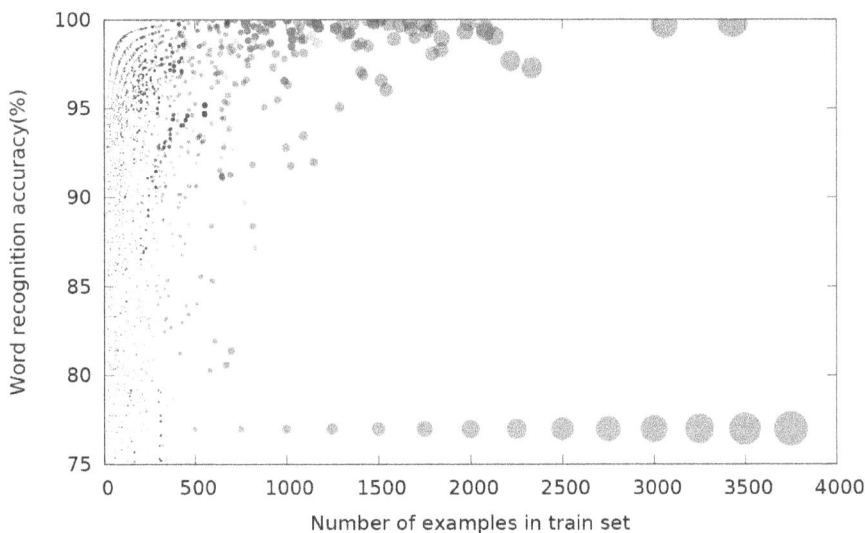

Fig. 12.6: Distribution of recognition accuracy as a function of labels, for a wide range of documents, script types and languages. Word classes will be moving towards the right and up over time, until a performance asymptote is reached. Some classes already have a decent performance with less than one hundred labels. On the other hand, some difficult shape classes remain just below 100% accuracy. The color of a circle denotes the manuscript group. The radius of the circle represents the size of the test set and is an indicator of the harvest.

for instance, the case were a class is performing suboptimally. Following 'old-school' precision thinking, the tendency would be to use, e.g., k-means clustering to separate style variants in the training set for that class, thereby zooming in to a more precise modeling of allographs and increasing the number of shape classes. However, as Figure 12.6 shows, this would entail an approximate halving of the number of examples from n to $\approx n/2$ corresponding to a large jump to the left on the horizontal axis, towards a point where the estimated expected accuracy (vertical axis) will be much lower. Indeed, we found that the performance will usually decrease after such an 'increased model-precision operation'. It is much easier to increase the performance by adding labels than to improve a given classifier on the basis of a reduced set of examples. There is no data like more data! Apparently, if the recognizer method is powerful enough, it is better to have mixed densities for style variants in one classification model, than have, e.g., two specialized models where each is trained on half the size of the original set of examples (Figure 12.7). We will only know whether the specalisation in modeling was worthwhile after our lifelong-learning engine has been able to harvest the original large number of labeled samples for each of the subclasses C_1 and C_2 that was present in the lumped set C at the onset, i.e., n examples.

In any case, by the time the final ball park of abundant labeling has been reached, a solid ground is present for constructing an index of a document. If linguistic models are present, an attempt can be made towards full-page transcription. Infrequent shapes and classes still pose a risk at this stage. It may be desirable to replace uncertain recognition results with an ellipsis ... instead of presenting uncertain text hypotheses. Presenting post-processed results introduces a new type of problem, especially if a recognized text is fluently legible, but unfortunately not what has been written. The user interface needs to allow the users to compare recognized results and handwritten image one on one. If this particular risk is not communicated to users, their disappointment with the system if they detect such output may be larger than necessary.

12.5 Technical Realization

Is the reading system offered as a stand-alone computer tool, running on the infrastructure of a library institution under local supervision, or is it constructed as a 'cloud'-based service, somewhere on Internet, with support from remote, possibly anonymous but expert-level staff?

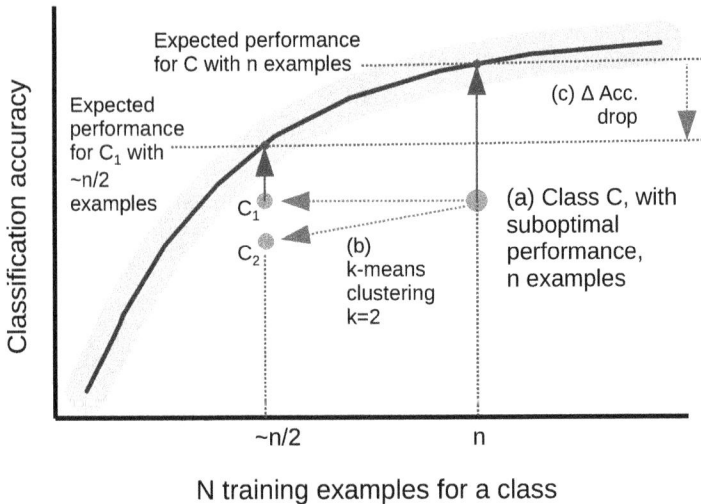

Fig. 12.7: Schematic representation of the effects of 'precise' modeling by splitting the training set for a class in style-based subclasses. (a) A class C shows suboptimal performance. (b) The idea is to use, e.g., k-means clustering with k=2 to zoom in on the shape differences and have two specialized models C_1 and C_2. (c) As a result of the smaller training sets, there will be a considerable drop in expected performance for the specialized models. On the basis of the large set of reference experiments, it is statistically questionable whether the supposed exactness of the models can counteract the large drop in accuracy due to the loss of examples.

12.5.1   *Work Flow*

Does the archive intend to perform a single-shot conversion of a given collection (from pixels to encoded text) or do they realize that continuous efforts in quality control will be required?

12.5.2   *Quality and Quantity of Material*

Will the be a preselection of materials and what are the criteria? What types of material are present: books, diaries/journals, shoe boxes with letters in their original envelope, written by diverse writers?

12.5.3 *Industrialization and Scalability*

Who is responsible for image preprocessing and layout analysis? A folder with 2300 scanned raw unlabeled images of papyrus texts is not well comparable to an academic benchmark test for machine learning that is preprocessed, packaged and prepared for k-fold evaluation experiments. How to handle the bad luck of success: "It works, now we need to process several hundreds of such collections within a year."

12.5.4 *Human Effort*

Who will be responsible for meta-data input, labeling, linguistic quality evaluation?

12.5.5 *Algorithms*

As the last consideration, the machine-learning methodology used: Will it be possible to enjoy improvements in algorithms, over time? How to select such method? Are current methods in deep learning usable in practical application settings?

12.5.6 *Object of Recognition: Whole-Word Approaches*

For an e-Science service in historical document analysis, it is important to strive for generic solutions wherever possible, given the large scale and huge diversity. Traditional speech and handwriting recognition usually rely strongly on linguistic resources. These are usually not present for unique documents that just enter the digital stage of their life cycle. The assumptions for 'optical character recognition' as 'classification of sequences of character classes' are not valid for a wide range of documents. At the same time it was clear in the period 2000–2008 that general image classification was making large leaps forward (Rath and Manmatha, 2007). In the document-analysis community, word-spotting techniques were being proposed. We found that biologically inspired neural networks provided very high word-classification rates on connected-cursive script (van der Zant *et al.*, 2008). As a consequence, a word-based classification approach was opted for in Monk.

12.5.7 *Processing Pipeline*

Ingest. - The processing pipeline starts with the *ingest* stage of a collection. It is verified that the users will have a long-term interest in the document, there is a responsible local 'editor' who instructs a group of volunteering labelers. The material needs to be sufficiently homogeneous, sufficiently large: much more than a hundred page scans, and of a manageable image quality. A choice is made for the basic text object on the scans that will be the target of recognition. This often requires a split in separate recto/verso images and a subsequent layout analysis to identify the major text columns in the document. Over time, a growing library of software scripts is collected such that new collections require just a variation on a known preprocessing scheme. This stage usually requires some additional programming using image processing tools. For instance, for a multi-spectral collection, a flattened image version that is optimal for ink/paper separation should be produced. The initial data transfer is realized using ftp, transfer web sites or hard disks sent via surface mail. We have experimented with allowing an upload of individual unorganized raw scans but this does not bring much to either party. Such isolated small projects do not benefit from the large scale of data-science approaches and the isolated material gives little chances to act as a multiplier for the solid coverage of a hitherto unseen script style.

Line segmentation. - Using horizontal ink-density estimates which are low-pass filtered, an automatic segmentation into lines is attempted. This is first done on a random subset of the scans, in order to find a proper parameter setting. Perfection is difficult to realize with a considerable portion of submitted collections. For difficult cases, curvilinear segmentation methods such as seam carving are applied (Surinta *et al.*, 2014; Chanda *et al.*, 2018b). Current approaches in machine learning favor end-to-end classification that starts with the original color image. However, the curvilinearly cropped text line requires an artificial background. Replacement by pure white pixels is not desirable, because it will introduce sharp non-text edges along the curvilinear cut. In Chanda *et al.* (2018b) an attempt is realized to construct an artificial background with the texture and color properties of the original image, replacing undesirable ascenders and descenders of the surrounding text lines. Even such an advanced method will not solve all possible problems. Collections with marginal notes and post-hoc corrections will be intrinsically unsolvable without some form of human intervention such as providing manual segmentations for deviant objects in the image. If the goal is a mere indexing (as opposed to full transcription) the attribution of a word to a particular line is less important. In many applications it will already be a great benefit if a target key word can be found and marked on the page, disregarding its membership to a line.

Word-zone candidates by over segmentation. - Using vertical ink-density estimates, candidate word zones are segmented which are of variable overlapping size. Widely spaced connected-cursive text is ideal: The number of word zones will be limited and wide white spaces prevent the occurrence of multi-word image crops. At the other end of the spectrum would be a faded typewritten text where even a single letter may consist of multiple connected components. Also here, some experimentation with a random subset of page columns is required. The segmentation is facultative. If at a later stage other word-zones are added by another word-segmentation algorithm, the resulting candidates are just added to the pool of word-zone candidates.

Word recognition. - At this stage, the document will enter the autonomous continuous learning cycle. Word classification tools will be applied to it, generating word-hypothesis lists for each word-zone candidate. The text hypotheses are added to a large raw Index. In the training of the word classifiers, data augmentation is performed using random elastic morphing [Bulacu *et al.* (2009)], which is necessary for all classes that have less than about 20 examples.

Word ranking: Hit list generation. As described elsewhere (van Oosten and Schomaker, 2014) we found that using the likelihood estimates generated by recognition engines, for instance the maximum a posterior likelihood $p(C|x)$ does not by necessity yield believable, intuitive hit lists. The task of separating an instance class from competing candidate classes, i.e., recognition, is another function than ranking, where one wants instances to appear sorted at the top of a hit list, with a strong similarity to a canonical model, i.e., optimizing the reverse probability, $p(x|C)$. Therefore, apart from recognition itself, an additional method is used that is optimal for ranking, yielding hit lists with understandable positive results and even understandable errors.

Presentation of recognition results to the user: per line, or per hit list for lexical words. At this stage, the user will be able to confirm text hypotheses or enter new word labels. This is detected by the event handler of the system, which will add a recomputation request for the class models at hand. This in turn will lead to re-recognition batch jobs, which generates new, improved text hypotheses, usually within 24 hours. At this point, the system will thus return to the Word-recognition stage, closing an iterative loop we have dubbed the 'Fahrkunst' principle. Closing of the loop to realize an autonomously learning system was realized in the summer of 2009. Controlling the feedback loop concerns the manual adjustment of computation policy parameters: Which books to focus the computation on, with which amount of delay time per cycle. A distinction is made between cold and hot books in the collection. Hot books are those where the user community has a great interest and displays a fruitful labeling harvest.

Construction of alphabetic word lists and provisional transcriptions. Finally, in this on-going process, there is a periodic selection of confirmed text hypotheses and manual transcriptions that is presented on internet as static files. A mechanism for downloading indices is also present, using download licenses with a limited time validity for end users. Together with end users, a 'work list' is defined for this type of objects. This part of the system is becoming more and more important and a large diversity of export formats is expected to be relevant at this level. For handwriting, the Alto standard is not optimal, but the Page XML format by the Prima group is an example of a usable output format for a range of further applications beyond this stage.

12.6   Performance

Although performance evaluation for recognition are straightforward, the same cannot be said of retrieval engines. The usual performance evaluation in machine learning assumes a train set, validation set and test set, all with labeled raw-data instances. Commonly, k-fold evaluation is performed to obtain reliable performance indicators in terms of accuracy, precision and recall. For the labeled portion of the data in a large document analysis system, a similar periodic evaluation can be applied to select optimal classifiers per script style, and so forth. One might think that the recall performance is a good predictor for the actual recall capability of a classifier in open-ended data mining. However, this is not straightforward while being in the middle of a continuous learning process. We do not know how many instances of a particular class are out there, in the mining pool? If an asymptote is reached in the accuracy for a particular class, does that mean that the pattern is 'mined out', i.e., that no more instances of that class exist in the pool, or, alternatively, is it the case that there is a particular problem at the level of shape representation and classification that cannot be solved by the current recognition method? In a lifelong learning context, new performance criteria are needed. For instance: where in the class space will additional labeling has the largest beneficial training effects?

An example of a new concept that was developed in this respect is the definition of the EUR, Equal Uncertainty Rate as a replacement for the EER, Equal Error Rate. In case of ranking instances of a single class, the labeled training examples are the basis for the computation of the False Reject Rate (FRR) curve. However, its counterpart, the False Acceptance Rate is less clear, since it is not known whether residual instances in a hit list are of the target class or not. Still, the EUR provides a good insight in the quality of instances as regards the likelihood that they are a member of the target class or not. By attracting the user to those classes where FRR/FAR curves indicate a good separating performance, human efforts are directed to where fruitful harvest are to be expected in the mining process. Figure 12.8 shows the effect of labeling on the False-Reject Rate and False-Accept Rate curves. The Equal Uncertainty rate should go down. In this real example, we see that the FRR rate (green curve, representing the target class) remains about the same, as well as the EUR value, but the False-Acceptance Rate curve (red, non-target samples) is becoming steeper. In lifelong machine learning, it is the goal to find the classes where these improvements are largest. In the Monk architecture, dedicated neural networks are trained to predict which classes give the highest improvement upon labeling. The users can then be attracted to these 'prospects', to confirm or disconfirm the label values for those classes. So basically, this constitutes a selective-attention mechanism of the learning system, answering the question: 'Where is the action?' in the learning process.

During the writing of this chapter, a large-scale field test was performed, comparing a traditional method and deep convolutional networks (Schomaker, 2019). The goal was to perform unmonitored end-to-end training of word, shape and character images in several hundreds of books with widely differing styles. Computing, using several GPUs, lasted from January 2019 to the end of April 2019. Although deep end-to-end training was able to obtain 95% word accuracy in many books, the training process failed several times for problems with more than 1000 classes in one-hot encoded classification,

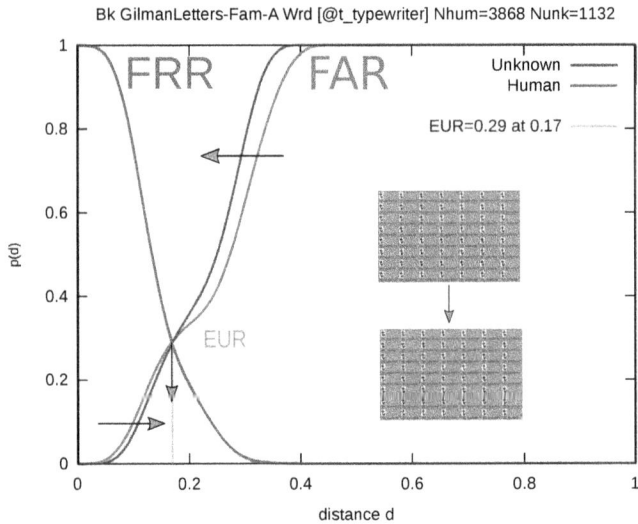

Fig. 12.8: Schematic overview of the effects of interactive labeling on the False-Reject Rate (FRR) and False-Accept Rate (FAR) curves for a class, in this example a typewritten letter 't'. By labeling a few candidates (light colored) in the hitlist, they become part of the training set and have an effect on the classification performance as indicated by the arrows. The samples and curves are an actual example of the consequences of adding nine new instances for the letter 't'. The Monk collection does not only contain handwriting: methods are also used for other classes of shapes. Equal Uncertainty Rate (EUR) is used instead of EER because the class labels of non-target patterns, i.e., the samples under the FAR curve, are unknown in open-set data mining.

even with a fairly small number of hidden units in the pre-final layer (150). Due to the fact that nearest-mean classification using bags of visual words is not limited by the number of (lexical) classes, the average performance over all books was higher for this traditional method (BOVW 87% vs 83% when failed CNN trainings were included). As we have shown (He and Schomaker, 2018), the problem of high numbers of classes can be solved using attribute learning, but this is a form of handcrafting of an output representation that would be required for different scripts and languages. For a system such as Monk, a pragmatic approach is chosen: For each book, the best-performing method can be selected.

12.7 Compositionality

The whole-word based approach has as advantage that it exploits the re-
dundance of shapes and has a diminished reliance on the well-formedness
of individual character shapes. The disadvantage is that there is a reduced
exploitation of the presence of stable pattern fractions corresponding to
letters and syllables. In the HMM-era this was addressed by 'state sharing'.
In the modern recurrent neural networks (LSTM, BLSTM, MDLSTM), the
training process will sort this out, automatically. However, this still requires
a sufficient regularity of character shapes to be successful, and many labeled
examples are needed, for instance 2000 lines of transcribed text. This allows
for compositionality and proper handling of words that were never seen ('out
of lexicon' recognition rate). However, not all collections lend themselves
to the use of LSTM, because spatial invariance is not its strongest asset
and is better dealt with using CNNs. Whole-word based approaches will be
able to handle unseen classes, if attribute schemes are used for constructing
class vector representations as targets for neural-network output. What is
most important for a data-mining framework, is that the harvest of labels
keeps the users motivated. Figure 12.9 shows the number of elicited labels
evolving over time. same collection are ingested. The growth curves show
non-linear speedup at points where labeling is facilitated due to the collaboration between man and machine. A detailed view on the growth curves
shows the 'snow-ball' effect at a smaller time scale: thirty labels are added
within a minute by a single user. Therefore, labeling of instances in hit
lists can be 'faster than linear', i.e., faster than begin-to-end, word-by-word
transcription.

12.8 Conclusion

In this chapter, an overview was given of design considerations, practical
solutions and problems encountered around a large-scale multi-user e-Science
service for text recognition and retrieval in a variety of historical-document
collections. The focus was more on text recognition than on document dating
and writer identification algorithms, which have been published elsewhere.
The major contributions of this chapter concern:

- A message to the machine-learning community that the current
  habits of algorithm evaluation entail the risk of a narrow view on
  pattern diversity and preprocessing problems in real manuscript
  collections;

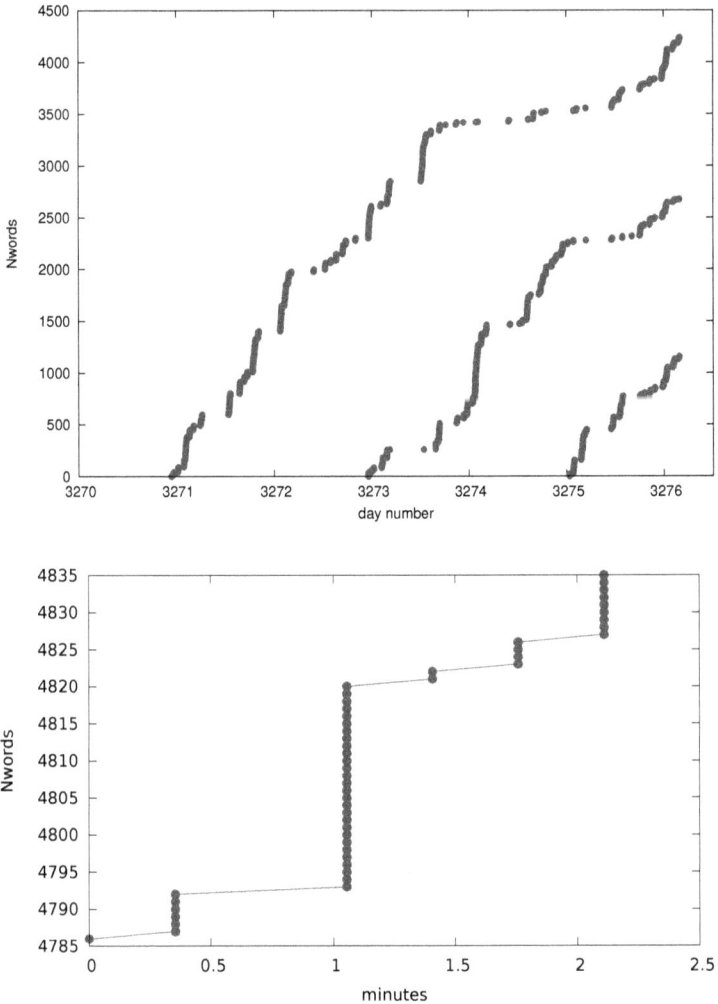

Fig. 12.9: Examples of label harvesting over time. Top: three books of the same collection are ingested. Note non-linear, steep speedups at some points due to hit-list based label confirmation. Bottom: zooming in on the growth curves show this 'snow-ball' effect at a smaller time scale: Twenty to thirty labels are added within a minute by a single user.

- Contrary to a separate laboratory and operational stage, continuous improvement requires lifelong learning, in an integrated manner, also called 'persistent cognition';

- An active label-harvesting engine that is running in autonomous mode needs new predictive algorithms to direct the investment of computational resources and human labeling labour to the data portions where the most attractive harvest prospects are to be expected. Such prospects are located on the fringe of a training front;

- When critical numbers of labels are reached, the label harvesting enters into a cascade of avalanche mode, such that ranked hit lists can be easily labeled, until the next performance asymptote is reached;

- The necessity for massive numbers of labels constitutes an intrinsic limitation of current deep-learning methods. The ball-park principle allows for exploitation of different types of methods which produce good results with a few or no labels, and then progressing to more advanced methods as more labeled instances are collected over time.

At this point, it also becomes important to add critical remarks. As a general method, a whole-word based method is very attractive. The task is very similar to general image retrieval, where a wide spectrum of algorithms is available to process greyscale and color images. In Monk, a single convenient general-purpose classifier is used to this effect. However, if individual characters actually *are present* and sufficiently regular, character-based methods and recurrent networks become applicable. In the methods described in this chapter, linguistic post processing did not play a role, because in most cases there is no suitable linguistic corpus. Again, however, if such a corpus actually *does exist*, it would be suboptimal not to use it. Current projects around the Monk system are directed at incorporation of linguistic and semantic resources to improve the classification accuracy. An intrinsic problem in document retrieval concerns the statistical distribution of terms: Many interesting target terms will be located in the long tail of the word distribution. A low frequency of presence implies a limited number of training examples. Also for these cases, letter or character based methods will be very important. An additional solution for this problem is given by the attribute-based methods which allow for zero-shot learning. Finally, a few words need to be spent concerning alternative projects, such as Transkribus (Kahle *et al.*, 2017) and READ. For historical reasons and due to different funding sources, the development of the Monk system took place in relative isolation. Still, a considerable number of users from the humanities are interested in the type of solutions provided by Monk. From their point of view, it would be very desirable if they could benefit from the advances in each of the different approaches. As an example, transcription data collected in Transkribus can be used to train recognizers in the Monk system. Alternatively, text-recognition results on word images could be cross checked by dedicated word classification systems on manuscript-processing e-Science servers, world wide, including those from READ, Monk and other projects. The ultimate goal would be to realize the type label-harvesting avalanches reported here, but over a wide range of document collections. In some areas, such as medieval European script styles, such a critical mass is about to be reached in the coming few years. The costs involved in maintaining large-scale computing and storage infrastructures will force all parties to cooperate. A good example is given by the astronomers, who have a similarly long-term perspective as the archives and humanities scholars, but who also have the tenacity to procure and maintain such long-term e-Science services (Valentijn *et al.*, 2017).

References

Bluche, T. (2016). Joint line segmentation and transcription for end-to-end handwritten paragraph recognition, in *29th Conference on Neural Information Processing Systems (NIPS)*.

Bulacu, M., Brink, A., Zant, T., and Schomaker, L. (2009). Recognition of handwritten numerical fields in a large single-writer historical collection, in *10th International Conference on Document Analysis and Recognition*, pp. 808–812, doi:10.1109/ICDAR.2009.8.

Chalmers, M. K. and Edwards, P. N. (2017). Producing "one vast index": Google book search as an algorithmic system, *Big Data & Society* **4**, 2, p. [unpaginated], doi:10.1177/2053951717716950.

Chanda, S., Okafor, E., Hamel, S., Stutzmann, D., and Schomaker, L. (2018a). Deep learning for classification and as tapped-feature generator in medieval word-image recognition, in *13th IAPR International Workshop on Document Analysis Systems (DAS)* (IEEE), pp. 217–222, doi:10.1109/DAS.2018.82.

Chanda, S., Pal, U., Schomaker, L., Chakraborty, A., and Basak, S. (2018b). Text line segmentation and background filling in historical document images using grayscale information, in *[Submitted]* (IEEE (The Institute of Electrical and Electronics Engineers)), p. [unpaginated], doi:doi.

Fischer, A., Keller, A., Frinken, V., and Bunke, H. (2012). Lexicon-free handwritten word spotting using character HMMs, *Pattern Recognition Letters* **33**, 7, pp. 934–942.

Gurjar, N., Sudholt, S., and Fink, G. A. (2018). Learning Deep Representations for Word Spotting Under Weak Supervision, in *Proc. Int. Workshop on Document Analysis Systems* (Vienna, Austria).

He, S. and Schomaker, L. (2018). Open Set Chinese Character Recognition using Multi-typed Attributes, *ArXiv e-prints*.

Hinton, G. E., Srivastava, N., Krizhevsky, A., Sutskever, I., and Salakhutdinov, R. (2012). Improving neural networks by preventing co-adaptation of feature detectors, *CoRR* **abs/1207.0580**, http://arxiv.org/abs/1207.0580.

Holley, R. (2009). How good can it get? analysing and improving ocr accuracy in large scale historic newspaper digitisation programs, *D-Lib Magazine* **15**, 3/4, p. [unpaginated].

Kahle, P., Colutto, S., Hackl, G., and Mühlberger, G. (2017). Transkribus - A service platform for transcription, recognition and retrieval of historical documents, in *1st International Workshop on Open Services and Tools for Document Analysis, 14th IAPR International Conference on Document Analysis and Recognition, OST@ICDAR 2017, Kyoto, Japan, November 9–15, 2017*, pp. 19–24, doi:10.1109/ICDAR.2017.307, https://doi.org/10.1109/ICDAR.2017.307.

Klijn, E. (2008). The current state of art in newspaper digitisation. A market perspective. *D-Lib Magazine* **14**, 1/2, p. [unpaginated].

Larochelle, H., Erhan, D., and Bengio, Y. (2008). Zero-data learning of new tasks, in *Proceedings of the Twenty-Third AAAI Conference on Artificial Intelligence*, pp. 646–651.

LeCun, Y., Bottou, L., Bengio, Y., and Haffner, P. (1998). Gradient-based learning applied to document recognition, *Proceedings of the IEEE* **86**, pp. 2278–2324, https://en.wikipedia.org/wiki/MNIST_database, leCun, Yann; Corinna Cortes; Christopher J.C. Burges. MNIST handwritten digit database.

Marti, U.-V. and Bunke, H. (2002). The IAM-database: an English sentence database for offline handwriting recognition, *IJDAR* **5**, 1, pp. 39–46.

Rath, T. M. and Manmatha, R. (2007). Word spotting for historical documents, *IJDAR* **9**, 2–4, pp. 139–152.

Sánchez, J. A., Schofield, P., Depuydt, K., Gatos, B., Davis, R. M., and Mühlberger, G. (2013). tranScriptorium: an European Project on Handwritten Text Recognition, in *DocEng'13, September 2013, Florence, Italy* (ACM Press), ISBN 9781450317894, pp. 227–228.

Schomaker, L. (2016). Design considerations for a large-scale image-based text search engine in historical manuscript collections, *it - Information Technology* **58**, 2, pp. 80–88, http://www.degruyter.com/view/j/itit.2016.58.issue-2/itit-2015-0049/itit-2015-0049.xml.

Schomaker, L. (2019). A large-scale field test on word-image classification in large historical document collections using a traditional and two deep-learning methods, *CoRR* **abs/1904.08421**, http://arxiv.org/abs/1904.08421.

Sudholt, S. and Fink, G. A. (2016). Phocnet: A deep convolutional neural network for word spotting in handwritten documents, in *Frontiers in Handwriting Recognition (ICFHR), 2016 15th International Conference on* (IEEE), pp. 277–282.

Sudholt, S. and Fink, G. A. (2018). Attribute CNNs for word spotting in handwritten documents, *Int'l J. on Document Analysis and Recognition* **21**, 3, pp. 199–218.

Surinta, O., Karaaba, M., van Oosten, J.-P., Schomaker, L., and Wiering, M. (2014). A* path planning for line segmentation of handwritten documents, in *International Conference on Frontiers in Handwriting Recognition (ICFHR)* (IEEE (The Institute of Electrical and Electronics Engineers)), pp. 175–180, doi:10.1109/ICFHR.2014.37.

Uchida, S., Ide, S., Iwana, B. K., and Zhu, A. (2016). A further step to perfect accuracy by training cnn with larger data, in *2016 15th International Conference on Frontiers in Handwriting Recognition (ICFHR)*, pp. 405–410, doi:10.1109/ICFHR.2016.0082.

Valentijn, E., Begeman, K., Belikov, A., Boxhoorn, D., Brinchmann, J., McFarland, J., Holties, H., Kuijken, K., Verdoes Kleijn, G., Vriend, W.-J., Williams, O., Roerdink, J., Schomaker, L., Swertz, M., Tsyganov, A., and van Dijk, G. (2017). Target and (astro-)wise technologies - data federations and its applications, in *Astroinformatics 2017*, Proceedings IAU Symposium (International Astronomical Union), pp. 333–340, doi:10.1017/S1743921317000254.

van der Zant, T., Schomaker, L., and Haak, K. (2008). Handwritten-word spotting using biologically inspired features, *Ieee transactions on pattern analysis and machine intelligence* **30**, 11, pp. 1945–1957, doi:10.1109/TPAMI.2008.144.

van der Zant, T., Schomaker, L., Zinger, S., and van Schie, H. (2009). Where are the search engines for handwritten documents? *Interdisciplinary Science Reviews* **34**, 2–3, pp. 224–235, doi:10.1179/174327909X441126.

van Oosten, J.-P. and Schomaker, L. (2014). Separability versus prototypicality in handwritten word-image retrieval, *Pattern Recognition* **47**, 3, pp. 1031–1038, doi:10.1016/j.patcog.2013.09.006.

Weber, A., Ameryan, M., Wolstencroft, K., Stork, L., Heerlien, M., and Schomaker, L. (2018). Towards a digital infrastructure for illustrated handwritten archives, in M. Ioannides (ed.), *Digital Cultural Heritage*, *LNCS*, Vol. 10605 (Springer), ISBN 978-3-319-75788-9, pp. 155–166, doi: 10.1007/978-3-319-75826-8_13.

Chapter 13

Conclusions and Future Trends

[1,2]Andreas Fischer, [1,3]Marcus Liwicki and [1]Rolf Ingold

DIVA Group, University of Fribourg, Switzerland
iCoSys Institute, University of Applied Sciences and Arts
Western Switzerland
EISLAB, Luleå University of Technology, Sweden
andreas.fischer@unifr.ch, marcus.liwicki@ltu.se, rolf.ingold@unifr.ch

Automatic text extraction from document images has been an important research area for nearly half a century. While printed text recognition has reached a level of maturity that allows commercial application for office automation, automatic transcription of handwritten documents remains a major challenge. The additional difficulty handwriting recognition is facing in comparison with printed text recognition can be explained by several reasons. An evident factor is the extreme variability of writing styles related to multiple socio-educative and cultural aspects. Additionally to these interpersonal variabilities, one can also observe significant intrapersonal variabilities related to psychological and aging factors. However, the latter being less important, writer models specifically trained for a given writer, can lead to acceptable transcription results.

Another characterization of handwriting is its cursive nature, which impacts the recognition process in two ways. First, the letter shapes are strongly influenced by the previous and next characters, thus increasing once more the variability. And second, character shape boundaries are hard to be determined; or stated differently, the word segmentation into characters is a non-trivial task reflected by the so-called Sayre's paradox: a character sequence cannot be recognized without being segmented first, and reversely, it cannot be segmented without previous character recognition.

Fortunately, Sayre's paradox can be circumvented by combining the segmentation and recognition tasks. Such approaches can be efficiently achieved by machine learning techniques such as hidden Markov models or recurrent neural networks, which both can integrate character models characterizing shapes with language models carrying contextual information, either in form of n-grams or of a complete dictionary.

Despite such strategies, universal handwriting recognition is far from being solved. Acceptable solutions can be provided for some restricted applications. This holds for instance for digit or isolated letter recognition or when the used vocabulary is reduced, such as in addresses recognition used for automated mail dispatching.

Another favorable situation occurs when systems can be trained for a specific writer. However, this requires enough training data that has previously been labelled. Fortunately, current modeling techniques do not require a transcription to be aligned at character level; ground-truth alignment at word level or even line level is sufficient. Nevertheless, the practical difficulty to get accurate transcriptions should not be underestimated, notably in case of misspelling or abbreviations that are often corrected or completed by transcribers and therefore do not match the real data. In any case, to build a strong writer model several dozen pages are usually needed and this is often a major hindrance for such recognition applications.

The research community is strongly dealing with all these issues. Regular progresses are reported, not only in terms of higher accuracy, but also by improved learning strategies reducing the size of the training data. A lot of effort is also put into interactive annotation tools, in order to facilitate manual transcription and alignment. Crowdsourcing can be used as a profitable alternative.

As long as automatic transcription is not available, mainly for indexing purposes, keyword spotting can be used as an interesting alternative. Several digital libraries provide search functionalities based on such approaches using as queries either text or sample images.

To further progress in historical document analysis, handwriting recognition is not the only obstacle; several complementary tasks have also to be improved. Complex layout analysis in case of ornaments or glosses is one of them; but we must also mention script classification or scribe authentication. All these techniques must rely on best possible image quality, obtained by adequate image pre-processing and filtering.

In a mid and long term perspective we can expect substantial progress in handwriting recognition. In this perspective, the key element is certainly to consider additional contextual information, including semantic knowledge. Considering the recent progresses made in natural language processing and machine translation we can anticipate that the integration of the same kind of knowledge with language models will effectively improve text recognition in the future. Combined with the still massive increase of computing power, we can expect a real breakthrough in this domain in the next 5 to 10 years.

Index